Other Books by Courtney McInvale:

Haunted Mystic

Revolutionary War Ghosts of Connecticut

CIVIL WAR GHOSTS
OF CONNECTICUT

COURTNEY MCINVALE

First Edition:
First printing

PUBLISHED BY HAUNTED ROAD MEDIA, LLC
www.hauntedroadmedia.com

Cleveland, Ohio
United States of America

I dedicate this book in memory of my father, John C. McInvale who introduced a love for history and supernatural to me at a young age and taught me the importance of the Civil War in our nation's history. A rebel at heart but a history advocate above all, I have felt his watchful eye through this ongoing Civil War journey.

I also dedicate this book to the memory of Corporal William Danforth Brooks and Private George Simon Brooks both of Company F, Connecticut's 16th Infantry and the men whose spirits sent me forth on this journey, guiding my hand through their story and the stories of their fallen comrades. They were gone too soon and too young, but their memory and sacrifice shall be carried forward.

To all my ancestors and the ancestors of those reading this, thank you for fighting with loyalty and conviction for your country and your beliefs.

ACKNOWLEDGMENTS

A book is never accomplished by just a single author; an entire support system comes together of family, friends, historians and experts who make the book possible and are integral to its success. The following people made this book possible and without them, this book would cease to exist!

I, first and foremost, want to acknowledge and express my sincere gratitude to my husband, Marty Reardon Jr. who encourages me to write, to follow my dreams and who believes in my ideas for books, tours, lectures and beyond. He never questions my ability or any idea I come up with and instead asks, "How can I help?" To have a spouse who takes their love and partnership above and beyond is something I am grateful for daily. Marty drove with me across the East Coast twice and through upstate New York for this book, walking battlefields and photographing every monument and grave I may need. He went to every museum and historical society, I suggested and enthusiastically participated in information-gathering. Marty did not hesitate to go out in 100-degree summer weather in the middle of Georgia for a photograph or in below zero temperatures in the cold new England winter to capture the perfect picture I had in mind. He stood in cemeteries with me and dark battlefields conducting investigations and even watched me run away from the Antietam cornfield at sunset with a hearty laugh. His heart is felt in every picture and without his assistance and support, this book would most certainly not be here.

Then there is my best friend and the lead tour guide of Seaside Shadows Haunted History Tours, Andrew Hill, who took on the bulk of our late season tours so I could focus on Civil War research and writing, who joined Marty and I on some of our road trips and did not hesitate to stand in battlefields or cemeteries talking to spirits and helping find unique information. No matter the day, Andrew says, "You know I'm here for you." When Marty went on photography trips while I wrote, Andrew would go with him. And most of all, Andrew was a sounding board for every fact, photo or finding that I had with this book giving me his excellent opinions and approval.

To the band members and singer-songwriters of Whiskey Myers and Tennessee Jet, I want to express my deepest gratitude for the profound and haunting lyrics and breathtaking delivery of the song, "Bury My Bones," that encompassed the stories of these soldiers, their identity and their tragedy in the most poetic way imaginable. This song, not only inspired a series theme but captured the relevance and importance of sharing the stories of these individuals and helping them to never be forgotten. I think I speak for the spirits as well as myself when I saw, we are all eternally grateful for the lyricism, poetry and melody.

I want to also acknowledge some fantastic historians and museums beginning with the New England Civil War Museum in Vernon, Connecticut. From the get-go, the Museum Director, Matt Reardon was accommodating and helpful, ensuring we got a visit as soon as COVID restrictions allowed. Dan Hayden of the museum gave us an excellent tour while Matt introduced us to the rifles and to the library. Matt, also, kindly shared the experiences of his third great-grandfather at Andersonville Prison and his life beyond by sharing his pension papers and letters with me for this book. He also shared his spiritual experiences as a descendant who visited Andersonville and answered questions of Connecticut Civil War men at all hours of the day. To Matt and the New England Civil War Museum, I extend my most heartfelt gratitude.

Then there is the beautiful Middlesex County Historical Society and General Joseph Mansfield House run by Director, Jesse Nasta. At first meet, Jesse had all the books and documents relating to Mansfield ready for me to go through at no rush. Be it photographs or copies, he did not hesitate, and he allowed us to conduct a paranormal investigation of the house for the first time in recorded history. Jesse gave wonderful book and landmark recommendations and has expressed a warm welcome for me throughout the entire process.

Then there is of course, the fantastic, Michael Amico, who wrote his dissertation at Yale University, entitled "The Forgotten Union of the Two Henrys: A History of the "Peculiar and Rarest Intimacy" of the American Civil War," exploring the friendship and romance of Henry Ward Camp and Henry Clay Trumbull and who answered all my questions about the two men to best understand and paint a picture. Now working and living in Germany, Michael would reach out to my requests almost immediately and with detail, always willing to offer more crucial insight to their story.

To the Friends of the U.S. Grant Cottage State Historic Site and our tour guide and site Operations Manager, Ben Kemp, there is an enormous thanks for the personalized private tour of the final home of Ulysses S. Grant. Ben gave enormous insight on Grant's mindset at the end of his life as he wrote his memoirs, met with Mark Twain and the Union men who came to see him in his final weeks and of his evolution from General to President to Citizen. The insight behind the scenes to Grant with such intimate interpretation of the facts gave an incredible feel for the entire Union Army and a close-up view of death practices of the 19th century.

To our tour guide, Mr. Aaron Bradford of Genteel & Bard Tours of Savannah, Georgia, there is a hearty thanks owed for his special information regarding Sherman's March to the Sea with the Union and making us laugh with his jokes about the local children who thought he had a devil's tail. He treated a couple "bonafide Yankees," with enthusiasm and an abundance of historical knowledge.

To the Madrigal Inn in Macon, Georgia and the Marshall House in Savannah, GA who served as Civil War Hospitals and provided a great space to spend a spooky retreat, I want to extend a thanks for the historic paranormal hotspots and excellent accommodations. Additionally to Vernell, the lovely Airbnb host at Antietam and all the wonderful hosts along the way who made our research possible with a personal touch, I cannot say thank you enough to these fine folks.

I want to thank Fran Freyocke, our Gettysburg Tour Guide for a personal four-hour tour of the Gettysburg battlefields specially focused on Connecticut's position at the battle.

To the National Park Service and American Battlefield Trust, I want to acknowledge the fantastic upkeep of the fields, the sharing of the stories and the enthusiastic and helpful park rangers met at every location.

To Sunshine Estar and her husband Jaeson Davis, who have assisted at Seaside Shadows Haunted History Tours taking away some of the workload while this book was researched and written and stood in the dark quiet of General Lyon's Monument and Birthplace reaching out with our paranormal devices, I want to acknowledge and express gratitude for their continued support.

To the authors, historians and paranormal researchers who came before me and documented their experiences and knowledge on topics, the value of all their work cannot be overstated.

And to my family, my sisters, my mom, my brothers-in-law and my siblings, thank you for your patience with me as I traveled and wrote on weekends and weekdays and bequeathed unsolicited information on the Civil War to at family get-togethers, they deserve all the gratitude for listening and for supporting this journey.

TABLE OF CONTENTS

INTRODUCTION

The Bury My Bones Series & The Civil War Ghosts of Connecticut

Growing up in Connecticut, the native state to my mother and several generations of her family before her, one would surmise my roots to be Yankee roots alone. However, the Nutmeg State was far from native to my father and his ancestors who hail from central Georgia in the Macon region. As such I had very dichotomous lessons in my household regarding the Civil War and was introduced to both sides of this bloody and brutal affair throughout my young life. Being a Connecticut native, myself, I was always glad of the Union's victory, the unification of our country, the fulfilling of the American dream and the ideas of brotherhood and sisterhood alike. I did, however, have sympathies for my Southern ancestors who fought with fierce loyalty and were fearful of loss of their farms, who had a sense of allegiance to their home that was unquestionable, and it was these loyalties, fears, desires and dreams that led to different views for a country. As I settled, upon writing this book, in many ways a follow-up to my previous book about the American Revolution, I looked to my ancestors as I did then…traveling with them through the centuries and reading of what they endured and fought for. Looking at my family tree during the Civil War, I found ancestors on both sides and it became clear at that moment, that it was that alone, that familiar division that made the war the entire heartbreaking and tragic affair that it was. It was ultimate haunting effect of the Civil War – knowing that the fight was brother against brother, American against American, pitted against each other in this desperate and ruthless landscape. When one thinks of a haunting, they think most often of poltergeist activity and unfinished business but to understand hauntings is to understand history, to immerse oneself in the stories of those lives changed the course of the future, whose presence made us all who we are and whose deaths could leave behind sobering reminders of the brief flicker of life. Oftentimes when a historic spirit, in regards to war, is encountered in a paranormal way, they are there for a purpose – perhaps not having moved forward from the tragedy of their shocking or violent death, or rather reliving a moment in time that was so impactful, the cycle of which cannot be escaped and sometimes, they are there to share their story, to be remembered. And that is precisely what this book series is meant to do – to share the stories of the boys, the boys become men by experience and pain, the men with labored life experience and those who loved and knew them. This book will focus on some of those who gave their lives to the Union cause, while the series will explore those who gave their lives to the Confederate cause as well – all of them sharing American blood and an unwavering loyalty to their family and homes. In this series, we will visit the places where hundreds of thousands of men would lose their lives, where their blood both literally and ethereally would stain the land. And we shall come full circle to visit the plots where they came to be interred.

"If I die young, write my mother/tell her that I love her but my soul's gone home/Tell my kin to pick up a shovel/wrestle that sugar sand and bury my bones/Wont you bury my bones beneath these pines/When it comes time for you to bury my bones?"

The Whiskey Myers song, "Bury My Bones," penned by band member, John Jeffers and fellow recording artist, Tennessee Jet is one you will read a bit more about in this book for it is one the spirits themselves seemed to place the radio, that described their turmoiled journey and brevity of life during America's most violent period of history. In fact, in this book, I will tell you when the spirits seemingly…put the song on the radio but no spoilers in the intro, right? The song was not written as Civil War poetry, (though it could have been,) however, it is the story of men, individuals, longing to come home and be remembered and that is what the *Bury My Bones* series is here to do – share those stories of those who gave everything for their country, their families, their homes – many of them far too young, others immensely experienced taken by surprise and all of them gone too soon. The series will take us through American wars, but more importantly introduce us to the people who were in them and lost to them.

Now, one may think that my motivation in writing this would come naturally after the American Revolution, but I am a spiritual person who believes that the right path will make itself known. In the recent pandemic in our country, I set forth to film some online videos for my customer base with my tours featuring local burials of note. One evening, in a dream, I encountered what appeared to be two Civil War soldiers, young, energetic and eager. I didn't remember much upon awakening, but I was immediately grabbing my phone and Googling Civil War burials near me – I remember having the distinct impression, that whoever I encountered hailed not terribly far from where I reside in Connecticut. Immediately, through the Connecticut Historical Society, I found out about a plot for two brothers who perished in the war, originally from the town next to mine, Haddam, Connecticut. The two boys, who had just transitioned into men were William Brooks and George S. Brooks, both enlisted into the 16th CT and both would become POW's during the war, one dying in the brutal conditions at Andersonville Prison in Georgia, and the other having been released Andersonville, perished upon returning to his unit in Wilmington, North Carolina being unable to survive the conditions of starvation and dysentery no longer, the same conditions that too claimed his brother's life. They would pass within a year of each other leaving their family without sons, their parents to grow into old age never seeing the smart young men they would send to university ever again. But one thing became evident in reading about their burial site and monument built by their father – that it was unclear where their remains were interred. Studying the brothers Brooks, I learned about the 16th Connecticut and their terrible runs at the Battle of Antietam, at Plymouth, their captures, their deaths and went on a journey to find the brothers and share their story. They selected this as their time to share the stories of the forgotten, the remembered, those who believed in a perfect union and who died among their brethren for that belief.

This book, focused on my home state of Connecticut, will take the reader on a journey that starts in our beloved Constitution State – a place of provisions, a home to abolitionists and a domain of brave men, introduce you to some of the thousands of characters who would leave an immeasurable mark on history and travel with them to and below the Mason-Dixon line where they will face hardship, brutality and war and back home, where few return and many come to be buried at some of the most prominent cemeteries in the Nutmeg State. Meet the men of Connecticut without whom there would be no Union, the men whose spirits call out from beyond, whose stories are awaiting to be told.

Brooks Monument & Grave Haddam (McInvale Photo)

Unrivaled Patriotism of Connecticut's Motivators:

The Provision State's Contributors, Inventors and Fierce Abolitionists Who Influenced the Civil War

"God created men, Col. Colt made them equal" – Samuel Colt

"A human soul is not to be trifled with." – P.T. Barnum

"I, John Brown, am now quite certain that the crimes of this guilty land will never be purged away but with blood." – John Brown

"Simply because I am investigating phenomena that claim the attention of the whole scientific world...now you dare to call me insane?" – Isabella Beecher Hooker

Inventors, Gunsmiths, Fighters, Circus Entertainers, Abolitionists, Authors, Suffragists and Mediums – are titles that belong to four Connecticut natives who would provide for and inspire the war...this is their journey and their haunting legacy.

When one thinks of provisions, they may find themselves thinking most often of food rations for weary soldiers and during the American Revolutionary War, the colony of Connecticut began earning it's nickname the Provision State for providing such food rations at an affordable price to the Continental Army. They were also able to provide clothing and other such goods but in a post-

Industrial Revolution world, the provisions that would come from the Constitution State would prove to be essential for the Union Army if they stood any chance at victory over the secessionists.

Connecticut had several motivations into joining the Union cause and supporting it so fiercely – sending her sons to the bloodiest and most action-ridden battles of all. Though, Connecticut was a bit more conservative in its ideals than its neighbors in Massachusetts. Even Abraham Lincoln won his election in Connecticut by only a small margin. Connecticut still had a solid idealistic seat in New England and for the Northern cause. By 1860, slavery had been abolished in the state for thirteen years. Some believe that in Connecticut, it was less about equality and more about stopping the dismantling of a government system was designed for those in well enough position to thrive – which was happening given the industrialization of the era.

Some may say, however, that the Civil War tensions would begin decades prior – and would link directly back to Connecticut – where the spark may have been started. Problems for the South arose quickly when Eli Whitney of Hamden invented the cotton gin in 1793. This miraculous invention lessened the cost of production of cotton cloth and increased the amount of people needed to produce it with demand – thus tying slavery into the American South for decades to come. The North including Connecticut natives like Harriet Beecher Stowe, author of *Uncle Tom's Cabin*, became vocal abolitionists and economists felt that the industrial movement and abolition movements were being held hostage by slave powers. One of the most famous abolitionists of all time is John Brown, who led the raid at Harper's Ferry in West Virginia, which was the action that, according to many historians, spurred the Civil War and was the first "gunfire" or attack in many ways. John Brown was Connecticut-born.

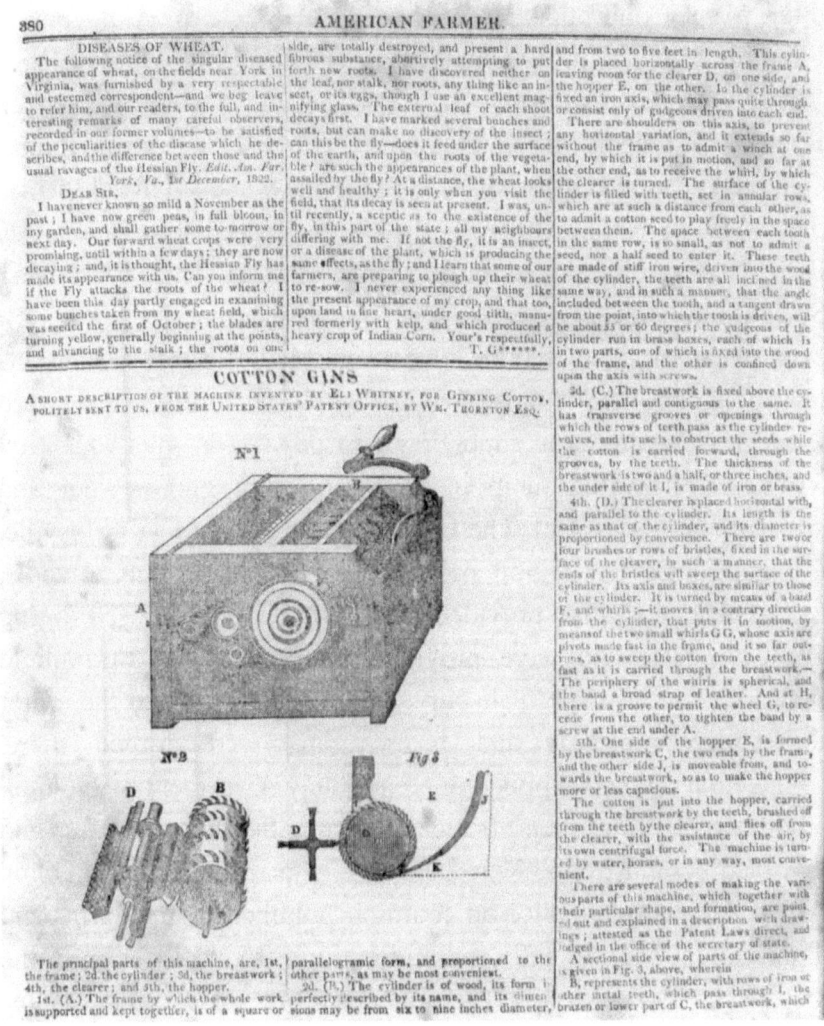

Cotton Gin Patent Eli Whitney (Courtesy Library of Congress)

Matt Warshauer, Professor and author of *Connecticut in the American Civil War: Slavery, Sacrifice & Survival*, describes the transformation of Connecticut upon seeing the need to support the Union in the war as a development into a "virtual arsenal unto itself." In this, Warshauer and historians refer to the shipyards of Mystic building ships for the Union blockage (i.e. Charles Mallory & Son and their nearly indestructible steamships; 56 steamers would come from Mystic), the gunmakers & entrepreneurs, 8 in total from Connecticut included Samuel Colt of Colt Patent Firearms Manufacturing Company in Hartford, Eli Whitney, Jr of Whitney Arms Company in New Haven, Savage Revolving Firearms Company in Middletown, Sharp's Rifle Manufacturing Company also in Hartford, CT and more new and small companies that were developing to meet the pressing need throughout CT. Rifles and revolvers were both popular choices. The Model 1861 Springfield Rifle Musket was a popular and common choice. Colt even would produce 75,000 Colt Special Model 1861 Rife Muskets to supplement the National Armory output at Springfield. Hazard Powder Company was supplying gun powder in great quantity. Samuel Colt would jump in to manufacture gun powder and supplement this as well. The Collins Company out of Collinsville, CT in the Canton region provided bayonets and cutting tools. Many believe Collins provided most of the bayonets used during the Civil War and were providing more than the Springfield Armory could provide. Salisbury, Connecticut provided the armor for Union ironclads and heavy guns were forged there. Connecticut, alone, supplied approximately 43 percent of the total amount of rifle muskets, breech loading rifles and carbines, and revolved bought by the War Department for the use in the Union Army. They also supplied an enormous number of small arms and ammunition. Musket balls and ammunition from utilization in the American Civil War can be found in gift shops in museums throughout the East Coast but spectacular examples of authentic Civil War weaponry and even uniforms found on the field can be found in the Museum of CT History near to the state capitol building. Examples of the 1861 Springfield muskets can be seen in the collections housed at the New England Civil War Museum in Vernon, CT. In sum, the Nutmeg State supplied almost 40 percent of the weaponry for the Union. In addition, Connecticut broke records for women's aid societies that would support the Union with supplies. Connecticut women would provide more support than any other Union State. There were over 70 local aid societies of women that reported under the Hartford Soldiers Aid Society to produce uniforms, flags and tend to physical and medical care for the troops.

Samuel Colt Portrait 1859 (Wiki Commons)

"God created men. Col. Colt made them equal."

Connecticut's patriotism was unrivaled as far as the American Union was concerned however one of Connecticut's biggest suppliers and rifle creator was the subject of much speculation and scrutiny. Samuel Colt, a man who played both sides of the dichotomous war up until it's very start and who had dealings with his family that remain under a shroud of mystery would have that dark shadow follow him to his untimely demise among the Civil War years. In fact, many believe in the "Colt Family Curse," which arguably could have haunted the weapons he designed and manufactured as well as the lives of all those in his family and on his stomping grounds. Many are familiar with the haunted Winchester house in California where Sarah Winchester built a house to trap and confuse the ghosts, she believed to be haunting her from having died by Winchester rifle. The Colt curse draws a couple parallels but also great contrasts to the famous Winchesters. Samuel Colt, above all else, was a salesman and many believe to be the father of modern marketing. His campaigns to sell his firearms were second to none and he was known most for one of his slogans,

No one questioned his ability to sell a firearm. Up through 1861 Samuel Colt supplied bot the North and the South with firearms as if he were selling them to Europe where he had often sold weaponry to opposing sides. But America was his own home and with the tensions rising, Colt decided not to build the armory down south that had considered building in 1859. But Colt had to be pushed into a sense of loyalty for the Union by the very own media that he had become the master of. When Colt sold over two-thousand revolvers to a Confederate agent named John Forsyth, the *Hartford Courant* and *The New York Times* blasted him in the news and called him a "Southern Sympathizer and Traitor to the Union."

Colt was furious to see the media frenzy turn against him in such a way and was commissioned as Colonel by the state of

Connecticut in May of 1861 – the 1ˢᵗ Regiment Colts Revolving Rifles of Connecticut. Colt had visions of grandeur for his regiment, the first to be staffed with the Colt revolving rifle in the war however the unit failed to take off, was never sent the field and Colt and his unit was discharged on June 20, 1861. The Regiment had been formed as Colt expressed his deep desire to Governor Buckingham, that only his arms be utilized as much as possible and have an entire Company with his new revolving rifle.

Union Soldier with Colt Revolving Rifle (Courtesy Library of Congress)

When the Regiment fell apart after many companies would not sign on to enlist in regular United States service for at least three years, the men who were enlisted, for longer the men that would form Connecticut's 5th were disheartened. They wrote that they really did not want to give up on the idea of "going out equipped with one of the most effective war weapons of the age, a "revolving breech gun" as described the Governor, enabling the soldiers to fire five or six shots in rapid succession, without the delay of loading, and which we had hoped would render us irresistible in a charge and surely immovable in case of assault, and so make the regiment very efficient and deservedly renowned in the annals of the war." There was also an impatience to go right away to war from where they were camped on the fanciful grounds of his home "Armsmear," without signing contracts or being prepared. The men were particularly disheartened to see proof of Colt's double-dealing nature and the smoke and mirrors of his showmanship when they met a company of Confederates that were taken prisoner. The rebels in a company of Ashby's cavalry were armed with the Colt revolving rifles that had been promised to the Connecticut men, to the Union men. The only revolving rifles that the regiment that would become known as the 5th, who were supposed to be with Colt at first, would ever come to have for the duration of the war.

Colt played both sides, until the very end. But it wasn't long after the disbanding of his regiment that the Colt Curse would come for the man himself. Colt would not live long enough to endure speculation or to play both sides throughout the war. Samuel would die of complications of gout less than a year into the war, in January of 1862. Colt's estate was valued in the millions at that time and the cause of his death was even termed to be one for gluttonous well-to-do men. Colt may have passed but his legacy was just beginning, and his weaponry was still being spread throughout the Union for the duration of the conflict.

Colt's mysterious past would not quietly follow him to his grave. On the contrary his dark tales would be talked about and spread throughout the region by soldiers and comrades of Colt alike—the tales of the Colt curse and the mysteries of his family – true crime, adultery, bastard children, hidden truths. Even Edgar Alan Poe would be inspired enough to write of the Colt family curse himself. Were his guns as cursed as he was? His wife, Elizabeth, would devote the rest of her years to building Colt's legacy as one of character and prominence and hiding the secrets as best she could – but the Colt family curse could not stay hidden. In fact, the Colt family saga is one of the darkest tales ever told of Connecticut residents and many would argue our Civil War ghost stories of Connecticut start right there.

Samuel Colt's armory was centered in Hartford as was the estate he had built in his later years called Armsmear ("meadow of arms,)" which is where he would be buried at first before being re-interred at Cedar Hill Cemetery. Armsmear was recorded to be "The most dazzling residence in Hartford and one of the most picturesque in New England," according to author, John Niven. He wrote that the "massive, rambling mansion by Colonel Colt in the middle fifties was a blend of Italian, Moorish and Gothic architecture, with domed conservatories and a prominent watchtower." Mrs. Colt would often illuminate the gardens and fountains with lanterns and host exuberant parties. His wife would inherit the estate not as long after its completion. It was built for her by all accounts and his son and nephew would be heirs to the rest of the family fortune…that was it. His son and his nephew would take over everything. Would they survive? And why the nephew? What happened to his Armory in 1864? Was it merely accident? These are questions that would open a proverbial Pandora's Box about Samuel Colt. It's hard to determine where the Colt Curse starts but many believe one of the biggest examples of the Colt Curse is the story of John Colt, Samuel's brother and the murder of a man named Samuel Adams.

The Colt boys, Samuel and John were native to Hartford, Connecticut. Colt spent some time in Glastonbury, CT and Ware, MA for indentured work and apprenticeships but the family seat was with Colt patriarch and matriarch in Hartford which is where

Armsmear Front Facing mid 1900's

Samuel would keep his legacy as evidenced with his residence and armory. John was about four years Samuel's senior and spent his adult life primarily as a fur trader and bookkeeper. His military endeavors ended with him forging a letter for his own discharge – some could even say that both Colt brothers had a romanced idea of being military men, but it was all pomp and circumstance. They were more successful in business. Nevertheless, let's start with the criminal story that would put a dark cloud over the Colt's in the 1840's. John struggled with his professional career except when it came to bookkeeping and he even published a book on double-entry bookkeeping when he was just 28-years-old in 1838. By May of 1841, wanting to pursue his career of writing about bookkeeping, John moved to Manhattan with a young woman, pregnant, who he said was his wife though she was not. He hired a printer named Samuel Adams for his pursuits. The pregnant woman was a part of the story...but her truths wouldn't be speculated upon until after the more sinister crime took place on September 17th, 1841.

Samuel Adams, the printer and John had a disagreement on the amount of money owed to Adams when Colt was summoned to his office for a meeting. Colt believed he owed Adams less than he was asking for. The argument over the disputed sum grew physical and according to Colt, Adam's took the next step and shoved him up against the wall twisting his handkerchief to cut off his airways. Colt would say, he had to act quickly when overpowered, and then he would state,

"I reached for a hammer, which was on my desk, and I struck him over the head until he released his hold and fell unconscious. He expired shortly afterward. Blood flowed in torrents from the wounds and after washing it up, I decided to notify the authorities."

First, John, decided against telling authorities and then John went to tell his brother who was having a nearby meeting but since Sam was still engaged in business, John took matters back into his own hands.

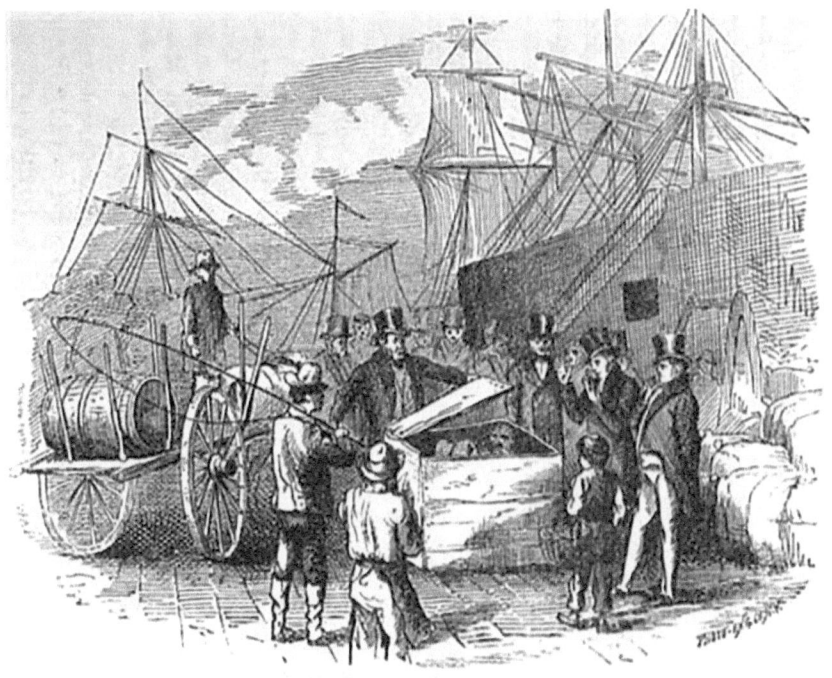

FINDING THE BODY IN THE BOX

Adams Body in Box – Colt Murder

33

Colt found an oblong box in his office that he felt the body could fit into. So, he stripped the body and placed it in the box – but being ill fitting, he stood on top of the box, hammered the remains a bit more into place and shipped the body off to a fictional man in New Orleans. One website on American Hauntings comments that Colt used towels to soak up the blood and while he did so, hog-tied the body of his victim to a chair upright so that he could lift the remains over his shoulder and force it to fit into the oblong box most effectively. When he performed the act of stepping on it, it was documented of that moment and testimony that he had "forced the stiffening corpse to form the shape of the container." It was only a matter of days before, John was discovered and brought to jail and then for trial. His neighbor heard the tussles, they exhumed the body off a ship and though John claimed self-defense – the treatment of the body showed there was a much more sinister side to the tale and John, was then sentenced to death by execution. Perhaps, you may all remember the pregnant woman, her name Caroline and she had just given birth to a son, named after John's brother, Samuel. John and Samuel requested that the couple be wed before his execution and Caroline, with strange, placid expression upon her face came to the jail before his execution for a wedding ceremony. They spent an hour together, and then John requested to spend time alone. During his alone time, Samuel and Caroline awaited outside the prison as smoke began to be seen and odors of burning building erupted into the air. The prison had a fire and, in the chaos, to extinguish the flames, prisoners were left to their own devices. John, by all prison records, took a knife and stabbed himself in the middle with it and committed suicide before he could be executed during this.

Many believe the fire to be a charade, smoke and mirrors by the intelligent and conniving Samuel. But this could not be proved. Stranger yet, the tales of Caroline began to be spread – the tales the young, illiterate German girl that was first Samuel's lover but being a woman of no means, a girl he could not marry. This and Caroline Henshaw who his brother married, could they be one and the same? Samuel would marry up into money and perhaps arranged the relationship between his teenage lover and his brother which would mean that Samuel Colt was actually the young child's true father and Samuel made sure that Caroline and young Sam were always provided for. Did John really die? The New York Police Chief believed he didn't and that Caroline and Samuel, put a different body in the cell and helped John escape – as people still received letters written in his hand.

Samuel would go on to live his life with Elizabeth and produce

Confederate Soldier Colt Revolving Rifle (Courtesy of Library of Congress)

a son, Caldwell Colt who would die mysteriously at sea at a young age as well. Illegitimate children, double marriages, young death, murder and intrigue are just a few common themes among the Colt family – a family of means who fell on to hard times and desperation. Theirs is a story of perseverance but also disturbance.

As for the Colt Armory, on February 4th, 1864, in the third year of the Civil War, fire would come to their corner of Hartford. When workers noticed smoke from the attic early in the morning, they tried to extinguish it bit failed when they discovered non-functioning water valves. The fire spread taking out the famous blue dome and the East Armory. Over nine-hundred men lost their work and two-million-dollars of damaged was assessed that Colt's widow was able to take care of later with the insurance policy. Suspicion remains that the cause of the fire was a Confederate sympathizer. Why? Well, Colt, though claiming he would support the Union cause and would provide weapons only to them, was still supplying for the Confederacy and theorists believe that the Confederates felt his allegiance and the Colt allegiance should be only to them and no weapons given to the Union. Colt's dichotomous nature followed him to his grave.

The Colt legacy haunts Connecticut, and their dichotomous energy can be felt around their burial plot at Cedar Hill and most peculiar of all is the spiritual nature of the Armsmear estate where locals for centuries believe that the appearance of the Virgin Mary depicts herself in one of the local trees. Spiritualism, you see, was at its height in the 1800's and it wouldn't have been strange if Elizabeth had tales of seances in her own home. Colt Meadows now sits on what was part of her estate and there is a shrine erected there to a vision of the Holy Mother appearing in a tree – a property that garners attention for its history and mysticism. Did the Holy Mother help Elizabeth in salvaging the family name? Some may think so. It's hard to be certain what the recurring supernatural phenomena may mean. Is it the Virgin Mary's Face,

Elizabeth Jarvis, or perhaps its Caroline Henshaw, lover to the Colt men and mother of the next generation? The mysterious face in the trees behind the Hartford baseball field will serve as a reminder of the Colt family's long-standing impact from the great beyond. More likely than not, the spiritual impact of the Colt's is forever embedded in the history of the Civil War and of Connecticut. Maybe Samuel comes back to deliver messages of hope and dedication. Walk in the footsteps of Colt in Hartford, and there will be an unearthly presence that follows you whether holy or not. Now some believe that the Colt guns could be haunted by the darkness of the family, but Colt himself would love nothing more than the publicity a curse could provide. So, believe what you will, Colt would support you. Colt's weaponry and past had an indelible impact on the American Civil War but when we look to Hartford, we find more than just provisions but motivations.

Similar in showmanship and a man who placed equal importance on publicity good or bad and playing both sides of the proverbial sense is another Connecticut businessman who rose to fame in the Civil War era. The man would receive scrutiny from both sides of the war effort and suffer, like, Colt due to this. In fact, their similarities both ended in fiery blaze. That man is known far and wide and his name is P.T. Barnum. P.T. Barnum is known most famously for his founding of the Barnum & Bailey Circus, but he also had a storied career as a politician. Barnum was, in many ways, like Colt a man of hard luck, a native of Bethel, Connecticut whose life throughout Western Connecticut provided home to his rise to fame; he came from nothing and was determined to be something, but he would do this at any cost according to some. Whatever "brought money into his own coffers" was on Barnum's list. He believed he could illicit money for any peculiar idea he came up with and didn't care whether he was seen as good or bad for it. He was at heart, an entertainer and during the Civil War, his museum in Manhattan, New York drew record audience numbers. The museum was a diversion from the horrors and depression that came on the civilians during war time and to see a Museum of curiosity and circus acts was a welcome relief. Barnum, however, had strong political opinions and served Connecticut as a local elected official at varying points in his life. Thus, he took the opportunity to place exhibits in the museum that were seen widely as "pro-Unionist." He had re-enacted dramas along the lines of supporting the Union cause and even hired an actress to perform for him who had been a Union spy. Pauline Cushman, the female spy, started working for Barnum in 1864. Barnum even became acquainted with President Abraham Lincoln during the war and brought one of his "Tom Thumb" performers to meet Lincoln at the White House. One well-known exhibit that started riling the Confederate sympathizers was something that occurred near the end of the war in 1865. Confederate President, Jefferson Davis, tried to evade capture and arrest in 1865. In doing this, he hastily put on one of his wife's dress to avoid being sighted. Upon being captured, he was wearing his wife's raincoat and shawl – showing that he was in a hurry. Davis, portrayed as a Southern Belle caught Barnum's eye. He offered to pay $500 for the dress and, in the summer of 1865, Davis was the Barnum Circus main attraction – Banner's of Davis as a lady were draped and Davis created the exhibit, "The Belle of Richmond," where he dressed a wax figure to match the images.

Barnum spoke out against slavery vocally at the end of the Civil War when he campaigned for the Connecticut General Assembly in 1865 where he served four terms representing the Fairfield region. He remarked of the equality of men by virtue of their soul by stating, ""A human soul, 'that God has created and Christ died for,' is not to be trifled with. It may tenant the body of a Chinaman, a Turk, an Arab, or a Hottentot—it is still an immortal spirit" At first glance, Barnum comes across as a hero, promoting the Union agenda and speaking out against slavery but Barnum revealed his dichotomous relationship with the matter during the same 1865 campaign when he revealed that when he spent time living in the south, he owned slaves and he did not treat them well.

Jefferson Davis Southern Belle (Courtesy of Library of Congress)

He said of this time "I whipped my slaves. I ought to have been whipped a thousands times for this myself. But by then I was a Democrat – one of those nondescript Democrats, who are Northern men with Southern principles." Barnum did indeed change his political party to Republican, aligned himself with Lincoln and promoted the Union but people were wary of what they believed. Benjamin Reiss, writer of *The Showman and the Slave*, is critical and skeptical of Barnum even despite his coming clean. In an interview with *Smithsonian Magazine* on the matter, he said, "With Barnum, you never know if that's part of the act or the contrition was genuine. People change and it's possible he really did feel this, although throughout his career as a showman there were many episodes of exhibiting non-white people in degrading ways." Reiss is perhaps referring to here, the man of diminutive stature and African descent that he called the "Monkey-man," but even more horribly he may be referring to the act that made Barnum famous. When Barnum was just 25 years old, he purchased and displayed on tour a blind and paralyzed slave woman named Joice Heth. He brought her around claiming she was George Washington's nurse and was 161 years old. Though he brought her throughout Pennsylvania and New York, and slavey was outlawed in New York, he used a legal loophole allowing him to lease her for a year for a thousand-dollars and he even used a loan to make it possible. When she died in February of 1836 at the approximate age of 80, after having worked for Barnum 10 to 12 hours a day, he made her autopsy an exhibit. Barnum sold tickets for people to come view the autopsy for 50 cents a piece to " see a dead woman cut up," as he revealed her identity to be that of someone other than Washington's nurse. This type of behavior does not reveal a man whose character we assume would be plagued with regret and change later. Whose side was he really on?

He wrote literal articles for the *Herald of Freedom* in Danbury Connecticut, campaign on equality and always know his treatment of others including the individual he called "Monkey Man," and the minstrel shows of white people wearing black face was behavior that carried right through into his later life and political years. The minstrel shows even included a stage version of Stowe's *Uncle Tom's Cabin*, where the slaves get freed perpetuating his vocal belief, at least, in equality. Barnum even went on to become the Mayor of Bridgeport, Connecticut. Reiss commented on his journey of respectability through the Civil War. "He owned this woman, worked her for 10 to 12 a hours a day near the end of her life, worked her to death and then, exploited her death. There's a shift in how he relays the story. His narration gets shorter and more apologetic to the end. Barnum's retelling rewrites history as if he didn't seem to know what he was doing, and this was just a little blip on his road to greatness. In fact, this was the thing that started his career. He had new ways of making racism seem fun and for people to engage in activities that degraded a racially subject person that were intimate and funny and surprising and novel." Who was Barnum really? Fun-loving? An entertainer? A man with real regrets? Or a self—serving man, focused on money and could care less about his fellow human being? Did he just have an impeccable knack for becoming who people wanted him to be. The Connecticut locals and Union sympathizers seemed to take him at face value – he had Union exhibits, he spoke with regret and changed his stance and they voted for him. The Confederates believed he was a traitor, they thought he was on their side and reason dictates that they had reason to think this.

The Confederate Army of Manhattan which was a group of Southern operatives who attempted to burn parts of New York City in late November of 1864. Barnum's museum was the site of one of their failed fire attempts. However, in 1865, "one of the most spectacular fire New York has even seen," happened at the Manhattan museum. The culprit has never been proven but some are still suspicious if it was Confederate sympathizers who started

Barnum Circus Fire 1865

the blaze.

The 1865 fire brought about wild tales of what happened all over New York City – animals jumping from the building and being shot by police, animals burning to death in enclosures, belugas boiling alive in their tanks, a fireman who killed an escaped tiger with an ax and carried out a 400-pound woman on his shoulders and more horrendous images came out of the fire where no human deaths were recorded. The wax figure of Davis would not succumb to the flames. A crowd took the bearded mannequin in women's clothes and brought it through the street. As the dress "revealed the statue," the crowd laughed and hanged the statue of Davis just as the songs of the time encouraged the deed to happen to the real man. You can still see the Davis statue dressed as a woman in the Barnum Manhattan exhibits To date, the mystery of who started the 1865 one was unsolved while the Confederates were known for the 1864 one and Barnum was heavily endorsing the Union, beginning a campaign with vocal anti-slavery sentiments, publicizing his prior visit to Lincoln and actively insulting the Confederate leader, some look to them as an incredibly motivated party that would want to burn it all down. After all, it was in 1864, that Colt's factory in Hartford was also burned down by Confederate sympathizers. Some believe that the circus fires haunt Connecticut. Barnum's Connecticut roots, home, establishments and more make him the source of many haunting legacies. Perhaps one of the most haunting is the Hartford Circus Fire in 1944, long after Barnum's death were nearly 200 people died, half of them children and their haunting cries are still heard in Hartford today.

Barnum & Lincoln Ghost (Wiki Commons)

The question remains, can we credit PT Barnum with an intro to the world of the paranormal? Perhaps we can credit him with the obsession of spirit photography. Barnum himself had a photo taken after Lincoln's death with himself posing for a portrait, where the photographer fabricated the appearance of the late President alongside Barnum. Though Barnum loved a good hoax, he loved his own and it was a set-up. The photographer William Mumler was held to trial for his fabrication of the evidence and Barnum spoke against him, as an expert on deception. Spirit photography was still believed in, but much more harshly scrutinized from that point on. Barnum passed away from a stroke at home in 1891 and is buried in a cemetery of his own design in Bridgeport, Connecticut – he Mountain Grove Cemetery.

Ah, PT Barnum, Hollywood's, *Greatest Showman*, and father of the entertainment industry – a Connecticut man of questionable morals whose influence indelibly came from the Civil War and the politics of the time may not be the hero we look for from the Nutmeg State, but an influencer, nevertheless.

If, however, you are looking for a man who stood his ground no matter what, and who history paints as heroic in belief it not in action, you may be familiar with one of the most famous of all abolitionists, John Brown, leader of the Harpers Ferry Raid who, himself was a Nutmegger and hailed from Tolland, Connecticut. John Brown, himself was quite familiar with death, and in fact, in the days preceding his raid at Harper's Ferry, he wrote to his wife and stated, that he does not feel any "particular dread," and that his impending death is a "great change." Symbolic of the Victorian era belief that death was nothing more than a transition – a move between worlds that must be honored but would never end the soul in its eternal journey.

The incident at Harper's Ferry has led to many purported ghost stories surrounding the old village, now part of the National Park Service. The events of the Harper's Ferry took place over three days of October 1859. Brown was a part of 22 men and the event was a list of who's who for the 19th century. Brown's goal was to initiate a slave revolt in the South and to do this it would be imperative to take over the arsenal at Harper's Ferry. A company of Marines defeated the Brown party. Then Colonel Robert E. Lee oversaw taking back the arsenal while future Confederate leaders Stonewall Jackson and Jeb Stuart assisted in Brown's arrest. The

John Brown's Fort 1885 (Courtesy Library of Congress)

Lincoln assassinator, John Wilkes Booth and writer Walt Whitman were spectators at the execution. A strange spiritual connection to think of Booth there -- the man who watched the execution, who would carry out his plan just some years later to murder Lincoln...the cards had been stacked. Lincoln even would go on to have premonitions of his own demise. Much like the raid at Harper's Ferry was credited with beginning the Civil War, does it stand to reason is that when fate started her hand on who would live and who would die? The raid itself started with gunshots from Brown and his men as they took hostages and took over buildings. The next day, Robert E. Lee and his troops stormed the building where Brown and his men were held. The storming of the Engine House where Brown and his men were, was brief but brutally violent. Lee had sent Stuart to negotiate surrender and to offer to spare the lives of participants if they did just that. John Brown refused via hand signal of a "thumbs down." It was shortly thereafter, that Israel Greene, the leader of the Marine Company present led the Marines to attack with fixed bayonets and breaking down the property doors with sledgehammers. Greene and some of the men used a ladder as a battering ram and once inside, pointed at John Brown and struck him with his "saber."

Brown was struck violently on the head and body but did not die. None of Brown's men would escape alive and free – they would leave the engine house, killed, wounded or imprisoned. The hostages Brown had taken the day prior had been freed. John Brown was never going to escape with his life, and he knew it. This wasn't the first attack he had led to slaveholders – having infiltrated homes with his men in months and years prior to murder slaveholders he found particularly horrendous. Over the entire raid several of Brown's own men, black and white and his own children would perish. Brown was charged with treason against the state and conspiracy to incite insurrection. Brown was executed in December of 1859, the gallows from Charlestown brought back in pieces later to Harper's Ferry along with, it would seem Brown's ghost.

But first, the body itself had to be dealt with. His haunting last words were in a guard's hand.

"I, John Brown, am now quite certain that the crimes of this guilty land will never be purged away but with blood."

So angry, so determined for justice, it was believed by some that his ghost still illuminated his vessel after death. When Brown was removed from the gallows, his eyes, still open had a twinkle and shine of being alive. The shine was so bright that the doctors continued to re-examine him to ensure he was dead as execution by hanging isn't always swift. Finally, certifying, he was dead but still being gazed upon by his glowing eyes, candle wax was poured over them. That was no matter for John Brown, whose soul it would seem would travel back to many places, not the least of which is where the Raid was and where he lost his children. It was recorded in the 1990's in the village of Harper's Ferry near the raid

Last Moments of John Brown 1885 (Courtesy of Library of Congress)

cite, a man appeared walking around the community. No one saw him depart a vehicle, but it was no matter, the man was clearly a John Brown re-enactor. His resemblance was unmistakable as Brown's facial features and lines...and those glowing eyes are unmistakable. Clearly this individual had taken their work seriously. As such, the re-enactor got a lot of attention from tourist who wanted a photo with the man they had come to learn about or honor. The man was asked throughout the day from varying folks, to have his photo taken with the visitors, and politely obliged each time. However, when the photos were developed later by each family (developed...because it was just slightly before the age of handheld devices that could take photographs at any given moment), the finished photos showed a smiling family, a family by monuments, a family by old Harper's Ferry, but that man that looked remarkably like John Brown? He was nothing but a blur in the photographs. Others state that the man that looks exactly like John Brown walks along the front of the old storefronts with a large black dog at his side, the ominous black dog is a legendary harbinger of death. When Brown reaches the fire-engine house door, both he and the dog vanish through the closed door. Many believe that the town of Harper's Ferry is John Brown, itself. His spirit all-knowing and all consuming.

Other ghost stories from the day came from the raid, itself. The Connecticut man, as mentioned, lost many of his own men and one of those was Dangerfield Newby, a former slave who was fighting so he could secure the return of his wife and children who were still enslaved. Newby had been trying to save enough money to buy them back. Whether he was shot through the neck or slain with a metal spike to the neck, he lost so much blood he died from the gaping wound and was left lying on the street for two days before he was dumped in a nearby alley and his body eaten by local hogs.

John Brown's Fort Harper's Ferry (Martin Reardon Jr. Photo)

Newby's ghost now walks around in his iconic slouched hat, baggy trousers and ripped out throat still searching and waiting for peace on the streets of Harper's Ferry.

Harper's Ferry was the precursor for the shots fired at Fort Sumter and the country would never be the same and John Brown's prophesy would come to be hauntingly true. The country would be almost purged away with blood. Adding to his haunting legacy, one of the popular tunes for Union soldiers to listen to and to sing together during the war was called *John Brown's Body*, and includes the refrain,

"John Brown's body lies a-moldering in the grave, but his soul goes marching on,"

Portrait Harriet Beecher Stowe

Yet another reference to his profound spirit, and the ghost of John Brown impacting the entire war.

To be sure, as weapons were created throughout Connecticut, the Colt Curse had settled in and John Brown lay groundwork for tensions to erupt into Civil War, there was still one more Connecticut resident who was blamed with starting the Civil War through her written work. That is the famous New England author of *Uncle Tom's Cabin*, one Harriet Beecher Stowe of Hartford, Connecticut and sister to Isabella Beecher Hooker, a suffragist and practicing medium who would conduct seances throughout Connecticut during the broad spiritualism movement. Harriet's herself held many seances at the home with and without her sister but Harriet's most prominent encounter with the other side was with Charlotte Bronte who she believed came and inspired her and talked with her. *Uncle Tom's Cabin* painted a picture for residents across the nation of the cruelties and sufferings of enslaved people and the inhumanity of slavery by depicting a story of "Uncle Tom," who is sold from a poor, destitute farming family to a slave trader and goes on to lead a life of torture separated from his wife and child who experienced their own horrors to escape.

The novel didn't set well with many who would deny the harsh realities that the country was living in and Stowe was sure to add a spiritual element to her work throughout the beliefs of Christianity offering absolution but also with tales of the supernatural spread throughout the communities of servants and enslaved being described in detail. There is even an entire chapter dedicated to a ghost story in the famous novel. This work comes from a deep belief and connection to the paranormal from Stowe, herself, whose house in Hartford, Connecticut is now fittingly deemed as a haunted location with phantom footsteps and flickering lights, herself sometimes blamed as the cause. But perhaps most fascinating about Stowe's relation to the paranormal is that she divulges her belief to another author of great renown, George Eliot, the pen name used by Mary Anne Evans. Eliot had reached out to Stowe after they had both received backlash for unpopular public sentiments or statements so that they could commiserate.

It was shortly after the end of the Civil war in 1872 when Stowe told Eliot about her "toy planchette," in reference to a Ouija board that she had used and a communication she had with one Charlotte Bronte, author of Jane Eyre and someone who faced great critique on her writing at the time. Stowe believed Bronte communicated and gave advice when necessary. Stowe would write in all her missives about the supernatural despite Eliot being convinced that the supernatural beliefs many Americans had were nothing more than a way of dealing with the fallout of the Civil War and grieving thus needing to validate the "invisible existence of the loved ones." Eliot, however, would be remiss to think it was just a continental divide, however, since she was living in Victorian England, she would be familiar with having a Queen who was frequently having seances in the palace to contact her deceased husband and some state the spiritualism séance movement was more English than American. Nevertheless, Stowe, knew too many stories, had too many experiences, she came from a family with mediums and communicated herself – so perhaps it's not so strange that now the Stowe house is haunted. Even paranormal TV shows have featured her house where shades open in the parlor and flashes of light emerge from the bedrooms.

Portrait Mark Twain/Samuel Clemens

It was just five years after Stowe's first correspondence about spirits with Eliot that her sister had a séance with Mark Twain, the Gillette family and several other notable folk and other mediums – a "party," at her house – she pushed boundaries, made Twain consider spiritualism with seriousness, even more so than his wife who was once healed by one and Hooker made it known that she would not be bound by restrictions – she would become a famous woman's suffragist and proponent of the paranormal. Twain would even go on to join the Society for Psychical Research and join in the endeavor to seek proof of the otherworldly. Isabella was perhaps more influential than she gave herself credit for. In her diaries, angry with her husband for daring to question her connection to the other side she wrote,

"Simply because I am investigating phenomena that claim the attention of the whole scientific world...now you dare to call me insane?"

Portrait Isabella Beecher Hooker (Wiki Commons)

Stowe and Hooker knew they were not insane...they knew all along that spirits communicated and made themselves known and continue to prove this from the other side. Where can you find the Harriet Beecher Stowe house today? Right next to Twain's of course, which despite his skepticism, is now also one of the most haunted places in Connecticut. And Twain, perhaps the most famous Nutmegger of all time, his birthname being of course, Samuel Clemens, would have his own role in the Civil War as the man who published Ulysses S. Grant's memoirs in his final days and ensured the former Union General and US President's family would never be destitute. One may ponder if the land of steady habits were the breeding ground for this eventful war as a home for weapons, abolitionists and the man who would streamline the industrialization of the cotton industry.

Harriet Beecher Stowe House 1905 (Courtesy of Library of Congress)

Today, you can visit the Harriet Beecher Stowe home in Hartford and seasonally, can even take a ghost tour of the haunt, where seances were conducted and where many people believe Harriet, herself continues to haunt the grounds. Perhaps Isabella will come by. You can also stop by her neighbor's house (Mark

Twain) and visit Isabella's burial at Cedar Hill Cemetery in Hartford, the same resting place as Samuel Colt and his wife. Colt's imprint is felt all over, but in Hartford, you can visit Colt Park, drive by Armsmear and witness the locations that perpetuated Connecticut's legacy as the Provision State. Be sure to look for a face in the trees. You may hop down to New Haven to the Grove Street Cemetery and visit the burial of Eli Whitney, the inventor. You can visit Barnum's re-built museum site in Manhattan, visit the Barnum Museum in Bridgeport, Connecticut or perhaps make your way to the Mountain Grove Cemetery where he lies in his grave alongside some of his performers. A unique cemetery is always worth a visit, particularly one built by a showman whose haunting presence can still be felt watching over his home state. Perhaps, if you're feeling up to a hearty drive, you may follow John Brown's journey to Harpers Ferry, West Virginia and stand where the abolitionist and his men (and women) stood, walk through the fort, what remains of the engine house, and stroll the museum from the National Park Service housing his weapons and the wooden beam pieces from where he was executed. But beware, whether you're driving through the land of steady habits or making your way on a road trip to sites of notes, spirits may appear and communicate at any given moment.

Spectral Soldiers of the Constitution State:

Select Spotlights of Connecticut Men Who Served the Union and Stories of the Spirit Energy they Left Behind

"As we behold the brave sons of Connecticut, one after another, falling on the field of battle, it may almost seem that our beloved State, doubly endeared by her abounding sacrifices in this hour of trial, is giving more than her part, in that richest of treasures – the blood of her children – to the war for Union. Yet, if she gives more than her part, she gives as freely as the light of heaven is this day poured down up on the world. Willingly she offers up her sons to die in the high places of the field; but oh, not without a pang – not without agonizing sorrow or regret... In that anxious hour he spoke of Connecticut and I never shall forget the warm and earnest words with which he expressed his love and veneration for his native State."
– Senator James Dixon regarding the death of General Mansfield and other Union men, 1862.

But how does one utterly understand the nature and effects of war without looking at humanity? Imagining the terror through the eyes of the human experience is a frightening prospect indeed. As historians and fellow human beings to all those who came before, it's impossible not to imagine this way. And in order, to best understand Connecticut in the Union and to meet the spirits of Connecticut, you must meet some of the men be they Generals,

Officers or Privates and get a small glimpse into their story while also realizing the immense violence, uncertainty and loss they faced. According to Connecticut History, 55,000 men enlisted for the Union and dispersed across the East Coast to serve. They witnessed their comrades died, risked their lives in encampments, skirmishes and battles that would be recorded the deadliest days in American history for the sake of a united country free from slavery. Who were some of these men? This chapter is intended to give you insight to some of the spirits who have made themselves known, many who never made it back to their beloved Nutmeg State having met untimely demise. Some are associated with ghostly legend others have communicated in paranormal investigation indicating their continual ethereal presence and yet others left a story so haunting and heartbreaking, their story remains residual and surrounds us with swells of sorrow and pride as we remember the sacrifices made.

Brigadier General Nathaniel Lyon

As we travel through the stories of the tensions that would lead to the Confederate fire on Fort Sumter, South Carolina on April 12th of 1861 officially launching America into the Civil War, it's important to note that Union Military leaders would arise from Connecticut having had strong influence from those notable figures and New England sentiments coming out of the Provision State and the surrounding area. Some of these men, already trained at West Point, served in the Mexican-American war, or both. They may have taken part in or witnessed military tensions and attacks that erupted when the iron was hot. One such Connecticut man of education and military experience, who was also influenced and motivated by fellow abolitionists within his own state Connecticut roots would find himself in Kansas and Missouri come the beginning of the war and that man is the one and only, Nathaniel

Lyon. Nathaniel was described in the *Hartford Courant* as a "tough, aggressive officer, short of stature with fiery red hair and a volcanic temper who was best whenever decisive action was warranted." His career commendations, fearlessness and leadership would eventually earn him the title of Brigadier General. His path would cross the paths with other notable war heroes and abolitionists including the one and only aforementioned, John Brown near to the time of the Pottawatomie Massacre in St. Louis. Lyon's beginnings were a bit humbler than one might expect albeit, genealogically impressive. Nathaniel Lyon, a native of the rural town of Eastford in the Ashford, Connecticut region was the 7th child of his parents and fourth son when he was born in 1818, and he grew up in a family that held each other dear, their farm work important and politics of immense relevance and discussion. Nathaniel's father, Amasa Lyon was an appointed elector for his town during Thomas Jefferson's campaign and his mother, Kezia Knowlton was the niece of the Revolutionary War hero, Thomas Knowlton and both his parents believed that he should be educated. Nathaniel had an inclination for academia and for fighting – and was described by his teachers as naturally vigorous and industrious from a young age however would often get into a bit of trouble for physically fighting with some of the other students. Fulfilling, a promise to his teachers and his younger self, after attending Brooklyn Academy in Connecticut, Lyon attended West Point in 1837, enrolling before he turned 18 but he was not well regarded by his peers. Lyon was inspired by the Knowlton side of his family, but this did not sit well with his father, a farmer who expected his sons to inherit his estate and be farmers. Nathaniel's brothers would fulfill their father's wishes, but Nathaniel would not, and his father was infuriated about this. Some believe Amasa Lyon's fury set in after his eldest son died at age sixteen and he took his anger out on his other sons to include the young man destined for a military career. Regardless of his destiny, Nathaniel was told that if he went to West Point and enlisted, he would not inherit any of the family property. His brothers would inherit, and he could have shares if he returned. Nathaniel was not stopped by this and his brothers were always willing to share. In quite a show of irony, the entire property is named after Nathaniel and is a state park today in Connecticut in his honor. The hearth of the family home stands in the middle – a beacon and remnant of what once was. The patriarch's spite lives on in history books, perhaps but not in legacy. Upon arriving at West Point, Nathaniel was keeping up correspondence with his sister, his brother-in-law and a young woman, only referred to as "Miss Tot," in correspondence with his family, though that not being her real name and her identity remaining shielded. Miss Tot is a fascinating concept for Mr. Lyon who died as a single man, never having been married. But for some years, he was enamored with a woman, who stole his heart. Lyon referred to her in his letters as "one absorbing object whom all other matters were of little importance in comparison." He also told his brother-in-law that even the most romantic poetry gave "poor index to his more intense feelings." The relationship as it were seemed to motivate Lyon to succeed in his studies and to ignore the sentiments of his peers who may not be so enamored with him as Miss Tot. His arrival at West Point was a rude awakening into perception from his peers. His father wasn't the only one who had a tough hand and Nathaniel's experiences were about to get tough, little by little. He had always been picked on for being a bit small in stature despite his large personality and West Point peers felt no different. time. William Sherman, a gentleman who would become one of the leading Union Generals, thought Lyon seemed scrawny, lethargic and not incredibly masculine. Records indicate, however, that Lyon, transformed himself from a teenager and twenty-something year old boy at West Point to a man by the time of his graduation where he graduated 11th out of 52 students. Also, notable, his vocalness regarding his opinions and his fury and distemper toward the idea of anyone being wronged. He would speak about the barbaric nature of duels and the need for communication. He would long for days with his siblings and talk about their ability to discuss all things. He spent his years at war writing to his family and visiting them if they were ever ill – a sensitive side not often talked about in the latter years or memories of Lyon's life. Upon graduation, Lyon even spent the summer at home before his first commission and described it to be a perfect summer.

As the years progressed, Lyon would go on to get the reputation of being hotheaded, a man of fury, a force to be reckoned with but his sensitive side seemed to always reign true to his heart as well. Those who worked under him would often remark dreading the sight of him because of his anger and toughness. Others mocked and called him "Daddy," for wanting to obey the rules. Some said, he was a curmudgeon, never having found a woman's love, destined to be cranky his entire life. So, what happened to the young, intelligent, lovestruck man? After West Point, his natural inclination to pursue justice along with his newfound strength drove young Nathaniel directly to the abolitionist movement. Nathaniel's military record was not completely clean – he has suspensions and even some arrests for getting into physical altercations with other soldiers and other such occurrences however also received a series of promotions and successes. Having gotten in trouble with his temper many times, it came to resignation or joining the Mexican War for which he picked the latter, was promoted to First Lieutenant and then subsequently Captain. Lyon was involved in significant action in the campaign to capture Mexico City in the Mexican American War where he was wounded and decorated for his courage. After Mexico, he served in California as a leader of an expedition against Native American Villages, which he ed and resulted in the death of hundreds of Natives in the Clear Lake region. At some point, his career, there was an abrupt end to his correspondence with and about "Miss Tot." Lyon's mother was distressed as he got older and remained unmarried so he would attend events and try to get the attention of the women he found to be beautiful. He said Mexico senoritas were lovely, but he wanted a fair American beauty. His shyness prevailed however and, according to women, he would blush to the ear tips in front of them. And women, did not love him in personality or appearance – disliking his red hair, his height and his shyness toward them. Lyon would continue for some time to impress when given opportunity but ultimately his romantic life would never return – Lyon was married to the military for the rest of his life. Nathaniel continued on into the ongoing Seminole Wars in the 1850's before he finally migrated to Kansas, a region that had voted for impartiality and unity yet would allow voters to have a say on slavery and repealing the Missouri compromise. It may seem hard to believe, however, when Nathaniel heard of his mother's aging and illness – likely dementia, he immediately requested leave to tend to her though he did not make it in time. His sensitive side and love for family, oftentimes covered by his rough exterior.

Nathaniel's furious and ruthless reputation began to precede himself on the battlefield. John Potter documents that Lyon was very much an eccentric in the pre-war army; he was a fanatical abolitionist and Congregational zealot and used corporal punishment for even the smallest infractions. The discussion of this repeal would reach Lyon's ear, and he abolitionist with a fierce temper like his predecessor John Brown, he was furious to hear of what was happening in his new home. John Brown, another Connecticut native was in neighboring Kansas and was a few years away from the raid on Harper's Ferry that would unofficially begin the violence precipitating the war, but another event would transpire near this border. The events were fueling the fires of both Lyon and Brown albeit, they both be men, of varying moral character but both sharing the same rage over slavery and being propelled into acts of violence at their own hand as they deemed fit. Missouri was a slave state with St. Louis being a Republican stronghold, filled with German immigrants and who would also be supporters of President-Elect Lincoln in 1860. By 1856, Ohio settlers, antislavery New Englanders and pro-slavery Missouri residents from other cities began to find themselves in Kansas fighting over the border. Violence against abolitionists and those with anti-slavery sentiments ensued. Soon to be secessionists raided the Free State stronghold of Lawrence and destroyed a local Hotel. South Carolina Representative physically beat a Massachusetts Senator with his cane and the tension were bubbling to the surface when John Brown made a move. On May 24th to 25th of 1856, John Brown and some of his sons attacked five pro-slavery men in their homes and hacked them to death. Historians described this preliminary warfare nothing short of guerrilla war tactics. Lyon watched this entire transition and began to write essays on what he witnessed, his support of the Free State of Kansas and for Lincoln. Kansas would officially join the Union before the ear in January of 1861. It was just days after this declaration that Lyon was ordered to protect the U.S. arsenal in St. Louis. In the years between, John Brown conducted his raid at Harper's Ferry and had been executed. The provision state and New England mentality, endured however, through men like Lyon who ironically, was not a big fan of Brown. He found Brown to be short-sighted and a simpleton. Lyon even believed Brown met his fate of execution deservingly. Lyon, though he agreed in sentiment, felt that the raid would fuel the South to blame the entire North and create more violence. Perhaps that sentiment wasn't all together incorrect. Lyon, in temperament and fire, was not much less impetuous. He had a controversial career prior to these tensions but he knew what he stood for and believed in and found himself in a split state – that he felt, only he could stop from joining the rebel cause. When Lyon, was placed in the region of Kansas, and Missouri, the main problem he would encounter lay with the Governor of St. Louis, a great Southern sympathizer trying to rally his forces and who had not much tolerance for the abolitionists as he himself believed in slavery, secession and using paramilitary force to ensure those things. The Governor was named Claiborne Fox and his headstrong support of the south would make the tensions in the St. Louis area continually fraught. When Lincoln was elected, he appointed a man named Frank Blair to be a Major General serving under William Sherman. Blair would be a political appointee to advise in the military and was immediately attracted to Lyon who was making himself quite known. Lyon could be seen a mile away with matted, shabby red hair and a large personality. Lyon would work on procuring arms for Blair's Committee of Safety in St. Louis. Missouri remained neutral with Kansas being a Free State for the Union into 1861 but that's what brought Confederate sympathizers there – that and their Governor. While everyone looked to the west, by April 13th, the Confederate attack on Fort Sumter arrived and Lyon took his opinions, his temper and his skills directly into the war. He saw this as a free pass for violence and to become a force to be reckoned with. When Lincoln called for volunteers, Lyon was ready. He would go on to write regarding the secessionists,

"Let them come. I would rather see the country lighted up with the flames of war…than that the great rights and hopes of the human race expire before the arrogance of the secessionists."

Blair and Lyon continued their work, Lyon was able to issue 5,000 muskets/rifles to the Union Home Guards but Blair received continual pressure to remove Lyon, a known hot head out of this leadership position. That didn't stop Lyon who went over their heads to the Secretary of War, acquiring permission right and left to arm other regiments coming from Illinois. As the Confederate raids began on St. Louis in April, Lyon and Blair started assembling their army. Four regiments came out of Missouri and Lyon was the Brigadier General with German man, Franz Sigel to the 3rd regiment. The war began, Lyon, with his Connecticut roots secured the provisions and with his New England sentiments running through his blood was ready to fight...little did he know that in just a couple months, he would meet his untimely demise and become the first General to die in the Civil War. Upon the beginning war, the lanky, mustard-loving general took his role from the provision state quite seriously and joined a pro-union military organization called the Wide Awakes – his intent was to arm them and include them into the Federal Army – knowing that Jackson would not provide the four outfits that Lincoln had ordered from Missouri – Lyon was committed to fulfilling that order. Jackson continued work on fulfilling his own military bill. He secretly armed them in the night and learned the importance of spy work. Legend states that he pre-emptively spied on Confederates during his moving of weapons that were not formally recorded and when he spied, he found an operation where Confederates were shipping captured artillery in Baton Rouge to the troubled and dichotomous region, he knew all too well in St. Louis, Missouri. Lyon and his men witnessed the crates and wagons filled with cargo being rolled into Confederate territory Camp Jackson. Being of slight frame, himself, Lyon dressed a poor farm woman, a widower who always wore black, and infiltrated the camp and was able to uncover Governor Claiborne Jackson's plan officially. Lyon called a meeting of the Committee of Safety on May 9th, 1861 and argued for attack. The local feud was escalating Lyon and his German immigrant friends wanted to maintain as much weaponry as possible for the Union arsenal were beyond furious about the Governor's, militia the Minute Men. The disputes were several in the month following Ft. Sumter, but on

May 10th, Lyon and his Wide Awakes made a move and became involved in a battle against the Minute Men. With 5,500 men, Lyon dispatched a messenger with an ultimatum. "Your command is regarded as evidently hostile towards the government of the United States," and he demanded surrender. Feeling outnumbered and outmanned, there was no choice. Lyon was able to force the state militia to surrender. This was not without loss. As Lyon and his men marched the captured prisoners back to the arsenal, those against the Union were growing resentful and rowdy and then there was gunfire. 35 individuals – civilian and military alike died in the violent disagreement between secessionist sympathizers and Lyon's army that day and the following day, nine more would meet their fate from the same outrage. This event was called the Camp Jackson Affair and it was Lyon's troops who effectively fired on the civilians who were sympathizers. Lyon would claim that he himself did not make the first shot, nor did any of his Wide Awakes. A drunken rioter was blamed by Lyon and his men. The rioters said they were unprovoked. It was following the events at Fort Jackson, that Lyon received lots of attention for him military superiors and within the week he was promoted to Brigadier General and given command over the Union troops in Missouri. He received congratulations from both William Sherman and Ulysses Grant who happened to be in the city that day. The capture outfitted the union with the captured booty which included two howitzers, several mortars, 500 muskets and considerable amounts of ammunition. Lyon paroled his prisoners in this time. And by the end of May of 1861. He was Commander of the Department of the West. St. Louis became a Union City.

The Southerners and rioters were outraged and referred to this event as the "Camp Jackson Massacre," and St. Louis residents sympathetic to the secessionist cause fled the city in droves. Many who stayed did not intend to make life easy on Lyon or any of the Union soldiers. And those who stayed were armed with a Governor

THE BATTLE OF BOONEVILLE, OR THE GREAT MISSOURI "LYON" HUNT.

Missouri "Lyon" Hunt (CT General) (Courtesy of Library of Congress)

with new power that would make things impossible for the new Brigadier General because Governor Jackson received his military request. Lyon did his best to manage this potential threat from the Governor and in June of 1861, still not knowing that his final months were upon him, he met with the Governor and the Major of this new Missouri State Guard. An agreement could not be made between the Governor and the Brigadier General. Lyon insisted that the Federal troops have free movement throughout the state and the Governor insisted that they would be restricted to the now Union city of St. Louis. Lyon could not stand for this and temper came back with the fire reflected in his hair. He proclaimed to Jackson, "This means War." The Governor was dismissed by Lyon and by law, allowed to go peacefully. When the Governor officially fled in the coming days, Lyon continued to conquer regions in his pursuit of Jackson and defeated part of his State Guard in the Battle of Boonville pushing the Governor in retreat southwest. The seat of Governor of Missouri was officially declared vacant in July of 1861, the same month Lyon had assumed company of the Army of the West. Lyon would continue in his pursuit of Jackson and nothing was holding him back. On July 13th in the sweltering summer of Springfield, Missouri and accompanied by 6,000 Union solders, Lyon would find himself a mere 75 miles from over 12,000 Confederate troops planning to attack the city he was in in just two weeks.

The two armies met up in August of 1861 at the Battle of Wilson's Creek just a few miles southwest of Springfield. Lyon faced tremendous violence and he would meet that violence in kind and reciprocate without question. Despite being outnumbered two-to-one, Lyon was ready to fight and he believed this readiness could fuel success. He was motivated, well supplied and knew who he had on his side. So, he led, what some would call an "impetuous attack." The General's comrades recall that the night before battle, Lyon made a bed for himself in a rocky holly to get some rest. When someone inquired as to his well-being in a seemingly uncomfortable place, Lyon thought with nostalgia on his home in Eastford and made a reference many Nutmeggers know well about their home turf.

"I'm quite alright, back in Connecticut, where I come from, I was born and bred among rocks."

The General got his rest in that rocky hollow and on the morning of August 10, 1861, he was ready for combat. The General led from the front where would become wounded at least twice– shot in the leg and shot in the head. His horse, as would happen with another Connecticut general in the coming year at Antietam was shot out from under him. Despite all these injuries, Lyon returned to his men on a horse from one of his majors. He was in the center of the combat on a mound called the "Bloody Hill." And led a countercharged of the 2nd Kansas Infantry on

Bloody Hill when he saw a gap forming in the enemy's line and ordered another advance. At this moment, having just mounted the horse and ascertained his next move, Lyon waved his hat in his right hand, turned to tell his men,

"Come on, my brave boys. I will lead you! Forward."

Portrait Gen. Lyon Horseback (Courtesy of Library of Congress)

And within moments, a shot rang through his chest. Lyon fell to the ground and died almost instantly as the fighting continued around his corpse for another hour and bodies piled around his. According to some accounts, his death came a different way just about 9:30 AM after Lyon had taken to fighting with the rocks that surrounded him. He struck a man named Will Morgan in the face and Will Morgan's relative promptly came up to Lyon and shot him in the heart at 9:30 Am with an "old fashioned horse pistol." The responding surgeon and medical exam would have to disagree with this seemingly Confederate fable. Assistant Surgeon Melcher who examined the body and remarked on the state of the injuries believed he may have been the only one to accurately be able surmise what happened with the death blow definitively and stated, "From the character of this wound it is my opinion that Gen. Lyon was holding the bridle rein in his left hand, and had turned in the saddle to give a command or words of encouragement, thus exposing his left side to the fire of the enemy." Lyon had died at age 43 and his body had been left on the field for about two-and-a-half hours before the Surgeon requested to examine the body and the Confederates brought his remains to the nearby Ray house at the Surgeon's request. After examination, nurses and soldier's wives kept watch over the body. And local women, Mrs. Kennedy and Mrs. Beal remained with the body until it was placed in a black walnut coffin which Mr. Beal had constructed under Doctor's orders. Mrs. Mary Phelps had the coffin taken to her farm via wagon which some believe is where he was buried before he was reinterred at his family plot in Eastford, Connecticut. Men told stories of the bold man, the temperamental man, the man of strong conviction who would never marry and would spend his free time eating an abundance of mustard-dressed sandwiches. They would talk of his fiery nature, his leadership and being one of the true men, who inspired himself by fellow Nutmeggers would lead Connecticut into its Union orders without hesitation. Lyon's body was transported to Connecticut with stops along the way for viewings before he would take his prominent resting place in the grounds now named for him – the General Lyon Cemetery. Thousands of attendees would come to the services and witness the marble monument erected in his memory and hear the eulogies of his heroism. Lyon would be buried, his legacy sealed by history and his energy would remain across the East Coast and in the hearts of all who knew him. On the Wilson's Creek Battlefield overlooking the Bloody Hill where Lyon perished is the Ray house where his body was brought. The Ray House, now part of the National Park Service had diligent caretakers over the years who preserved the bed Lyon was laid out on and the counterpane placed over his body before transport – items that can still be seen in the house today, with his mark of death. In St. Louis, Lyon Park boasts a large tribute to Lyon. The nearby St. Louis Arsenal at the site of Fort Belle Fontaine, has tale of a ghost in a blue Union uniform that many liken to be Lyon wandering about still performing his

Wilson's Creek Fall of General Lyon (Courtesy of Library of Congress)

soldierly work, but does his spirit come home as well? The aforementioned hearth and stone walls of his childhood home and family property remain in Eastford, Connecticut at the Nathaniel Lyon Memorial State Park. His body, interred just a couple miles up the road from his childhood home leaves us with a hot spot for General Lyon's spirit to roam.

His story written in books since the year after he passed. His spirit – everywhere. For all of Lyon's controversy, his legacy is undeniable yet for a man whose story is so well preserved, he left an awful lot of unanswered questions. Who was Miss Tot? Who fired the first shot in the Camp Jackson Affair? Did his fatal blow come as he called for his soldiers on horseback or while throwing rocks? How does one get answers from a General long since passed away? That is where the presence of a ghost of the man himself comes to the forefront. Myself, a practicing medium, my husband, a paranormal investigator and tech operator, Sunshine Estar, a local psychic medium and Jaeson Davis, a paranormal investigator and sensitive all set out on a brisk January evening to investigate the childhood home and final resting place of the General and to ask him questions. Armed with an offering of mustard to leave in his memory and for him, we ventured first to his burial. His monument is on an incline and surrounded by cannon – intimidating yet gravitational. The marble has an engraving of the brave soldier in his final moments, the lists of his battles, an eagle atop the monument and he is surrounded by American flags and the burials of his family. We set upon a paranormal investigation to see who was present. There is a quiet in the woods near Eastford on General Lyon Road, aptly named, a sense of being watched, few homes in site and the haunts of eastern Connecticut and the surrounding areas of Windham being close. As we came to the monument in the cemetery, we needed to figure out if the General was present. I felt watched from atop, and as we creaked open the gate, despite being seasoned in ghost hunting trips, a feeling overcame me that for a moment, made me fearful. I looked around, told the group I was spooked, and we walked together. We approached the monument and settled in, presented the mustard, adjusted the flags and we set up the equipment. Our SB-7 Spirit Box which generates white noise through radio sweeps was on and our EMF detector was out. Marty held the Spirit Box in one hand and EMF in the other – pointed in opposite directions. Sunshine sensed a presence nearby and her husband, Jae sensed someone, perhaps the General watching from the corner and gravitated to that spot. Standing facing the monument, I asked aloud, "General Lyon, if you are present, can you tell me the color of your hair?" I knew the answer to be "red," and being a "redhead," myself, I thought we could find some common ground. "a few moments later a deep male voice boomed the voice, "Red." Marty said, "My hand is getting hot, like something is touching it." We were all freezing but took this to mean he was close. "Where did you attend school?" I inquired of the spirit that had answered before. A few seconds later, the same deep male voice tone, sounded, "West Point." I jumped up and down – two, non-coincidental audio responses, physical sensations and EMF fluctuations confirmed we were in the presence of a spirit and that spirit had to be General Lyon. We asked if he liked the mustard and an indiscernible voice responded, which we took to be a positive response. Now, that we had his attention, or at least seemed to, I asked, "What brought you to Missouri." "War," he responded. I then asked, "Who fired the first shot in the Jackson incident?" The voice that answered was male but again, indiscernible. We took video of the EMF, "Please touch the lights, if you fired the first shot," I asked. The EMF stayed quiet, no lights. "Please touch the lights if a rioter fired the first shot," The EMF lit up like a Christmas Tree with lights. We repeated this process three times. The same – silence upon self, lights upon the other side. The wind blew, the flags around the monument whipped and suddenly, as we stood on the cold hilltop, we all began to sense that other voices were coming through, perhaps from the other spirits we had stirred awake and we took our journey to the park, to the Lyon property to ask more questions. Sunshine sensed that Lyon would want a place where we would be more uninterrupted.

As we drove down the dirt drive to General Lyon's home, it's almost as if he was waiting. Sunshine and Jae believed that there were family remnants or letters perhaps still to be found on the property, hidden in time. We walked around the hearth, remarked on all the fireplaces that remained, saw the beehive oven. Stonewalls marking old fields surrounded us. Marty turned on the equipment and I asked the General, "Do you come here?" The male voice responded, "At night." I asked of him,

Lyon Grave Eastford (Reardon Photo)

"Pray sir, tell me, how did you die?" "War," he repeated. "Were you on horseback? Whose horse?" "Other," he replied – again, true. "Were you throwing rocks?" "No," he answered quickly. I assured the General, I wanted to know more about him. "What did you think about in those final moments?" "The one," he replied, his voice echoing in the cold night air, the haunting memory perhaps of the "Miss Tot." We proceeded to get evidence that wasn't as clear, but we knew we had found proof – proof that the

General was aware of all he'd done, proof that he hears us and proof that his ghost walks his burial site and the site of his family home in Eastford, Connecticut and as for the love of his life's identity? He took that to his grave. Perhaps she attended his funeral with the throngs of others. Of the estimated 15,000 attendees that were present at Lyon's funeral, one stands out among the rest, a young aspirational Connecticut native, who would come to be known as the "Knightly Soldier," Henry Ward Camp, who performed escort duty at the service as part of his membership of the City Guard. Attending this funeral and hearing of the cause for which General Lyon gave his life, only added fervor to then 22-year-old Camp's desire to join the war efforts and confirmed his early enlistment was the right decision.

However, before we get to Camp's troubled journey that would cause his even more drastic and untimely end, there are yet other leaders and prominent Connecticut men who would not leave the early years of the war unscathed or …better yet, alive.

Commander James Harmon Ward

One of the earliest losses for the Constitution State, even before General Lyon was Commander James Harmon Ward of Hartford, the first officer of the United States Navy who was killed in the war. A scholarly gentleman who had received his education from the American Literary Scientific and Military Academy at Norwich, VT in the 1820's, Ward was appointed as Midshipman in the Navy by 1832 and served on a frigate in the Mediterranean for four years before continuing his education at Washington College which Connecticut residents may be more familiar with today as Trinity College. Having found a home in education, he became a Professor at the Naval School at Philadelphia and then ventured just a bit further south to Annapolis Maryland. It was here that Lieutenant Ward became of the five founders of the Naval

Academy and continued to educate up and coming sailors. He was considered one of the most educated and academically minded officers of the Navy and held office as Executive Officer. Today this Office is referred to as Commandant of Midshipmen. The war with Mexico, much like with Lyon, would take Ward's skills and he took command of a ship called the USS Cumberland for the war. Later he commanded another steamship. As he ventured from steamship to steamship and continued to each, he even had his own abolitionist work he involved himself him when he commanded the USS Jamestown to hunt down slave ships departing the African coast and during this venture, he became a writer – publishing Manuals of Naval Tactics.

By the 1860's, having settled back close to home in New York, and the siege at Fort Sumter having taken place, Gideon Welles summoned Ward and assigned him to go to Fort Sumter and provide relief. This plan was canceled when General Scott believed this effort would be in vain. Ward came up with his own plans to form a "Flying Squadron," to use against Confederate Naval and Armed forced that would come near the capital. The steamship Thomas Freeborn

Portait James H. Ward (Wiki Commons)

became his flagship and worked in conjunction with the ships Freelance & Alliance and several coastal survey ships. They became known as the Potomac Flotilla and on June 1st the Flotilla led by Ward was able to silence the Confederate ships in Virginia at the Battle of Aquia Creek and later that same month endeavored to dislodge Confederates at Mathias Point in Virginia. This would not be easy. When a sniper and several cannons aimed fire at their ships, Ward and the Union sailors gave up their attack and retreated. It was during the retreat, as he was sighting the bow gun in his flag ship to provide gunfire support for the retreating landing party, that Commander Ward was shot – the bullet going directly into his abdomen. Ward collapsed on to the deck and died within an hour's time on June 27th, 1861, less than two months before General Lyon would meet his untimely death, also by gun fire at the Battle of Wilson's Creek, Lyon, of course, the first General to die in the conflict. Ward's body was brought back to his hometown of Hartford where he was interred at the Old North Cemetery under a beautiful monument to his service. That fateful June day, at 54 years of age, Scholar and Commander Ward became the only Union casualty that day and the first Union Naval Officer death of the war. Connecticut men were becoming the most notable figures to die and the first to die. That was not a track record Connecticut could keep.

Major General Joseph Mansfield

Ward and Lyon made Connecticut proud and fueled Connecticut residents across the political spectrum to support the boys in blue – her pride and joy, her educated, motivated and skilled men were now on the frontlines, vulnerable, injured and dying. We needed unity, we needed a moral compass and we needed to come together if there was to be victory. However, the war that everyone believed would be brief, less than a year, less than a few months' time would stretch out for four more years and Connecticut's bereavement had only just begun. Perhaps nothing cut quicker to the heart of Nutmeggers than the loss of one General Joseph Mansfield of Middletown, Connecticut. The tale of General

Mansfield's demise upon the battlefield in Sharpsburg, Maryland in September of 1862 and his honorable service would be told not just throughout Connecticut but throughout a morning nation and Union territory. General Mansfield's death would continue to empower younger generations of men to devote their service to the cause for a united country as the war experienced the loss of greatness and the deadliest day in our country's history at the Battle of Antietam. Antietam, which will we detail further into this book, remains until this day in 2020 at the composition of this book, the second deadliest day in our nation's history, coming only behind the casualty toll of the 1900 Galveston Hurricane. Antietam, at the time of its occurrence was something never seen -- the casualties, the wounded, the prisoners was an unfathomable number. Over 22,717 would be marked dead, wounded or missing on September 17th, 1862 and among those thousands was the oldest General to serve and die in the Civil War, a man of experience and fortitude, General Joseph Fenno Mansfield. General Mansfield's beginning was in New Haven, Connecticut where he was born in

General Joseph Mansfield (Wiki Commons)

1803. though his adulthood would bring him to Middletown where he would settle. General Mansfield had an astounding military career. At just fourteen years old, Joseph entered the Military Academy at West Point, the youngest in his class, graduated with high honors in 1822, coming in second in his entire class. It was mere months later that

Mansfield was appointed as Brevet Second Lieutenant of Engineers though his first commission would not come for a decade until 1832.

The 1830's being a time of relative peace, made promotion in the military increasingly difficult to come by in one's career. In 1838, Mansfield was promoted to Captain and that very same year was quite eventful for him as he also married Louisa Maria Mather, the love of his life. You may recognize her surname from the Salem Witch Trials of which she was distantly related, centuries later. Over the first six years of their marriage, Louisa and Joseph had four children, one that would die in infancy. Coinciding with the start of his wonderful family life, Mansfield's career would continue to take him in interesting directions. During the 1840's, Mansfield was transferred to Texas where he served as General Zachary Taylor's Chief Engineer. Yes, this is the same Zachary Taylor who would go on to become President of the United State of America. Mansfield's claim to fame at this time during the Mexican war was his design of the earthworks along the Rio Grande known as Fort Brown. It was here in May of 1846, that one of the first battles of the Mexican-American War took place. The Captain was just shy of 35 years of age, Mansfield when he was promoted in 1838 promoted to Captain and had just entered his 40's when he became a leader in the Mexican-American war as a Chief Engineer of the Army between 1846-1847. For his bravery during the Siege of Fort Texas then known as Fort Brown in May of 1846, Mansfield received the brevet of Major for distinguished service. Just months later in September of 1846, another merit-based promotion came Mansfield's way for gallant conduct during the storming of Monterey where he was promoted to Lieutenant Colonel. He was severely wounded during this time and took about five months to recover before he went back to his post and fought in the battle of Buena Vista in February of 1847.

Mansfield served alongside several notable men during the

Mexican War to include Ulysses S. Grant, Jefferson Davis, Stonewall Jackson and James Longstreet – three of those men who would become Confederate Leaders and one that would be the General of the Union Army though of none of them could see that coming at that time. Throughout the early 1850's Mansfield continued his military service as a Captain in the Corps of Engineers and 1853 fulfilled the post of Inspector General with full rank of Colonel, resigning from the Corps of Engineers. In the 1850's while he was still third in the Corps of Engineers, he had distinguished associates including the man who would become the leader of the Confederacy, General Robert E. Lee. He had been familiar with Robert E. Lee and even served with him in 1831 before his first commission at Fort Pulaski on the Savannah River when Lee was still a Lieutenant. This post would be Mansfield's home for service until the outbreak of the war in Spring of 1861.

Period Charcoal Mansfield's Injury Mex-Amer. (Courtesy Warfare History Network)

Less than a month after the siege at Fort Sumter, Mansfield was nominated by the president for one of the new Brigadier General positions in the army that Congress had just established. He was sent to Washington upon being summoned and assigned to the defense. He fortified Arlington Heights and assisted in the engineering of all the forts around our nation's capital. He took some leadership over Newport News and captured Norfolk. In

Norfolk, he received orders to take command of Bank's Corps which was in the service of General McClellan. It was in this service that General Mansfield, anxious to reach his command and become involved in service of the Union army in a highly active capacity once more, led the army to Sharpsburg, the night before the battle of Antietam. Mansfield's reputation among his peers and those who he commanded was one of great rapport – a man seen with respect, gallant nature, fairness and bravery. For some thirty years, rumors would swell regarding the nature of Mansfield's death on the field, what happened, where it happened, who as responsible and after much investigating from journalists and other soldiers alike, facts were confirmed.

There were approximately seven rumored spots where General Mansfield and his beloved horse were taken out by the Confederate Army and most of this was chocked up to confused memories, inaccurate memories and lack of witnesses. However, the 10th Maine Regiment witnessed Mansfield's mortal wound. Mansfield and the 10th Maine were uniquely placed apart from many of the other soldiers in what was a remote section of the battlegrounds, nevertheless, enough men of the 10th Main recall vividly, the death of General Mansfield and even attended the site in 1889 for the first time in 25 years since they had been there to identify the fighting position. They would recall the story of the 12th Army Corps, commanded by Mansfield marching on the Boonsboro Pike on September 16th to the farm of George Line where they would rest. General Mansfield had a bed of grass and a blanket roof as many soldiers would create. Some of the younger men recalled that the General asked them to lower their voices when they were loud into the night. Other brigades rested nearby. Mansfield and the 10th Maine were the advance and began their march before dawn near to the Poffenberger Farm which can be seen on the field 'till this day. They encountered Hooker's Corps in the Cornfield, a bloody region we will address later in the story of Antietam. The 10th

Maine continued with Mansfield to the East Wood. They witnessed him upon his horse where her hurried the men to the front and downhill through a field where several piles of stone lay. The enemy hidden to the south and west, many among the woods throughout the ordeal. As morning settled upon Sharpsburg, Maryland, Mansfield had barely entered the bloody cornfield when he immediately beckoned the 10th Maine to go their left. They marched "left oblique," but Mansfield did not feel they gained ground enough to the left. It was apparent that he found their movement "unsuitable." A Colonel Beal commanded "Left Flank," aloud, his voice bellowing to try to hist the General's point home and turning each man to the East where they would parade through and knock down fences enroute to the Poffenberger field. General Hooker rode forward with haste of warning about the Confederates coming through the East Woods near to their location. They crossed the road at that moment, and it was matter of seconds before he bullets from the hidden Confederates began to fly through the Union men. The Colonel Beal tried to turn them around to the right, but this was in error. Mansfield's left was where they still needed to go but as they marched right in "double column straight into the enemy at half distance."

Battle of Sharpsburg/Mansfield Ex Rt. (Courtesy of the Library of Congress)

The men had turned left, until they couldn't, and turned right back to square one, and to certain death. With Confederate advantage, Beal suggested taking the risk of imminent death, but

Mansfield wanted to protect his men, he was a man of war. He thought on this and said no and remarked that the regiment could be handled "in mass," and that they should get out of line.

General Mansfield rode out of sight after these orders. Half the companies ran left and half, ran right. Though a fellow General, as soon as Mansfield left put some of the men back in line. Confederate Major, William Robbins of Alabama did not recall the Union regiments being dispersed, despite some appearance of it, nor did he recall exactly which road the ruthlessness would ensue on though Robbins recalls ordering his men to fire into the unit which caused the dispersion to the left that Robbins witnessed, never witnessing the companies that went right. Thus, this placed the men of Major Robbin's command squarely with the 10th Maine and General Mansfield. The Confederates in the woods were recorded to have been "well aimed, as the distance was between us (the 10th Maine and Confederates), only about one hundred yards, we had a bloody time of it." Only a few rounds were fired by the Federal Army before attention was drawn to what was happening with General Mansfield and Crawford and several officers. Mansfield had come back into sight with haste galloping downhill into the men shouting, "Cease firing, you are firing into our own men!" He was "fearless," as he rode through with his urgent revelation.

It was then that Captain Jordan pointed to Mansfield at the rebels in the woods with the higher ground who were less than fifty yards away. Jordan summoned Mansfield for a moment to converse, and some historians believe it was in this conversation that Mansfield received the fatal wound. The Confederates had been well staged, rifles on the fence to pick off the Union men – and in the open on a field would make Mansfield a prime target. The General appeared pale, unwell for a moment but proceeded to go forward with instructions for his men after his discussion with the Captain however his horse, who appeared slow moving and fearsome refused to go near the broken fences or to jump. General Mansfield dismounted his horse to tend to him in the Poffenberger field as much as he was able. Colonel Beal was also dealing with an injured horse who refused to carry him. They gestured to each other though the men of the 10th Maine could not sort out what they were saying. As Mansfield approached back on his horse, the horse still unable to carry him and Mansfield dismounted once more when the wind carried his coat open and the men saw the blood streaming down the right side of his chest. Having not noticed the men's reaction to him, Mansfield walked his horse through the fence and tried to re-mount but could not hoist himself up. The men surrounded Mansfield and told him he must receive aid and brought him to the surgeon. This would be the last that the General would see the battlefield. Some accounts of Mansfield's death differ than that of the 10th Maine and their recollections some decades later. Initial letters show varying reports and at his home, which is a museum and historical society, they believe that Mansfield was shot while upon his horse because of the mistaken assumption about the direction into which his own men were firing and upon noticing his error receiving a fatal blow. One soldier recollected,

"The General was in a most perilous position. The bullets and missiles were flying like hail and no one upon horse could survive. It seemed as if the very depth of the pandemonia had sent their furies and such a tornado of missile screaming through the air baffles all description."

One may wonder, if the Confederate sharp shooters were using Colt's rifles – if that residual two-faced energy was coming back and firing on Connecticut's own at that moment. Mansfield's fatal wound was a shot through his lungs.

Mansfield Monument Antietam (Courtney McIlvane photo)

Due to conflicting reports for so long, upon conducting a paranormal investigation of Antietam, one of the first places that I as a medium along with my husband, Marty and team member and fellow paranormal historian, Andrew Hill decided to "investigate" first was alongside Mansfield Ave on Antietam so named for the one and only General and to reflect upon the large monument built for him, the cannon marking a supposed nearby spot to his fatal

83

wound and to ask him, if he was able to communicate, where he was shot from, where he was. We were armed with the SB-7 Spirit box that sweeps through radio stations at a rapid rate so as to create white noise in which spirits may communicate, the EMF detector to pick up electromagnetic field fluctuations in the area that would be anomalous and theoretically, associated with a nearby ghost, a regular audio recorder to record our session, a camera for photography of the area, a Thermal FLIR camera to pick up heat/temperature disturbances and visuals as well an SLS camera, able to show shapes of figures visually on a Windows tablet using Xbox Kinect technology and a tablet. These items would come with us throughout the battlefield journeys. Upon walking the road and looking into the woods where we believed a strong energy was residing from, we proceeded to ask General Mansfield if he was present – first, we must know if the spirit energy we felt was indeed the man, we were seeking to contact. When we inquired if General Mansfield was present, the fields and spirit box fell eerily quiet and there was a feeling of stillness – something we would come to note on multiple battlefields and cemeteries – no sounds of birds, animals, wind – just the silence that is the calm before a storm, the dull roar of a stampede of men in the background that you could almost hear charging, the echoing that rings in your ears as you leave a crowded concert halls from the long experienced noise is how to best to describe what our human sense can detect. As we listened, leaning over to the spirit box in front of the cannon as if it were a phone call with a direct line to the other side, we introduced ourselves to the General as Connecticut natives of the 19th century that may be present. It was sudden, when a male voice responded quickly back, almost as in the distance. We all dispersed around the area, so that we could hear and discern its direction without overwhelming one area, but decided ultimately, it would be more fruitful to see if we captured evidence in any particular spot around the cannon marker. I proceed to ask, knowing his fatality was caused by gunshot, "From which direction were you shot, sir?" Suddenly a booming male voice responded,

"TO YOUR LEFT,"

with urgency. Andrew and Marty came back, and we faced our left to which a voice sounded to say "shot," and enemy before he responded. "TO YOUR LEFT." The session took us by surprise. His urgency, his dismay, the thick energy that clung to his desperate voice as if a part of him was left on that battlefield to urgently try and change the orders and change the outcome was beating in our ear drums and in our hearts.

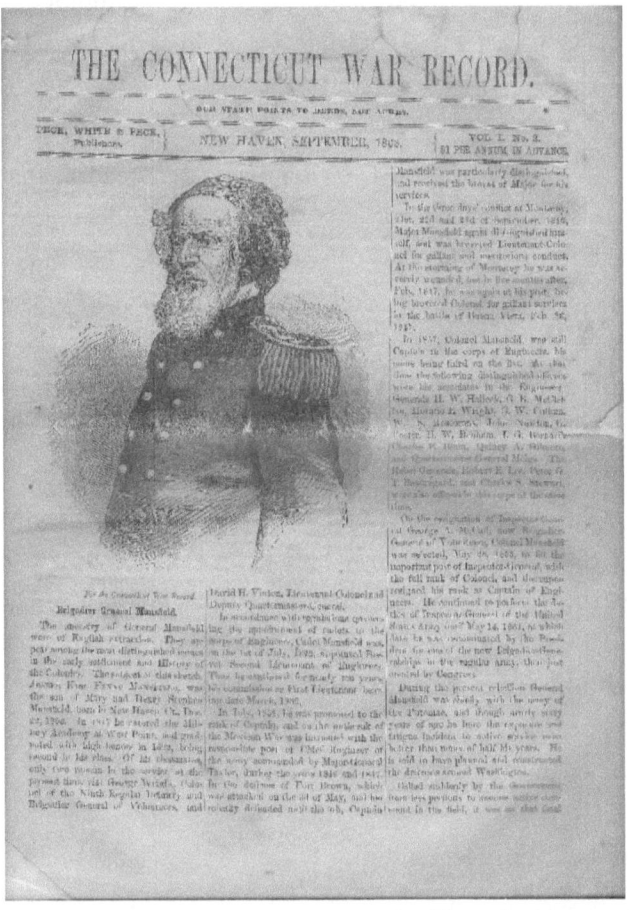

CT Civil War Record with Mansfield 1863 (Middlesex Co. Historical)

We left with heaviness but this marvel at the specific verbiage and answer he gave us. A couple weeks post-investigation, back in Connecticut, I began to review news clippings and accounts of the General's last moments. And the words from the 10th Maine jumped off the page, about his orders of Left flank, to move left, to go toward the enemy, his repeated urgings. Chills ran up my spine because it immediately struck me that what I had just read confirmed that, without a doubt, it was General Mansfield who spoke to us that day. The National Tribune of 1906 had a special edition dedicated to Brigadier General Joseph K. Mansfield in May of that year and consulted John Mead Gould's narrative written in 1895 on the matter – Mead being the Acting Adjutant of the 10th Maine and Major of the 29th Maine. Gould wrote of Mansfield's position at the final blow,

"The 10th Maine as guided by General Mansfield in person. We had all seen him for some time previous sitting on his horse at the northwest corner of the East Wood marked W on the map. He hurried us, first to the front downhill through a field where several piles of stone lay, the Smoketown road still being on our left. We barely entered the 10-acre cornfield when Mansfield beckoned us to move to our left. We then marched a few steps by what tactics call "left oblique," but did not gain ground to the left sufficiently to suit the General, so Col. Beal commanded "Left flank," whereupon each man faced east, and we presently knocked over the two fences of the Smoketown road and marched into Sam Poffenberger's field. While going across the Smoketown Road, Gen Hooker rode from the woods and told Col. Beal, "The enemy are breaking through my lines, you must hold these woods." After crossing the road, bullets from the enemy began to whiz over and around us…"

Gould's chilling description verified that what we had heard on the battlefield were indeed General's Mansfield's last orders, his last concern, the direction he'd been fired upon from was all from the "Left." Mansfield was on that field at Antietam by the cannon and monument of his name on Mansfield Avenue when he took that fatal blow, and he was there in spirit as well. Was his ghost destined to sit upon the lonely fields of Sharpsburg, Maryland trying to relive that moment? Trying to change history? Trying desperately to be heard? Or did the General make it home in body as well as spirit, able to visit the sites of his life as well as his death. When that fatal blow occurred on September 17th, 1862, Mansfield did not take his dying breath straight away. He lingered for the remainder of the day and most of the night under as much medical care as could be provided to him.

Immediately, after the fatal shot was discovered, a telegram was sent to Mansfield's wife telling her of his injury, but that he would be receiving care. There was an air of hope to the letter that just perhaps, he could survive. That telegram and the ones that would follow subsequently are housed at the Middlesex County Historical Society in Middletown, CT on Main Street is the Mansfield collection. It is of course, quite fitting that the Historical County is in Mansfield's Home on Main Street and the collection houses many original records including the telegrams, letters sent to his wife, Louisa and other such effects which can be viewed upon request. It's a humbling albeit surreal experience to touch the telegram that eventually told Louisa, her husband would never return. One telegram from Edwin Stanton on September 18th made it's way to Mrs. Mansfield and stated, "I regret to say that the sad intelligence of the death of General Mansfield is true. He fell in the battle of yesterday gallantly leading a charge." the letters from his doctors and those who were by his side letting her know that her husband spoke of her in his last moments and to recount to her about his insistence upon being wounded that he could not die as he had to make it home to her during those last breaths. Just three months after the war, Gould wrote a letter describing his last sight of the General,

"I saw the General put into an ambulance and then started forward for my regiment. The General was shot by the enemy whom he took to be the Union forces, from their nearness to our lines and distance from all other rebels. It is now known to have been the Twentieth Georgia regiment. Sergeant Merrill went with him to the hospital and made him as comfortable as possible. But I did not see the General again."

The surgeon, Patrick Flood wrote a detailed letter to the widow about Mansfield's injuries and his efforts. He assures her that due to the injuries inflicted by a *minié ball*, he could conclude that it was a rebel that struck him, not friendly fire. The surgeon encountered men trying to carry him in a blanket but "the jolting motion made him bleed so fast, they were afraid to move. I found the clothing around his chest saturated with blood and upon opening them found he was wounded in the right breast, the ball penetrating about two inches from the nipple and passing out of the back near to the edge of the shoulder blade." When Mansfield deduced it was a surgeon he was with and Flood confirmed that to be true, he said,

"For God's sake, do all you can do for me and stop the bleeding and get me to some house."

He was scared, he knew death was possible and he was not ready to leave this world. The surgeon set to work and did compressions, tried to stop hemorrhaging and brought him to a white house they had passed before, nearly a mile away in which he was carried in part and then ambulanced the remainder. The house was full, but the surgeon found a bed for him and had him placed there. The surgeon and doctor cleaned the General, removed his personal clothing and effects and examined the wound, no longer bleeding and a small portion of lung protruding from his chest. The surgeon described Mansfield "almost as white as paper, his pulse small and quick," yet describes him as talkative and excited – still talking of stopping the men from firing at each other as he had believed was happening in error. As the hours passed, excited chatter lessened to an indiscernible muttering, but the surgeon recalled his desperation enroute to hospital. "Oh my God, am I to die? "Get me to my poor family." Other accounts and letters to the widow, recall how he was asking on battle updates, mourning the erroneous news of General Hooker's death and then rejoicing in the news Hooker was simply fine and that the Union was winning all as he fought for his life. He referred to the news of the lost or injured as "Poor fellows," saddened for them more than himself. General Mansfield died with his final prayers, with grace and dignity, wishing only for his family to be here. To read the eulogies, memorial booklets and accounts of Mansfield as well as to read his own hand while sitting in his Middletown home, that he did not make it back to alive is to know Mansfield in what feels like such an intimate way. As you stand there and hold his collection or peer upon these letters, you can almost hear the desperation in the surgeon's voice, the sorrow in the soldiers and feel Mansfield himself standing behind you, arms folded, looking over your shoulder, shaking his head as if he meant to leave that battlefield on his own two feet and he still feels frustrated that he couldn't. Death on the battlefield was likely inevitable for the General and part of him knows that, but part of him would always desperately desire that his end would be peacefully in his own home.

The Mansfield home in Middletown, originally the seat of his wife's family homestead, the Mathers has exhibit space set up in the old parlor and dining room of the home, though the feel of the Mansfield's walking around is palpable. General Mansfield's children and grandchildren owned the home and it stayed with his direct descendants until the home was sold to the Middlesex County Historical Society in the late 1950's. Perhaps, its' the sense of knowing that direct connectedness to the most recent residents of the home makes them feel more alive, as if it's them you'll see opening the front door or descending the staircase from the archival holding. Historical Society and Museum Director, Jesse Nasta, allowed us to spend a cold January afternoon in the homestead to gather any potential evidence of spirit activity relating to Mr. Mansfield. His being new to the position, he hadn't become acquainted with too many resident spirits yet, but the old house seems to cry out their consistent presence. We began investing in the front left parlor or dining room, with spirit box, REM pod, EMF detector, audio recorder and photography. The REM pod beeped to detect temperature drops as male voice echoed in response to Andrew, "Is there anyone else in the house with you?" "No, I'm alone," a deep male tone responded that we assumed to be the General. He whistled. "Is this your house?" Andrew inquired. "My wife's," the voice said. Clearly, we had an intelligent spirit in front of us, General or not. "Can you make a sound to let us know you are here?" I asked. "Clomp, clomp," as if someone descended a couple steps. "That sounded like footsteps," Marty concluded. The three of us looked around, the camera picking up on anomalies trying to photograph them but the pictures coming out clear. The male voice was intelligent and commanding. We knew that someone was looming over us – the similarities to the voice captured at Antietam were eerie to say the least. Suddenly, the man's voice cried out, "I don't know why." We proceeded to the other parlor and the voice stopped, we came back into the dining room and the General's voice was picked up again though somewhat indiscernible. Was he still upset about how he died, thinking it was friendly fire – hence the "I don't know why?" We took the investigation to the back yard by the old stables, much of the brick structures original to Mansfield's time. We asked him if it was his favorite place at the stables. He corrected us – see chapter on Museums to see what his favorite room was. He answered us about his funeral procession being around "North Church," where his body was indeed displayed. And then his voice grew distant. He appeared to almost be resuming work outside, still talking and we, guests of the home, could hear him moving around, going about his chores and business. The General, we confirmed, was there as a visitor and former resident of the home, but he confirmed that he does still spend time at Antietam Battlefield and his final resting place at Indian Hill Cemetery. Mansfield's story did not end at his death. His funerary services in Connecticut were historic.

Mansfield's horse had perished in the battle as well, his wife was given compensation shortly after her husband's passing and was given word that her husband was too decomposed quickly in the heat to be embalmed and would therefore have to be transported in a metal coffin which his son would end up paying for the corpse's long journey back to Connecticut for funeral and burial. The train with his body made varying necessary stops along the way. It was on September 21st that the General's remains had made it Meriden, CT where they were then transported by carriage to Middletown. The body was placed in the Town Hall under guard of a detachment from the 24th Regiment of Connecticut militia before being moved to the North Church vestibule. When the General's body arrived home to Connecticut, a state he held so beloved, the entire state mourned and came from surrounding towns to attend his funeral, deemed to be one of the most impressive funerals ever conducted in Middletown, Connecticut. The funeral took place on Sept. 23, 1862 at the North Church. By then, the entire town of Middletown closed for the day, not one business in operation and the Main Street was draped in black. The funeral service began at his home with prayers for his family and close relatives and then to the First Church where they surrounded the casket, and the eulogies were given from men such as Senator Dixon and Governor William Buckingham. Senator Dixon notes General Mansfield's peers and the sadness of Connecticut's loss.

"As we behold the brave sons of Connecticut, one after another, falling on the field of battle, it may almost seem that our beloved State, doubly endeared by her abounding sacrifices in this hour of trial, is giving more than her part, in that richest of treasures – the blood of her children – to the war for Union. Yet, if she gives more than her part, she gives as freely as the light of heaven is this day poured down up on the world. Willingly she offers up her sons to die in the high places of the field; but oh, not without a pang – not without agonizing sorrow or regret. Beginning with a Lyon and Ward, now she closes the list – would that we might hope for the long, sad list were indeed closed – with the name of the oldest and most distinguished of her military heroes."

Oldest and most distinguished indeed. Mansfield's death was a shock to all including himself, a career military man of great renown. Dixon went on to say.

"Cool, collected, self-reliant, he seemed to me all that could be imagined or desired in a military hero. In that anxious hour he spoke of Connecticut and I never shall forget the warm and earnest words with which he expressed his love and veneration for his native State. As he honored her in life and in his death, so she, this day, standing as a mourner by his grave, honors him."

Mansfield was eulogized as "upright, scrupulously just, conscientious, domestic and religious," and Connecticut remains proud of him 'till this day. The singing of the quartette club, the slow tolling of the bells and the firing of minute guns signaled the beginning of the funeral procession that Connecticut's sons and daughters would witness in both grief and awe, the funeral procession including the Governor's Boot Guard of New Haven, Colt's Armory Band, the Governor's Horse Guard units of New Haven and Hartford, the Third Artillery Band, the Mansfield Guard, the Town Authorities, the Governor, the faculty and students of Wesleyan as well as Berkley – Divinity School and they made their way to the cemetery. His burial first took place at Mortimer Cemetery and five years later in 1867, Mansfield was moved where he is interred today with family and comrades at Indian Hill Cemetery in Middletown. Mansfield is buried underneath an ornate Connecticut Valley Sandstone monument, unique for it's kind with elaborate carvings of a U.S. flag, a sword and a hat remains today overlooking men of the same army he gave his life too as just diagonally across the street from him is the GAR monument and his brothers in arms from Connecticut's Regiments and Companies. Does Mansfield's soul keep watch over his final resting place and the resting place of so many Union men? His burial has the same silence, calm and peace felt near the site of his mortal wound and a young buck, that the cemetery staff jokes is always there keeps watch over Mansfield, perhaps a symbol of who he once was – brave, energetic, thoughtful and if you follow the young buck as we did, he will take you to the General and the men and then disappear into the woods.

Major General John Sedgwick

Lyon and Mansfield were two of the most prominent Generals and Connecticut residents to perish in the war. However, an exceptional man, and the highest ranking Union General to perish was in the Civil War is no small story. This man is certainly not to be forgotten of the Nutmeg State and he was lost at the Battle at Spotsylvania Courthouse after much experience and bravery throughout the war. That man is Major General John Sedgwick of Cornwall, Connecticut who also graduated from West Point. He finished his education there in 1837, became a second Lieutenant in the U.S. Army and was sent to "Clear the Seminole Indians," out of Florida, he fought in the Mexican War under Zachary Taylor and received two brevet promotions. He fought in Utah, raising to the ranks of Colonel and at the beginning of the Civil War received orders to report to Washington and serve as assistant inspector general for the Military Department before he was promoted to Brigadier General of Volunteers just months later. He was given command of the 2nd brigade of Heintzelman's Division, received injuries and always recovered with positivity. His men respected and adored him. There is even a statue and memorial of him at West Point. I will let you read of his end at Spotsylvania in the chapter on Battles. Sedgwick was the highest-ranking Union death in the Civil War and is now interred at Cornwall Hollow Cemetery in Cornwall, CT, of course, not far from the famous haunt of Dudleytown. George William Curtis spoke of the legendary, figure, General Sedgwick, best at the dedication of his monument at the battle site where he died.

"In all that great army, struggling in the slimy toils of the Peninsula, there was no officer more trusted and beloved than this most unobtrusive man, this most ideal American soldier. In person not tall, with dark hair, dark, almost still eyes, with the tranquil aspect of reserved power, a man who did not talk much or loudly, but who was always gaily chaffing his associates, who was smilingly suspicious of newspaper fame, and never went to Washington; a man of iron will, promptly obedient, and therefore requiring exact obedience; in council clear and swift, in action every faculty nimbly alive, his powers intensely concentrated, his soul glowing with eager purpose, as at a white heat, but not mastered either by victory or defeat—he had all the cardinal soldierly qualities, the positive masculine manly traits, but with them that depthless tenderness and sweet humour which complete the finest natures."

The death of General Sedgwick was so shocking, that General and future President Ulysses S. Grant reacted with horror and asked to verify several times, repeating, "Is he really dead?" Grant went on to say that Sedgwick's death was "greater than the loss of a whole division."

Sedgwick's home remains in Cornwall and it is now a private residence on Hautboy Hill Road. Sedgwick commissioned the building of the house just before the start of the war in 1859 and 1860 and then immediately went to war and hoped to retire to the home built on the property and farm on which he had grown up. A lifelong bachelor, he had no wife or children that would move into the home. The home is an expansive example of Italianate architecture popular of the Federal period. His childhood home, was built by his Revolutionary ancestor in 1818 but had burned to the ground in 1859 motivating Sedgwick to build the new structure as the family homestead. The house has a feeling of waiting to hit, a feeling of knowing it's owner never came home and one can't help but wonder if he still pays it a visit from time to time in his spectral form, wondering what could have been and honoring the relatives who raised him there.

Major General Alfred Terry & Brevet Major General Joseph Hawley

Not all Generals meet tragic ends. Connecticut had it's fair share of award-winning Generals, some who would even survive the war, to include Alfred Terry of Glastonbury who led the Union troops to victory at Fort Fisher, ending the trade of goods for the Confederacy through Wilmington, North Carolina. A native of Glastonbury, Terry grew up in New Haven. He received a Thanks from Congress for his part in the capture of Fort Fisher and was considered one of the most capable generals of the war despite having no military training. His military career continued after the

Civil War where he went to fight in the Battle of Little Bighorn, Custer's last stand and became a military governor of the Third Military District and a strong opponent to the rise of the Ku Klux Klan. He became a Major General in 1886 and is buried in New Haven, CT at the Grove Street Cemetery. Alfred Terry was one of the only exceptional native Connecticut Generals in history's eye that would go on to survive the Civil War. General Joseph Hawley was another General who survived the war and became 42nd Governor of Connecticut after the war. He served into the 1st Connecticut infantry and participated at the First Battle of Bull Run and was an assistant to Terry in raising the 7th Connecticut infantry where ehe served as Lieutenant Colonel. He had a storied career in the war and Hawley commanded a brigade in the Battle of Olustee. Terry was his mentor and as such Hawley joined him in North Carolina as Chief of Staff for X Corps and took command of forces in southeastern North Carolina after Terry's capture. He returned home to Connecticut and Hawley was breveted as a Major General. Hawley practiced law in Hartford prior to the war and made his post-war career for many years in Connecticut, the home of his ancestors as Governor and Representative in Congress. Both Terry and Hawley have statues at the Hartford State Capitol.

Private Daniel Tarbox

Here we are, in September of 1862, a year and four months since the beginning of the war at Fort Sumter, and two of the most prominent and fearless Connecticut men whose experience made them Generals and inspirations to all along with the most scholarly and accomplished Commander of the US Navy had passed away with the Civil War raging furiously after just over a year, no signs of tensions letting up and hopes dwindling for all involved. The idea of this being a quick conflict with a safe return home had been dispelled, barely a memory. And these just three of the countless lives lost – many without high ranks and little to military experience would be killed, wounded or fall to disease that ran rampant through the camps and battlefields. The average age of men in this war was recorded to be about 25 however many young men lied of their age and there were thousands of teenagers, fighting in a war with no idea that they were not immortal. One young man, from Connecticut took to the cause before he turned eighteen and had it not been for the communication of his spirit during investigation, clarifying his name and confirming his presence at the site of his death, his name may not have even been remembered in the books. Hell, the monument at Antietam to the fallen of his regiment even has his name incorrect. This young man's name is Daniel Tarbox. Daniel Tarbox, born March of 1844 in Brooklyn, CT was just eighteen years old when he would meet the wrong end of a Confederate rifle. Daniel's father a well-to-do farmer and his son shared his name. His mother, Lucelia managed the homestead and raised her young boy. Daniel's family had qualms about the young man serving – his youth, his need on the farm, their protective nature. They perhaps sensed that the war was to be more dangerous and frightening than anyone could have ever imagined.

Daniel enlisted in October of 1861 into the 11th Connecticut, Company F and mustered for a three-year enlistment on November 14th, 1861, less than a year before he and his comrades would encounter the deadly final attack at Burnside's Bridge on Antietam. He and his company moved around the Maryland and Virginia region beginning in December of 1861 for various placements and saw battle for the first time just a day before Antietam and it was a small skirmish, nothing that could prepare them. Unlike the generals and many officers, Private Daniel Tarbox did not attend any military school or learn how to be a soldier, fire a weapon, march orderly. This would all be learned by experience over a short amount of time under harsh weather and among others equally inexperienced. Young Daniel bravely continued with his commitment and remained in correspondence with his family through letters that he sent home during his time away. It was just eleven days prior to his death, when he penned a letter to his father with morbid undertones, perhaps a residual psychic energy had been communicating to him in some way. He wrote,

Daniel Tarbox

"I expect that we are going into it now for good. Right where grape and shrapnel and chain shot fly thick. And whole company's and Regiments are mowed down at one volley. If we go in, we can't think of coming out. If I do fall, you take what money I have sent home and get my bounty and appropriate it to yourself as a present. But I hope for the best."

Hope and inclination to believe in the reality of the violence you are facing are two vastly different things. The Battle of Antietam had many different skirmishes and attacks. One, the final attack was Burnside's Bridge then known as Rohrbach Bridge, where the 11th Connecticut would be on September 17th, 1862. 500 Confederate Soldiers from Georgia were trying to hold the bridge from the Union Army's IX Army Corps led by Major General Ambrose Burnside. A brigade from Ohio attempted to get the bridge, however, they got lost upstream. Next the 11th Connecticut with Daniel Tarbox, engaged the men from Georgia but suffering heavy casualties and injuries had to withdraw. Daniel Tarbox, part of that first brave attempt to take the bridge but still heavily outnumbered would be shot, at least once. It was reported to his father that he was shot through the bowels and that he lived until the next day before he passed. The "particulars" were to be provided in a later letter. Daniel Tarbox Sr.'s motivation quickly turned to getting his son's remains home. And what of the bridge? The 2nd Maryland and 6th New Hampshire tried to capture the bridge but were stopped by Confederate sharp shooters. By the end point the Confederates had held off almost 14,000 Union soldiers despite there being only 500 of them. Back to Daniel, who was buried in a shallow grave in a town called Middletown, with a small placard above his head to be identified and easily removed. Daniel Tarbox, Sr. assigned his son Louis, to bring back Daniel's body with haste to be buried at home in Connecticut. Louis, Daniel Jr.'s half-brother would bring a zinc coffin to transport and preserve his remains as best as possible. Daniel was brought back to Brooklyn, CT where he is buried in South Cemetery alongside his beloved parents.

Our investigation at the site of the memorial to the 11th CT down the path from Burnside's Bridge in Sharpsburg, Maryland led us to meet young Mr. Tarbox. As we stood on the hillside and listened to a squirrel chattering and eating in a tree, there was the deafening quiet of nature overtaking history. Myself, my husband, Marty and Andrew introduced ourselves to any spirits that may be near to the spot or were part of the 11th. A few minutes of eerie silence resonated even on the spirit box. Then a voice came through, a young man, somewhat indiscernible. Andrew understood, "It sounds like he's telling us his Company." Company F is what it sounded like of which there were just a few men listed on the monument. "Is Mr. Weeks here I asked, inquiring for one of the killed." No answer. "Is Mr. Tarbox here?" I asked after. "Yes," the young man's voice responded. "Can you confirm, is this Mr. Tarbox," I repeated, he was clear – but I really wanted to confirm such a strong spirit who would identify himself. "Yep," he confirmed affirmatively. My husband, seeing his forename as "David," on the marker addressed him as such, asking if he needed to tell us anything. Silence…I asked again for confirmation and he said it was him. Perhaps, the erroneous addressing of his name on the stone startled him. "Can you tell us where you're from," The audio, less clear, but still projecting in the same voice, said, "Brooklyn," it was Mr. Tarbox. He was still there, at least in spirit, at that spot by Burnside Bridge where he had clung on to his young life.

11th CT Monument Antietam Back Names (Martin Reardon Jr. photo)

Lieutenant Colonel Henry Czar Merwin & Captain Jedediah Chapman

Tragedy continued to come for Connecticut's officers and soldiers when just over a year later, nearly 1,300 men from Connecticut over six infantries/artilleries would descend upon the battlefields at Gettysburg, Pennsylvania over 3 sweltering summer days in July. Nearly a third of all Nutmeggers present would meet their death on those devastating days. When, one visits Gettysburg they may wonder where the most casualties were, where the greatest sadness lies. And each location over the nearly thirty square miles has a piece of tragedy – be it Pickett's Charge, the Devil's Den, Little Round Top, Culp's Hill, Cemetery Hill near the Eternal Flame or, if you ask a paranormal investigator, the Wheatfield. While we discuss a bit more of the loss and tactics of the haunted battlefield as a whole later in this book, we bring you to the Wheatfield to introduce you to two men, officers from the 27th Connecticut who are honored with small, almost hard to detect monuments. Men, who both happened to be just 23 years old, already battle experienced, promoted to officer ranks and hailing from New Haven, Connecticut – those men are Lieutenant Colonel Henry Czar Merwin and Captain Jedediah Chapman. On the Wheatfield there were engaged thirteen small Union brigades against six larger Confederate brigades with a total of over 20,000 men engaged on and around the Wheatfield over a period of three hours on the second day of Gettysburg, July 2nd, 1863. Of the 20,000 that would fight on that field in those hours alone, over 6,000 men would become casualties marking it in military history as one of the darkest engagements in Civil War history. Many would put this on par with the Cornfield at Antietam – which Mansfield barely saw before his death less than a year earlier, but thousands of other men would see and meet their end.

After the battle at the Wheatfield, bodies were left where they lay for days on end, many still believed to be in that field, especially from the Confederate side where bodies were not hastily brought back for burial. Experiences with spectral soldiers began when visitors felt a strange wind blow, or a feeling of being watched from behind, a closeness, whispers nearby. Those who would find themselves closest to this were reenactors who would go so far as to camp on the sites overnight. Story tells that some years ago, some reenactors endeavored to camp on the Wheatfield – but as they began to see the shadows move and feel ghostly touches as if they were laying where someone died…which to be sure, they likely were, one by one the reenactors departed the Wheatfield, excepting one, wanting to prove his bravery and skepticism about the paranormal. Needless to say, the lingering reenactor lasted some time but woke up a changed man, having seen apparitions, having felt their grabs and heard their cries for help. Could any of these specters be Lieutenant Colonel Merwin or Captain Chapman? The spots where they were mortally wounded were marked by survivors in the years that followed and you can stand where they met those fatal blows and feel them, their lives unfinished. Merwin, in life, left some record of his personal life, albeit through letters, almost of a day-to-day and familial nature that were maintained in family records. One of note, was to his sisters whose descendants continued to tell the story of her brother and preserve his tale. This letter was composed in January of 1863, less than seven months before Merwin would make it to Gettysburg. At this point, Merwin, as mentioned, was already battle-hardened. At the outbreak of the war, he had volunteered to serve for three months with the 2nd Connecticut as a Sergeant where he saw combat during the Battle of Bull Run.

By the summer, Merwin was recruited by Company A of the 27th where he was elected Lieutenant Colonel and would serve in combat at least

Henry Czar Merwin (HistoryNet)

twice more at Fredericksburg and Chancellorsville. He even suffered becoming a POW, of whose experiences we will detail as well, shortly after Chancellorsville. He was part of a prisoner exchange, returned to his regiment and was able to lead them into the Wheatfield. It's almost hard to conceive that Merwin was only twenty-one and twenty-two years old as he saw these battles, became imprisoned and received such titles of experience. Barely twenty-three at Gettysburg, he was a leader among men. The letter composed to his sister, Ruby Sophia Merwin Osborn, with bits of transcript here was in response to her, suggesting regular correspondence and was written with intent to ease her worry, that she must have presented in her letter by assuring, "do not believe all you hear," he wants to let her know that business is as usual as much as it can be in war and their hopes for good leadership to get them through the coming months. Likely, they were waiting to hear news any day that they could emerge victorious from this war that was carrying on for far too long already. He worries for his family, requests a word from them and shows, what any of us might be thinking when so far from home.

"My Dear Sister,

…I am very glad to hear you have sent a box to Uncle John for it will do him lots of good. He is very lucky to be in such a good place this winter. I hope his regiment will not have to move…

I hope you do not believe all you hear. I see by the scrap of paper you put in my letter our army had moved and we had no doubt whipped the enemy. Do not believe all you hear. We hear Hooker is in command of the army and that Sumner and Franklin are relieved of their commands. We hope the day is not far when George B. McClellan will be in command of the army….

Love to all. Tell Mother to write often and give me my box in letters. Is Father's health as good as usual? Have him send a word now and then by you if he does not write.

Your affectionate brother, — Hen

He does not mention his comrade Chapman, in this letter, though one might hope being of similar age and home, that they are close to one another even in death. Chapman's brother, Frank, two years his younger was also enlisted in the same regiment. There is no documentation regarding whether he witnessed his brother's death, but it is quite possible that he did, though he would survive the carnage and the war for decades, reminiscing about his brother and what could have been. Frank was serving in Merwin's Company A. His brother had a new charge. Prior to Jedediah's untimely demise, he had served honorably and admirably at the battle of Fredericksburg before he took ill during Chancellorsville which left most companies of the 27th in tatters. Chapman was given charge of a new company carved out with the survivors of the eight that had been dismantled by death of their peers. Due to this he had won the commission of Captain, however, he would tragically die before receiving the good news as he was leaving the company of detached members in the Wheatfield.

THE TWENTY-SEVENTH

JEDEDIAH CHAPMAN, JR.,

CAPTAIN OF COMPANY H.

Jedediah Chapman (27th CT Regiment History)

After the battle at the Wheatfield had concluded, the men of the 27th Connecticut met for roll call at a location called Cemetery Ridge. Seventy-five of them had entered the Wheatfield to fight, only 37 returned and they recalled the loss of their officers. Some

Henry Merwin Mortal Wound Mon. Gettysburg (Courtney McInvale photo)

remarked that they heard Merwin's last words to a comrade from another region, as he said,

"My poor regiment is suffering fearfully."

Chapman was recorded to have been brave and fearless as he marched forward leading his men in deadly charge, marching until he was shot down at the forefront of his men. The same was said for Merwin, though some may think he was just a boy himself, his friend says he was a man for the boys...an example. Lieutenant Thomas remarked on Merwin's nature in his condolences sent to his brother, Samuel. Thomas wrote,

"A frequent recipient of his kindness myself, I had learned to look upon Col. Merwin as the head of the regiment -- the father to the men and the friend to all. In camp, on the march or on the battlefield Col. Merwin was the man for the boys. It was he whose kind words and kinder deeds cheered the sick and encouraged the wayworn -- it was he who inspired us in battle and who looked to our welfare when the battle was over. We had hardly a comfort -- but it was associated with his name, and we never had a sorrow that any exertions on his part could banish. Any proficiency in drill which the regiment may have attained is due in a great measure to his personal attentions, which to him I am directly indebted for what knowledge I have gained of military. Both officers and men will ever cherish the memory of Lieut. Col. H.C. Merwin, as they would cherish the memory of a very dear brother."

Jedediah Chapman Grave New Haven

Once back on Cemetery Ridge the men of the 27th Connecticut met for roll call. Of the seventy-five men that went into action 38 fell in the fight for the Wheatfield, "eleven killed- among them Lieutenant- Colonel Merwin, and Captain Jedediah Chapman; twenty-three wounded, and four missing."

Both Merwin and Chapman are interred back home in the same burial grounds, in New Haven, Connecticut at Grove Street Cemetery. Henry Czar Merwin's funeral was recorded to be quite the affair as it was with many officers of higher ranking with thousands of visitors.

Chapman's funeral is not as spoken of, but we can surmise that it too would have brought out much of the public, showing their loyalty and support for the Union cause, their sorrow at the loss of one their own.

Myself and my small investigative team including my husband, Marty and friend and colleague, Andrew Hill investigated both the Wheatfield in Gettysburg and conducted a small audio recording and discussion at the burials of Merwin and Chapman in New Haven. Our investigation of the Wheatfield will be detailed more in the discussion of Gettysburg in the chapter on battles. The Wheatfield was perhaps one of the most tragic and spookiest of all the places at Gettysburg. There were experiences there not just captured with devices but felt and seen with the body – all experiencing a similar "grab," around the ankles. In New Haven, as we visited the graves of these two young heroes one chilly, sunny morning we sought to communicate with them and find if they too, like Mansfield, were home and where they met their end. We captured evidence of male's voices at each of their burials at

Spirit Photo Wheatfield Gettysburg (Courtney McInvale photo)

Grove Street Cemetery tucked behind the stunning Yale University. Our "investigation" implied, however, that it may have been Chapman who was seeking our attentions, more than Merwin that day as it seemed it was Chapman who rested less easily.

Henry Czar Merwin Grave New Haven

Merwin's burial was easy to find, within moments we looked at his grave, envisioned his funeral, thanked him for his service and promised to bring a flag to his stone. The audio, while quiet, showed his awareness that we were there. It was after this in search of the young soon-to-be Captain, where we struggled, to find his grave for some time. Suddenly and quite unexpectedly, our car hit a large tree root in the road. We all lurched forward and looked out the window to see his stone. His presence was strong, and he led us to him. We immediately felt pangs of guilt and regret as the spirit box played the sound of a male spirit who said he wasn't done. Both men informed us that they still visit each other on the other side.

Private George Warner

Tragedies at Gettysburg were beyond number and would even affect those who would leave the battle alive but far from intact or unchanged. Case in point is Private George Warner, who has in many ways become a Connecticut icon from the Civil War, an icon for the monument placements at Gettysburg and in his home state, a prominent placement in parades and beyond. George was with Company B of the 20th Connecticut Infantry. Perhaps the most tragic part of George's story and the reason so many bestowed honors on him was indeed part of his courage and patriotism but even more from the fact that his loss of limbs and injuries were sustained in friendly fire. Private George Warner served in the 20th Connecticut and like the men of the 27th Ct, at the time of his enlistment, he hailed from the New Haven region as an area farmer, and records indicated that he resided in Bethany, CT. Warner was born closer to Hartford, CT in Glastonbury and began working as young as age 12 for a large farm on the Connecticut River in which he was a laborer. George's Dad died when he was young and leaving his mother alone with 10 children, the prized cow he had purchased as a gift has to be sold and the family had to take up work in a local cotton mill.

At age 30, in August of 1862, Warner enlisted in the Union Army. At this time, he was married, with his own children and would leave them behind to fight for the cause. Warner, himself, wouldn't see battle until Chancellorsville in May of 1863, in which he, would escape relatively unscathed. He remembered his knapsack being shot off his back as he ran into the woods from the Confederate artillery. It was about two months later at the battle of Gettysburg, that Warner would make it out alive but not unscathed. On the morning of July 3rd, Warner and the 20th were making their way up the area known as Culp's Hill at Gettysburg. There were earthworks they had constructed on July 2nd, that they were attempting to take back as they had been commandeered in the night by the Confederate Army. Suddenly a fragment of artillery shell coming from nearby Union batteries fired in the direction of the 20th, striking Warner and severing his right arm just below the shoulder and doing so with such power that his arm was propelled several feet away from him. Simultaneously, as this shocking event happens, another piece of fragment hits his left arm shattering bones and causing intense blood loss. The continued firing into the 20th from their own allies even caused injuries to Warner's leg and scalp. Lieutenant Colonel William Wooster became incensed when he deduced the direction from which they were being fired upon from was indeed their own division, seemingly the 123rd New York. Wooster was ready to fire into his own division when after two attempts to get them to cease fire and realize they were aiming not at Confederates but at their own, they continued to fire until the realization came upon them. 1st Brigade Commander, Archibald McDougall of the 123rd would look upon this day with great regret for his erroneous orders.

George Warner & Family 1869 (Courtesy of the Library of Congress)

In the meantime, Warner was enroute to receive medical care and within an hour, the surgeon treating Warner realized that his left arm was not salvageable and would have to be amputated as well. When Warner awoke, he remarked with shock and exclaimed that he thought he had only lost but one arm, not both. Despite the apparent shock and immediate dismay which is to be expected, Warner continued his recovery in a local Gettysburg hospital for the next month. Though he continued to recover, it was officially

20ʰ CT with Warner Culp's Hill 1885 (Gettysburg Daily/PD)

deemed some months later that Warner could not even serve in the Invalid Corps and as such would be sent home. His wife, Catherine attended Gettysburg to escort him back home.

He immediately applied for a pension and received it and learned to navigate his new life with no arms. He and his wife were immeasurably close, and his wife was his assistant in navigating a world without limbs. They continued to grow their family. Having had five children, prior to the war, Catherine certainly had her work cut out for her on the home base, and then upon his return, they had three more children and he sold books and photos of himself to help support them along with his pension. Warner was often asked to be in parades with the Grand Army of the Republic and to attend memorial erection services in his home region but also on the battlefield Gettysburg where he was asked to raise the flag. If you're like me, you may be asking yourself, "But, how could he do such a thing?" Well, if we've learned anything from Mr. Warner it's that he was a man of positive attitude and resilience. He had no regrets about his service or what happened to him and was creative about how he would live his life, open to suggestions that may help him to navigate the world. At Gettysburg, for the dedication ceremony of the 20th CT monument in 1885, in order to raise the flag, which was the duty/position awarded to George, a pulley system was utilized and tied around Warner's waist so that as he moved backward the flag would raise.

Today, a boulder placed by the monument near where he was shot and that he sat upon at the ceremony is named Warner Rock. Warner Rock and the monument sit upon the 20th's position at the battle on Culp's Hill. Meanwhile, back home, in New Haven, when he unveiled a monument, another pulley system was used, and Warner removed the drapers with his teeth. The family had door devices attached at his home so that he could open doors with his teeth. His son, William assisted in

George Warner Grave New Haven

the book writing and his son, Charles built an elevated box that would allow his father to play cards. Warner led a very full life and even outlived many of his children and his wife well into his 90's. His story is still told throughout Connecticut, especially among his descendants in the New Haven region, where he is now buried now in Evergreen Cemetery

Though stories of ghosts and deaths and the feeling of unfulfilled life can be overwhelming as we meet the characters who so often met an untimely demise during this war and in this book, it's important that you also meet the men who heroically were able to show the power of human capability while being an ever-present reminder of what we as a country and as a people so violently did to one another and how close, we can be to committing such acts again. The thing, that I, find most fascinating about Warner is that he housed no chip on his shoulder and no bitter feelings about the mistake that would change his life, making his life an ever-trying event. He sallied forth with a smile on his face, a great love for his family and a pride for his service. When one thinks of Connecticut in the Civil War and gets a sense of pride, I hope that they envision the face of George Warner. And, dear reader, that is my wish for you as well.

Major Henry Ward Camp (Chaplain Henry Clay Trumbull)

Gettysburg, the turning point of the Civil War according to many military historians. Gettysburg, where Merwin and Chapman would be just two of the 23,000 Union men would lose their lives over the course over those three days in the fields of a small, rural Pennsylvania town. 51,000 men would lose their lives in total at that fateful battle where the winds of change were blowing for any possibility of Confederate victory looking like a marginal dream for the secessionists, yet one they and Robert E. Lee would not give up on. Ulysses S. Grant led the Union to a victory in Vicksburg the day after Gettysburg. Robert E. Lee lost all hope of taking over any part of the Northern States and the war would take a turn to be fought further south. Rations would be limited on both sides, the battle became intimate and personal as more and more soldiers would die from disease than battle, as the prisons would fill beyond capacity and the war in many ways was an experiment of human torture. As we journey from a year that saw two of the deadliest battles and days in American history, we make our way to a somber journey of smaller battles, impoverished journeys and prisoners, who wished death would come and relieve them of their torture, or who may make it out only to meet an alternate end. In fact, the sorrow and inhumane treatment of the prisoners in the south became one of the most unspoken tragedies in the war, one of the only ways that any soldiers were held accountable for war crimes was if they managed these prisons. National cemeteries were established nearby by Clara Barton and Union allies over the shallow trenches were emaciated, sick bodies were tossed away like rubbish after suffering starvation, dysentery, scurvy and deplorable living conditions. The most notable prison and burial was in Andersonville, Georgia. Together, we will journey to the prisons in this book, haunted by those who perished there, those whose guilt keeps them tied there for running it and the overwhelming residual horror that palpates through the earth of suffering.

One Connecticut gentleman, who left an impression on his regiment suffering imprisonment yet surviving imprisonment and still meeting a violent end, is a gentleman known better in legend as the "Knightly Soldier," Major Henry Ward Camp – the young man who felt the cause deep in heart and enlisted after attendance at General Nathaniel Lyon's funerary service. Camp, like Commander Ward and Samuel Colt came from Hartford. Camp was born in 1839; His ties to Hartford's abolitionists and spiritualists alike ran deep, as he received his education in law alongside Isabella Beecher Hooker's husband, John Hooker, Esq.

This was, subsequent, to Camp's graduation from Yale University – a well-educated man, likely influenced by his classmate's abolitionist and feminist views – and the forward-thinking nature of the prestigious university. He finished his law education in 1861 at the young age 22 and enlisted in the Hartford City Guard in 1861 just one month prior to what was then the inevitable tensions coming to war in May of

Portrait Henry Ward Camp (Yale University)

1861. By December of the same year, Connecticut's Governor Buckingham, whose home still sits in Norwich, CT, commissioned Camp as a 2nd Lieutenant in Company I of Connecticut's 10th. Camp's motivation perhaps came from his companionship with Hooker and the abolitionists of Connecticut. Throughout his deployment, Camp would seek to assist the escaped enslaved peoples trying to make it north or the enslaved that he would see at camps or in town, listening to their stories, hoping to bring their families together and building his horror at the institution of slavery's existence. He was firm in his stance that that was is what they were fighting for, but they had to say it was for the government of the union, but it was really to rid of the ghastly legality of slavery in the south. To read his firsthand accounts of his encounters with the enslaved and mistreated, will bring a tear to your eye as you feel the simultaneous sympathy and rage that coursed through Camp's blood at these moments. Camp was young, motivated, handsome, intelligent and according to his peers stood out among the ranks for his strong build and attractive look – almost a beacon in the night – the perfect picture of a Union soldier. Camps promotions continued to 1st Lieutenant in Company D and Adjutant of the 10th by 1862. With academic skills and described bravery, along with several promotions by mid-July of 1863, Camp was well aware of what had happened in Gettysburg, about the rising death tolls and the dark turn that was coming in the war. He was especially aware because he participated in the assault on Fort Wagner, shortly after which he and his comrade would be captured, and he would have time to think on it.

Camp had previously been dancing around much of the danger and engagement, by no choice of his own. When the 10th Connecticut saw combat, firsthand, he was often summoned away as he was in Roanoke/New Bern, to go get ammunition and supplies at the 11th hour or on a trip up North when no combat was expected and following orders, this was the right time for him to journey – but that was in late 1862 when the 10th saw combat at Kinston, Rawl's Mills and Goldsborough. While he was present at Fort Wagner – he did not take part initial armed assaults as he had to manage men at camp, provide orders and take on other responsibilities. Additionally, much of the assault at Fort Wagner was managed by the Naval forces. The most successful in the assault, were not the 10th who were diversionary, but rather the African American troops of the 54th. Not seeing combat, up close, yet again, was disheartening for Camp who felt that his purpose was to fight for and die for the abolishment of slavery and preservation of the Union and to be the leader he was promoted to be. At times he even turned down promotions, and requested they be placed with men who saw action. His friend, Chaplain and biographer, Henry Clay Trumbull, wrote of his repeated dismay at not having been involved in the frontlines. Camp stated about Kinston,

"So I am about a week too late, I would give more than that of life to have been in that bayonet charge. My absence from it, like that from battle of Roanoke – much more, even, -- will be a life-long disappointment and regret. When the war is over, what shall I Have done? It is hard…I have nothing to reproach myself with, only I feel like a man who had unfortunately lost a magnificent opportunity."

Camp was as involved as possible in the Fort Wagner Siege, the 10th playing a crucial role and importantly going to assist the injured and dying in the terrible morning that would follow the wake of another active day at war. As Camp and others from the 10th were on the battlefield the next day after the flag of truce had been seen and were gathering their dead, they met a Confederate

Portrait Henry Trumbull (Wiki Commons)

sergeant with a squad of men who halted them and called out that they were prisoners. Though Camp and the others protested that they could not be captured under truce, the Captain who had detained them, also happened to be a defected Northerner and their General Haygood did not want to get involved and so they were held by General Ripley at Charleston while their case reviewed. Camp and the men imprisoned with him including his Chaplain and biographer were blindfolded and walked along the beach past Fort Wagner until sundown, and since their fate was undecided, they along with the other prisoners and wounded were taken up to

Charleston with a stop at Fort Sumter. They were marched in the city with the colored regiment of the 54th as if it were meant to disgrace them, and they also were told to spend the night with them to disgrace them -- but that did no such thing as their mind was focused on being in prison. Camp took to his pen.

"Strange sensations are those which man experiences during his first hours in prison. The consciousness of helplessness under restraint produces a feeling of absolute suffocation, a nightmare oppression, with a nervousness that makes it impossible to sit or stand still, to concentrate the thoughts on any subject, or to do anything but pace up and down the longest possible beat which the narrow limits of confinement will afford."

The one sense of relief for Camp through the sufferings of imprisonment was that for the first weeks and months, he had the company of his best friend, Henry. In fact, Camp and his best comrade, after receiving the decision of the General were moved with the other prisoners to the Richland Jail in Columbia, South Carolina together. Richland Jail is referred to also as "Jailhouse Prison," and was a three-story building, seventy by fifty feet – the third story belonging to the Sheriff leaving the prison to be easily overcrowded though perhaps not as deplorable as other more well-known prisons of the South. The two Henry's settled in. For Camp, having Trumbull's company made things not just bearable but sometimes enjoyable – he expressed joy at the company of reading with someone, writing with someone, playing games, talking – that they did all things together – eating, breaks when they were provided. The confederate guards as well as their Union peers referred to them as the "two Henrys" or "the twins" for their inseparable nature. Both Henrys were likable, kind and exhibited leadership in their own right – and it wasn't hard for them to gain respect among their peers. It was clear to those around them and the historians who would read their letters, that the friendship was far more than a brotherhood, but a love that these two men shared and suffice to say, they were in love with each other. This did not diminish their reputation with their peers. Their character, their Christianity, their intrinsic values of God and Country as well as protective nature of their fellow soldier made them leaders both by appointment and by choice. And their peers understood, on a human level, that love was the driving force for all men, especially during times of war. Love of country, love of belief, love of brotherhood and the love for those families at home that they deeply wished to return to – wives, children, parents, peers – the two Henrys were no different and were an example of love in the face of the worst situation a man who could find himself in. General Sherman would later comment that he believed it was their love that gave Camp and by default Trumbull's legacy. In reading of the biography on Camp by Trumbull, Sherman wrote, "I thank you for the volume commemorative of the life and ser- vices of young Camp. These personal narratives add a special charm to the story of our great war and seem to illustrate its inner history." Michael Amico, who holds a PhD in American Studies from Yale University completed his dissertation in recent years, entitled *The Forgotten Union of the Two Henrys: A History of the 'Peculiar and Rarest Intimacy' of the American Civil War*, regarding the romantic and intimate relationship between Camp and Trumbull, diving into their letters and came to find several details about the two men and more importantly, about the nature of those around them being defined by unity, support and respect. While Camp and Trumbull spent some time together in prison, Trumbull was released earlier. Camp, being a higher-ranking officer, was someone that the Confederates saw as giving them leverage and that was worth holding on to. After a few months, which is longer than most officers were jailed in Columbia, Trumbull was sent in early November for release in Richmond. When Trumbull, was separated and returned to his comrades in the 10th Connecticut, they reported his distress at being separated from Camp, his collapse to the ground, his tears and he would set forth on a mission to ascertain release terms for his friend. Meanwhile, Camp, who found life in prison without his other half, unlivable, was concocting a plan with a friend, Captain V.B. Chamberlain of the 7th Connecticut to escape the confines of their prison. The scheme, detailed in writing by Camp, after being completed was detailed and meticulous and was carried out successfully…somewhat. Camp and Chamberlain escaped the prison and traveled on foot through treacherous swamps, wetlands and dangerous conditions over the period of about one week and over a hundred-some odd miles on their way to Union territory in Tennessee before they were ultimately captured and returned to prison. They were captured near Pinckneyville, South Carolina where word had traveled about escaped officers and when locals caught sight on the side road of the two men, it didn't take long for them to deduce who they were, and the two men confessed to their identity upon confrontation. They were held by their captors, by which they were treated well and then escorted back to Columbia, and back to prison. Camp spent the winter in prison when he received news in the spring that his regiment was enroute to St. Augustine FL for recruitment for a season and that his good friend Henry was with them and they would be safe rom combat. Meanwhile, Camp, pondered on how much of his life he was losing confined in an increasingly demoralizing state. There were several false hopes given to Camp that exchanges could be negotiate but many times nothing would happen.

"We feel like the three egg-gatherers of the Orkneys, whose story used to be in the school-readers, -- our rope seems to be parting while we yet swing halfway down the precipice a, and it is a desperate chance whether the last strand holds long enough to bring us to the top."

Camp considered escaping again with the navy officers when the orders finally came for his release in the middle of April 1864. First, however, he was moved to Libby prison in Virginia, this was in Richmond, where he met his brethren from the Nutmeg state and was placed in a room with Connecticut officers. But this was not a refreshing experience. At Libby prison, Camp saw the contrast in prisons from where he was in Columbia to where he found himself. In fact, Libby prison would go down in infamy for some unlivable prisons throughout the Civil War history – Civil War prisons were often the cause of death by starvation, confinement, vermin, disease and cruel treatment. Camp was only here for a small amount of time to the standing room only quarters before he was summoned to go enroute to Annapolis for release. They made a stop briefly in Virginia, where the other Henry was waiting for him. They had a brief help, before Camp had to take his voyage continuation to Annapolis. Camp wrote to Trumbull immediately after with a gratitude to God for the immeasurable blessing of being able to see him and him not being in St. Augustine – but there to see one another.

"I am a thousand times happier than I deserve to be – almost as happy as I could be. My cup is full. I won't ask to have it overflow."

Camp was gleeful for the sight of Trumbull and for his freedom. But then worry set in, would he be able to rejoin the regiment before they were engaged in combat? He couldn't miss it again…his concerns for missing prior still coursed through him. By mid-May, Camp was officially declared "exchanged," though he had been away from home 18 months and ten of them imprisoned, Camp shortened his stay with their family to rejoin his men. Trumbull wrote, "But with Henry Camp, the cause of country was the cause of God, and for that cause he was willing to leave father and mother and brother and sisters, and to lose his life for its sake." Camp missed a skirmish near Drury's Bluff by just a day, but he arrived on May 16th and battle ensued. The 10th Connecticut succeeded in their attempts and mission to take City Point and Bermuda Hundred with Camp's leadership. They also engaged in the fight for Fort Darling at Drewry's Bluff but were not successful and suffered many casualties though they were able to help Union troops continue to make their way to Richmond. Camp was the leader the men needed. Just months later in September, for his efforts and bravery, Camp was promoted to Major. They were enroute to Richmond by way of Appomattox and were near to the Darbytown Road by October 1854. The 10th was about to become engaged in the final campaign of the war, the Richmond-Petersburg Campaign, which h would have a series of bloody attacks on the Darbytown Road in which Camp, Trumbull and their comrades were headed. By mid, October, in fear, due to intelligence from deserters, that they would soon encounter Lee and his troops up close, orders were received for the regiment to move at once in light marching order. On October 7th, there had been a successful Union attempt nearby at the New Market and Darbytown Roads where the Union was able to withstand Robert E. Lee's strike force on the capital region – the region where Grant was determined his men should be infiltrating. The 10th had participated and were ready for round two on October 13th, and Camp had ensured that he would not be separated from his men but would lead them. He had demanded discussion with his General that this be the case. Lee had demanded work on new defense lines and Grant determined that this would not be allowed which sent the Union troops on the 13th including Camp into the skirmishes of the day, and this day the Union and Camp would not emerge victorious. Just after noon that day, the 10th was in remnants and assault was imminent. When Camp and Trumbull briefly saw one another, there was a sense a foreboding and finality to their encounter. Trumbull was afraid to see that Camp would be leading the left of the assaulting column in the battle lines when casualties were already high. The 10th all seemed to sense a death march was coming and the Henry's…the twins, in their own way said goodbye and remarked of what was to come in the afterlife. Trumbull remarked,

"If we don't meet again here, we will hope to meet in heaven,"

and Camp responded,

"Yes, and yet I have been so absorbed in this life that I can hard realize that there is another beyond."

They clasped hands, the battle energy palpating, they said goodbye and Trumbull asked his friend quickly, "You do not doubt your Savior, do you?" Camp turned with a smile, "No, no, dear fellow. I do not doubt. I do trust Jesus, fully, wholly. They then said their final goodbye for this life. Major camp struggled with his men through the thicket to reform a broken line that was fallen apart in the tangled wood. The rebel parapet was close to their front during this re-assembly. Camp, not seeing them, waved his sword and called to his men,

"Come on, boys, come on!"

And when he turned, made eye contact with the color sergeant just as a bullet from the Confederates pierced his lung. Camp fell to his side and he was struck once more. Trumbull wrote,

"His eyes scarced turned their glance at the tattered, dear old flag, ere they were closed to earth and opened again beyond the stars and fields of blue."

Major Camp never knew they were walking into the parapet with the Colonel and Lt. Colonel having already retired. His body was left where it fell and Trumbull was not allowed to recover it as the Confederates stripped his body of clothing, took his sword, pistol, watch, ring, money and anything of any value. The next day, urged by Chaplain Trumbull and accompanied by Lieutenant Shreve, the two men with Colonel Rockwell of the 6th Connecticut negotiated a truce with the Confederate forces including the return of Major Camp's body. The Confederates returned his remains, expressed regret for the state of it having been ransacked for valuables and upon Trumbull's request, returned Camp's journal. In the days that followed, Trumbull accompanied Camp's remains back to Hartford, where Trumbull would deliver remarks and tribute at the funeral service on October 21st. Colonel Harris Plaisted of the 11th Maine Volunteer Infantry, who wrote in his official report "Major Camp was killed: he fell among the foremost of his comrades and within a few yards of the enemy's line. Our cause cannot boast of a nobler martyr than Henry W. Camp. His name will be recorded with those of Ellsworth and Winthrop, youthful heroes who have given their lives for their country". Camp was interred at Spring Grove Cemetery and both the written and oral tributes in his honor from peers and fellow comrades were countless – he was remembered as a gentleman, a friend, a knight, a man of integrity, kindness, courage and Christian virtue. All who spoke of him expressed gratitude and honor for knowing him. His body that had been accompanied first by his friend all the way home, was reinterred just two years later to the remarkable and brand new (at the time) Cedar Hill Cemetery where Samuel Colt is also buried. His epitaph on the monument reads, "A true knight; not yet mature, yet matchless. Erected by his fellow citizens of Hartford as a tribute to his patriotic service, and to his noble Christian character." His friend, his intimate companion and partner went on to lead a life away from Connecticut where he had once served as a Sunday school missionary and moved to Philadelphia and traveled the world. He lectured at Yale Divinity School, authored dozens of books and lived with his wife, Alice Gallaudet Trumbull and saw his children grow but never forgetting Camp and living as if tomorrow is not promised with those you love, because he learned that indeed, it is not.

The grounds in which Camp is buried in Hartford, Connecticut at Cedar Hill are breathtaking for any visitor -- truly one of the most beautiful and profound examples of a rural landscape cemetery in all its Victorian era glory, lays outside the state's capital city. One afternoon, visiting Camp to thank him for his service, we did a small audio paranormal investigation session to talk. We asked Camp, first for his first name to which he said, "Henry." "What other Henry may be with you? Who is

Henry Ward Camp Grave Hartford

your best friend?" We could make out two syllables on the SB-7 Spirit Box. We asked once more, "Trum-bull," he repeated. How many Henry's are here right now, I asked. "Three," we all looked around at each other. Three? Henry Ward Camp, Henry Trumbull...and then we looked at the stone next to Camp where his father was re-interred as well. His father's name? Henry. Unlike the reaction's we got at the burial for Chapman or Lyon, there was a peace to Camp, a sense that despite his young age, he was ready to die. We know he said his goodbyes, he assured that he would be able to participate in battle, that he would not miss standing with his men once more and that in his short life, he was very loved and loved all in his family and inner circle. So, perhaps, at age 25, Major Camp was able to rest and our short conversation with him, confirmed that notion. Or perhaps, any restless, residual energy would not be in peaceful home burial but on the Darbytown Road where his body was stripped of all his belongings and attire or at the Richland Jail site where he spent so much time as POW. His story, however, will be with us in Connecticut forever, the haunting of the Knightly Soldier who broke down barriers to leave an eternal legacy.

Captain Thomas Wolfe

By 1864, the losses for the state of Connecticut were immense from battle, disease and injury. The losses for the Union often seemed insurmountable. How could an army that outnumbered the rebels two-to-one find themselves in such a long and violent conflict? How could our most experienced officers continually be taken down by guerilla warfare tactics that they could not anticipate? Bravery, courage and intelligence was in no short supply and the men would not give up, but imprisonment would challenge the hearts of even the bravest men. As Camp and Trumbull demonstrated, prison can be harrowing for even the most well treated but what was it like for those who weren't treated well at all, who were treated cruelly, starved, left with remnants of clothing, forced into standing room only quarters, made to live in their own filth. The Confederate prisons that housed the Union prisoners of war became "Hell on Earth," for those who would walk through the stockades and oftentimes never walk out. The descriptions are nothing short of horrific and graphic yet, the Connecticut men, so youthful many could justify calling them boys, endured this agonizing imprisonment for weeks or months at a time. Some of the imprisoned were enlisted men and some were men that manned Union ships providing necessary provisions to those in encampments and at battle sites. It's important to meet those who would survive and those who would not in order to utterly understand the haunting effects on a soul and a land after such an experience. Another prison survivor who still met a dark end was a seaman delivering provisions who would become captured and imprisoned in the notably dark, Salisbury Prison, was Captain Thomas E. Wolfe. Salisbury, the second most contemptable of all the prisons (second only to the brutal Andersonville Prison in Georgia), was nothing he could have expected. A man of intellect, ambition and life experience, Wolfe had never seen anything like. Captain was Thomas E. Wolfe of Mystic, Connecticut. Thomas' early life in Mystic began with learning the art of celestial navigation by the age of fourteen when he was out at sea as a "ship's boy." Thomas' time participating in whaling expeditions helped him learn the navigational arts and gave him the ability to go back home in Mystic, to school and impress both teachers and classmates with tales of his worldly adventures.

The late Groton town historian, Carol Kimball, shared stories with Carol Sommer of the *New London Day* of how Thomas fulfilled a writing assignment at school about his travels, writing a paper entitled, *The Isle of France, Indian Ocean as it appeared to me in 1846*, the most exciting assignment submission in the class. When Thomas completed his studies, his ambitions took him West for the Gold Rush. He and two comrades from Mystic made it to California after sailing around Cape Horn. He became involved in trade work and worked hard, however, never found Gold and decided to come back home. The weary gold seeker however missed his sailing connection at Cape Horn and had to cross Nicaragua on foot to reach his transit back home. Despite not finding the gold he sought, after his return home, Wolfe did well for himself in his maritime career and was able to acquire and reside in a stately home in Mystic with his wife. They attempted to raise a family here as well though only one child, his namesake, would survive to adulthood. His career and beliefs aligned him with the Union when the Civil War began in 1861 and he began the shipment of supplies for the Union from New York to New Orleans. His ship, the Texana, was captured by Confederates near the mouth of the Mississippi River in 1863 and burned. Wolfe and his crew were then taken to prison. Though the prisons, arguably, hadn't reached the harshness of 1864 and 1865 quite yet, they were still quite unlivable, and Thomas was held in prison for well over a year and saw firsthand the deterioration of the conditions. Thomas and his men were brought to Salisbury Prison in North Carolina. The prison was built to hold about 600 men, however, by 1864, there were 10,000 men kept there. This caused lack of food amid the obvious overcrowding. Men were living in holes in the ground and both at Salisbury and Andersonville, some ruthless guards used the prisoners for target practice. It was estimated that fifteen to twenty men died every day at Salisbury. Diseases related to starvation and various other fatal epidemics as well as the cruel abuse caused the death of thousands of prisoners held by the rebels during the war. If one tried to escape Salisbury, they weren't typically brought back like Camp was to his prison. They were executed for their attempt.

After a year in prison, news made it to Thomas that a stricter commandant was going to be taking over the prison. The odds of escaping safely were even less if a crueler commandant was going to take charge. So, in the dark winter of 1864, Thomas and four of his fellow prisoners and friends decided that they would escape or

Escape of Salisbury Prisoners (Project Gutenberg Ebook)

face death, but they would not continue to live in the barbaric conditions of Salisbury Prison. On one cold December night, Thomas and his friends deceived the guards through carefully obtained "medical passes," and escaped the prison. They decided instead of fleeing straight away, which is how most had previously gotten caught, they would hide in plain sight, as it were, right under the noses of the prison guards. They fled with nothing with the clothes on their back and hid for the first night in a barn, having been guided by a silent ally after leaving the other gate and stayed within sight of the prison. A sympathetic Confederate officer brought the men water and another Confederate officer helped to usher them off the grounds the following day and brought them an additional prisoner to travel with and gave that prisoner a Confederate uniform to assist in the journey as well as written directions to a Union settlement. The men had hoped the Uniform would provide safety, but they encountered sharp-shooting Union sympathizers on their journey would take aim at them, leading to a narrow escape once more enroute to Tennessee. The reason the men survived this perilous journey? An enormous network of men and women that assisted. Locals sympathetic to their cause who would house and feed them. Enslaved people and farmers who would assist even using the Underground Railroad connections. One unnamed woman, a heroine for the men in need was the wife of a Confederate Officer. Thomas was battling a sprained ankle for the entire journey but remained an optimist and continued to lift the men's spirits when they were cold and hungry with humorous stories and despite several slips on the ice from his injured ankle, consistently picked himself back up. One humorous story, Wolfe shared with his friends on a cold night on their journey was a story about Southerners having tea rather than coffee for the first time. Wolfe said that one time, his father attended a log-rolling in South Carolina where,

"As a rare and costly luxury, the host regaled the workers with tea at the close of their labors. But unacquainted with its use, they were only presented with the boiled leaves to eat! After this novel banquet, one old lady thus expressed the views of the rural assembly, "Well, I never tasted this before. It is pleasant enough; but except for the name of it, I don't consider tea a bit better than any other kind of greens.""

They all had a hearty laugh on this and admittedly, I have that same laugh now as the Southerners are quite known for their iced and sweet teas! The laugh was needed, the miles were treacherous, their diversions many, the men suffered from typhoid and pneumonia. Wolfe was also relied upon to keep them on track – he had the art of celestial navigation in his back pocket and his comrades would often get lost. One of them stated that for a full mile Wolfe, continually repeated that they were on the wrong side of the "North Star," and, of course, they had to turn back around and retrace their steps and take rest at the home of a black family living in a cabin. Cabins and barns every night, the reliance on strangers, the men became a spectacle for those wanting to see "genuine Yankees," and onward they went. The extra mileage and hard walking conditions made Wolfe lame by the end of the trip, but he never ceased moving forward. The journey is a remarkable one and it ends with the men arriving safely at Strawberry Plains, Tennessee where it's documented they "bowed their heads and wept." Thomas arrived at home in Mystic, Connecticut on his birthday, January the 20th, 1865. He would recuperate here and received the good news of the Union victory at home with his family. Journalist and prisoner, Albert Richardson of Massachusetts, correspondent for the New York Daily Tribune and future biographer of General Ulysses S. Grant went on to write a book about the harrowing experience that would take them 340 miles over a month to Union territory. His book about the war he witnessed, his life in prison and escaping prison in North Carolina is entitled *The Secret Service, The Field, The Dungeon and The Escape*, was published in 1865, his memories fresh to mind. The details of the journey read as if watching a dramatic movie with combat, fears, near-death experiences and characters of tenacity, resilience and strength making it through.

Thomas Wolfe & Prisoners Escape Sketch (Project Gutenberg Ebook)

What became of Thomas is bittersweet. After he recuperated in Mystic, he took on work for the local Mallory Steamship Company. However, just about a decade after his escape from prison while delivering lamp oil on the steamship Waco off the Gulf of Mexico in Galveston, Texas, Captain Wolfe's vessel was tragically struck by lightning and he was catapulted by the explosion miles down the water. His ship burned and sank, no one escaping the event alive. His wife and at the time, two living sons would receive his body and have him buried in historic Elm Grove Cemetery overlooking the Mystic River. According to author Lisa Saunders, he was one of the only bodies recovered from the wreckage. As for Thomas, the question remains, did he have unfinished business? A reason to haunt his hometown? If you ask the visitors of Elm Grove Cemetery, his beautiful obelisk monument engraved with a steamboat on the riverfront is the first one you notice upon entering the cemetery housing over 13,000 bodies. His energy calls to you – a man with an amazing story, who endured every tragedy and never gave up. His soul calls and it's easy to feel swept away standing in the plot. Feelings of dizziness are often reported by his stone and the infamous "Lady in Black," that haunts the cemetery grounds when weather events are to come or souls are nearby is often seen walking by his stone. Is it his betrothed? Is she waiting for him to arrive home safely? Or is Thomas telling us that he has yet more of his journey to complete? I suggest a visit to Elm Grove to meet him and see what story he must share with you. But remember, no matter how sad, Thomas will find a way to make you laugh and take heart, that our journey is never over on this side or the next.

Corporal William Danforth Brooks & Private George Simon Brooks

Thomas' and his friend's story, albeit a tragic one was the end many prisoners may have hoped for but couldn't receive. Our journey through haunting prison experiences with many Connecticut natives brings us further south to Andersonville, Georgia, in the middle of a rural, agricultural and sweltering, landlocked region where the souls of thousands of Union Men and Connecticut men would take their last breath. Andersonville, Georgia, a prison once built to hold ten thousand men would swell to a population of three times its capacity at one time, a prison that held over forty-five-thousand Union soldiers, a prison where thirteen-thousand men would lose their lives due to disease and cruelty. Many regard Andersonville as one of the darkest pieces of the entire American Civil War, a chapter many don't want to talk about, a chapter that delves into the depths of the evil that humanity is capable of. The darkness and haunts of the prison will be delved into more the coming chapters. You may recall that in the introduction, the stories and souls of two spirits in many ways inspired this book, and Andersonville brings us to these two young men, William Danforth Brooks and George Simon Brooks of Haddam, Connecticut. William was the elder brother by only about one year. Both brothers enlisted for service on August 12, 1862 and mustered out on August 24th, 1862. Prior to their enlistment they had been raised as hard-working young men by their father George Brooks and Abigail Turner Brooks. Their parents were just 22 and 20 when they married in 1841 and it was only a year later their wedding that William was born and just over a year later that young George was born. Their middle names were inherited from their maternal Turner grandparents. Their father George was a blacksmith by trade and would have been of great necessity to their community where they resided not far from their Turner family. Just two years before their enlistment, elder brother William, age 17 to 18 years old was living with his parents and serving as a joiner apprentice, meaning that he was studying woodworking occupations. Younger brother George was living with his

Grandfather, Danforth Turner and serving as an apprentice to his shoemaking trade. Both young men were industrious and helping to support their family.

The young men had no notable military experience of which to speak of nor military education. They had received no training prior to their enlistment in August of 1862 and it was just three weeks after being mustered that they would find themselves at Antietam, perhaps some of the young men being handed muskets, rifles or swords for the first time in their lives the night before the battle. The Brooks survived Antietam and followed their regiment through Maryland and Virginia where they engaged in the Battle of Fredericksburg, endured Burnside's second Campaign the Mud March, moved further south into Virginia to the Siege of Suffolk, and move on varying expeditions around the Commonwealth of Virginia before moving to North Carolina in early 1862, New Bern and then Plymouth. The Battle of Plymouth was a Confederate victory, perhaps one of their most notable.

When the Carolina region had been occupied in 1862 near to Plymouth and New Bern, North Carolina, frequent raids had occurred and the Confederate vessels Albemarle and Neuse had not been completed, which they would have needed for their rebel defense. But by 1864, the ships were completed and three brigades of Confederate infantry, estimated to be about 10,000 commanded by Hoke made their way within five miles of Plymouth. They wanted to take back their town, their region from what the Union army. There were only about 2,834 men at the Union Garrison when Brigadier General Hoke and Commander James Cooke of the rebel forces led their attack. The lesser numbered Union had a good defense with a fortified post and were able to fight off the first day of attacks. The 16th helped to hold the fort on the 17th. By April 18th, Union vessels were sunk and gunfire wad abundant. The U.S. navy boats were not able to assist the Union boys. By the 19th, the Albemarle destroyed the Union ships and a double envelopment attack on the town began. The attack was renewed by the 20th of April and forts were captured as the Confederates descended upon the town and forced themselves into the Union stronghold of Fort Williams. Cannons from the Albemarle and artillery fired upon the fort. Plymouth residents took refuge in the Latham House. Brigadier General Henry Wessells looked around him, saw the 16th and his other regiments and companies and infantries -- and knew there was no chance.

THE REBEL RAM ATTACKING FEDERAL GUN-BOATS AT PLYMOUTH, NORTH CAROLINA.

Battle of Plymouth Sketch (Wiki Commons)

He wrote to General Hoke, of the moment

"I was now completely enveloped on ever side...this condition of affairs could not be long endured and in compliance with the earnest desire of every officer I consented to hoist a white flag and at 10 am of April 20th I had the mortification of surrendering my post to the enemy with all it contained. General, this is the saddest day of my life."

General Henry Wessells

Wessells, another strong Nutmegger, West Point graduate, Seminole War veteran and battle-hardened man since 1861 was no stranger to combat, he had fought gallantly at the Battle of Fair Oaks, has participated in several engagements and defended the town and his men for three days. He knew upon surrender that imprisonment was inevitable and that he would stand a better chance than the boys and young men around him. Commissioned officers, especially high-ranking ones, often got taken to different prisons than the men they commanded and guided. And when he surrendered, prison was inevitable for them all. Wessells went first to Libby prison in Richmond, VA and was transferred to Danville, Macon and Charleston and would finally be exchanged in 1864 and became Commissary of Prisoners. Wessells recollected the day of capture as the worst day of his life. The General would survive and return home to Litchfield, Connecticut, but the hundreds and thousands of men captured in Plymouth, most would not. The non-commissioned officers and enlisted men would be sent to a place they would only come to know as hell, and perhaps that is even an understatement. Those enlisted men and non-commissioned officers included the Brooks. The Brooks were there for all of it. One of their companies engaged in assisting civilians out of the area and escaped the inevitable imprison, the Brooks and the other companies of their regiment, however, stayed at the fort. They had served at New Bern until the Battle of Plymouth on April 17th through 20th, 1864. It was on April 20th that the 16th was captured including both William and George and then taken prisoner and walked through the gates and stockades of Andersonville for the first time. The Brooks and their comrades of the 16th would be known as the "Plymouth Pilgrims," at Andersonville.

While there are no records in historical collections that we've found about what the Brooks brothers specifically felt upon this experience, others in their regiment, left us an idea of what they encountered and how they were feeling. Sgt. Major Robert Kellogg of Wethersfield, the same age range as William and George upon entering the prison, scribed,

"As we entered the place a spectacle met our eyes that almost froze our blood with horror, and made our hearts fail within us. Before us were forms that had once been active and erect; -- stalwart men, now nothing but mere walking skeletons, covered with filth and vermin."

He said of their first night, "There were ten deaths on our side of the camp that night. The old prisoners called it 'being exchanged," and truly it was a blessed transformation to those who went from such miserable existence on earth, to a glorious one above." Sgt. Oliver W. Gates of Co. F, the 16th Connecticut recorded of his time, "And if any sight would make a man's heart sink, the middle of this pen would. Twelve thousand men turned into this place just like so many cattle, not a tree or shelter of any kind to protect from the sun or rain or cold…it was the hardest trial of my life." The night of their entrance, the 16th was divided into groups of ninety men each for different parts of the prison camp. Since both Brooks were in Co. F, there is hope they may have been together though no proof. Kellogg described the center of the prison camp as "a swamp, occupying about three or four acres of the narrowed limits, and a part of this marshy place had been used by prisoners as a sink, and excrement covered the ground, the scent arising from which was suffocating. The ground allotted to our ninety was near the edge of this plague-spot, and how we were to live through the warm summer weather amid such fearful surroundings, was more than we cared to think about just then." The details of what the various Connecticut men experienced are to be detailed but the Brooks sentiments can be deduced by that of their companions.

William survived three-and-a-half months in the squalor before he perished as recorded in prison records from dysentery and by his parents by starvation. Elder brother, William, died on August 8th - 9th, 1864. It was recorded that though their regiment was doing well despite all horrors to begin, the first death two months after their imprisonment on June 20th was the beginning of the horrors. Men started dying daily from the 16th from there on out. The 16th was already considered the "Bad Luck Regiment," for their lack of training and their high death count and Andersonville would see the death of 85 more of them.

George survived the prison conditions for months after his brother's death, surviving ten months in Andersonville and other southern prisons. George was recorded officially released/exchanged from the rebel prisons on February 22nd, 1865. Reports of men in the 16th state, that starting in the fall of 1864, many of the men were moved from prison to prison throughout the south to include Charleston and Florence. A lot of the motivation to move was due to the fear that General Sherman would soon liberate the prisoners. The outbreak of Yellow Fever in Charleston made their stay their brief and the shooting of prisoners who came hear the "deadline," was still daily as was the abysmal lack of food and provisions.

Officers were moved before enlisted men, so the exact timeline for the enlisted prison movement is not well recorded. It was February of 1865, that the men started to hear more rumors of exchange thanks to General Sherman having arrived so close to their new imprisonment in Charlotte, North Carolina. Through their movements to Camp Necessity, their rebel captors confirmed that their exchange as imminent. Young George was likely with his comrades on February 28th. The 16th Regimental history states that when they came in sight of the "Boys in Blue," they saw a "Welcome, Brothers," sign with a wreath from the 6th Connecticut, the released and their comrades were cheering loudly for Lincoln, Grant, Sherman and the General Exchange and finally at Cape Fear saw the U.S. Flag that some hugged and kissed as *Hail to the Chief* played. They received a full meal. Relief at last or so it would seem. However, George and 17 others perished within just days of their arrival – the effects of the dysentery and the starvation were too much, and their bodies could not take it anymore. One of the men of the 16[th,] Corporal Charles Lee, who passed away in Wilmington, the same day as George, remarked of their condition, some months prior,

"Again I am called to bid adieu to the passing year, but under very different circumstances from any in which I have ever been. During the year 1864, 1 have passed eight months in the most degrading imprisonment. In that time, our inhuman captors had not furnished shelter of any kind; and we have repeatedly been for two and three days at a time without a morsel of food; and even that we have received would at home have been generally thought unfit for swine. We have not had a particle of meat for forty-two days, and but little molasses, or anything to take the place of it. Our rations chiefly consist of about a pint and a half of coarse cornmeal, and half a teaspoonful of salt daily. Now and then we receive a few beans or sweet potatoes. Many a night have I lain awake because I was so hungry that I could not sleep."

George Brooks took his last breath on March 6th, 1865." The stories of the "Bad Luck Regiment" and rebel prisons are haunting to one's core and the Brooks seem to be ensuring their tale is heard. They are not mentioned by name in regimental histories and, in fact, other than beautiful grave markers, may have been lost to history. Their parents had no other children, and they have no descendants. Their hometown has no sources on them. But, as mentioned in the intro, the Brooks inspired this story.

It was when I was filming a virtual history segment for my company, looking for notable burials when I dreamed of two young boys in Civil War uniform one night, out of the blue. When I awoke and researched who it could be, feeling as if they were close to my hometown, the monument for them became known to me. It was then that I went to their burial site. It was chilly, rainy

Andersonville Stockade Close-Up, Courtney McInvale Photo

and their shadows appeared on either side of it, pointing to the monument and to their names. I read about them on their stone as a chill overtook me and knew I had to find out more about these young men. Old records were even unsure if they were ever reinterred back at home. I knew I wanted to feature them straight away. My husband assured me, that we could film more about them later, that it didn't have to be THAT day despite my insistence that it did, there was something about that cold April day. Nevertheless, I had to learn more before we did any filming and I settled on doing it a week later. But I was right, and the spirits of the young boys awoke me on just the right day. April the 20th, the day of their capture, the day of their imprisonment, the beginning of the end. Coincidences are funny things, but when it comes to something as clear as this dream and their pointed shadows, coincidence and spirit communication are two different things. I told the young men that I would endeavor to find them. I took a road trip, with my husband and went to Andersonville and Wilmington, found their burials, told them I hoped they could be together. I also decided to use my recorders and SB-7 spirit box to see, if they knew that I had found them, to confirm that they were still there with this me on their journey from Connecticut through the South, if they knew that they had not been and would never be forgotten. Thanks to Clara Barton and Dorence Atwater, the small and shallow ditches and trenches where the remains of the Union men were so callously thrown or buried were turned into a National Cemetery at Andersonville and each grave carefully marked with the identity of the individual buried in those grounds. William's headstone is easy to find as they are all numbered and he lays at #5152. I sat with the young Corporal in the hundred-degree heat in the middle of a summer Georgia day with no cloud in sight and thought of him, how he must have felt and the unimaginable horrors there, what he may have said to his brother. After moments of quiet, I decided to talk aloud with him, knowing any other spirit there may very well choose that time to speak as well. I started asking questions, but something didn't feel quite right. I knew what the spirits needed, the starved, diseased, confused and sad needed to know they weren't forgotten or looked down upon for not having been battle-hardened.

"I want you to know you died with dignity, grace and are very loved. WE are so sorry for what happened to you. You endured the unfathomable."

I felt a sense of acknowledgement from the thousands around me and then William, I could feel near to my hand where I quietly held the audio recorder. "Were you at Antietam?" I inquired quietly…the audio recording gets still. "Was it you that came to get me?" A male voice breathes deeply, groans. There's a sound of gunshot in the distance though I was the only one in the area under the blazing son. A man's southern accent could be discerned in the back of the audio. Was the man yelling at them? Not allowing them to speak? The quiet and birds chirping resumed. "I'm so

sorry you didn't see the Union victory that happened," and the birds sang joyously taking over the audio in response as if the men gathered there rejoiced how they could not in life. I only used the spirit box for a moment, something seemed more willing to contact in the silence of the cicadas and pine trees in the distance. "William, did you try to get my attention?" "Yes," a male voice whispered. "Was it you that

Grave Corporal William Brooks 16th GA came to my dreams." "Yes," the voice whispered again on the spirit box. "Are you with your brother again?" There was silence as if they were separated but trying to be together. I knew there was almost this need to reunite them, bring them together. William had longed to look after George but was unable to. Sitting in the stillness by William's stone, I put my hand to the earth and felt the heat of it and the small breeze that came by. William stood behind it, ever present, longing to be back in New England just one last time. Further on the road trip, we made it Wilmington, NC, to investigate battle sites but perhaps, even more pressing find George. I sat with William a while longer that late June day. I thought of a song that seemed perfect for him, entitled *Bury My Bones* and played it for him as we drove out of the National Cemetery and throughout the trip,

"If I die young, write my mother, Tell her that I love her but my soul's gone home....Won't you bury my bones beneath these pines when it comes time... if I die young..."

The Whiskey Myers song echoed with what I imagine was the sentiments of so many of the 13,000 young men buried in Andersonville, having died so young and looking up at the Georgia red pines in their final resting place...their legacy forever haunting the hearts of all those who hear their story. In the coming days I made my way up the coast to North Carolina, to see the younger brother who almost escaped alive. George is buried in the Wilmington National Cemetery, likely not far from where he took his final breath. Another hot summer day, it was more difficult to find George's burial with the numbers not being as clear, but my husband called me over to his stone when he found it. I reached out my hand and took a few photos hoping to catch an image and then I turned on the audio recorder for a couple moments and subsequently the SB-7. George's energy was less solemn, perhaps

Grave Private George Brooks 16th NC

as he passed away with the idea of hope still ringing true, George was ready to communicate. First on just audio, I introduced myself in front of his headstone and asked, "Are you here?" A male voice, in the tones of a whisper with a Connecticut dialect that could be heard, said, "I am." There was quiet for a few questions until I informed, "I want you to know the Union," won. The audio picked up a clapping of hands. It was time to go to the spirit box. I continued, "Where are you from, George?" "Haddam," he replied, a loudness to his tone. "Do you know that I am from the next town, "Yes! Home!" He cried out. "Who came to get my attention in April?" "IT WAS ME!" he exclaimed, and my husband took a step back. "I went to see your brother," I continued, "I hope you are both together now. I'm so sorry for what you went through." "A more hushed tone," came over the SB-7 and I shut it off for a more quiet, spiritual session. In some ways George was almost more visible, seemed a dark-haired young man, and cheeks that once held a prominent dimple, a floppy blue hat and the sensation that he almost made it back to share his brother's story, to keep his parents from mourning two sons, but he just...couldn't hold on any longer. It was nothing short of a miracle that he held on as long as he did. I promised the brothers once more that they were loved and let them know that the Union did indeed win. It was then that I envisioned in a way holding hands talking to me, that I would share their story, that the two of them would not be lost to history. And with that I could see them give a half smirk.

Nearly 55,000 men from Connecticut enlisted in the Union Army, nearly 55,000 boys, young men and grown men with stories, labors, family, loved ones, hopes and dreams each leaving a remarkable imprint on this earth that can never be replaced or forgotten. Whether a high-ranking officer or a young private being handed a rifle for the first time in his life, the men were brave, inspired and patriotic. Their souls leave a legacy and to know them is to love them and to remain haunted by all that was lost and all that could have been. Should is often thought to be a "dangerous," word but if you ask me, they should have all lived to tell their tale but since they could not, their ghosts share the story of a country divided and their sacrifice to keep us united no matter the cost. Whether you visit their hometown, their burial, the prison sites or the battlefields, their spirits will find you and know that you are seeking them.

This intimate view of over a dozen men and some of their acquaintances gives us an idea of the courageous and intelligent men that the Nutmeg State provided for the Union cause. Through this book, you will meet many more soldiers, be they privates or officers, each single one who left a significant impact. Let the number stay in your heads and your hearts – 55,000. 55,000 men from Connecticut who were fathers, sons, husbands, brothers, lovers and remarkable individuals who gave themselves to the Christian God they believed in and to the Union cause with their whole heart never knowing if they'd ever make it back home. 6,000 men from Connecticut alone, maybe more, would meet their end in this conflict and every one of them has a story and a soul. Each burial site, battle site, encampment site and family homestead still maintain the heartbeat of their energy. Feel them, know them, honor them and know their spirits are with us always. Together, we will journey into a broader view of the regiments of men and the battles they engaged in that left such a haunting mark; the stories of men who worked together, fought against one another on opposing sides of the field and sometimes on the same, men who lifted each other up and mourned each other and the unfathomable danger that brought them all together.

Fierce Fighters: Remarkable Regiments and Ethereal Energy that Lingers in Connecticut's Bootsteps

"The friends of the dead of your regiment are more than of the living, and my heart was sad as I saw the tears start in the eyes of the little child, the tender maiden and the mother with her little ones, as they looked in vain among your passing ranks for their friends. But they will never again watch their returning footsteps, or hear the sweet sound of their voices. No words of mine can heal their wounded hearts. I can only say they have the highest claim upon the nations' gratitude. The noble deeds of their martyred dead will ever live in the archives of the State, and their memories will be embalmed forever in the feelings of the American people." – Ezra Hall

Connecticut men were enlisted in one of thirty regiments, regiments each divided up into companies. Connecticut had twenty-eight regiments that were made up of local men from across the state as well as neighboring states, many of them, young, white men in their 20's and most regiments existing of an average of one-thousand men and ten companies. Notably, in Connecticut, one new regiment that formed was populated by the relatively new Irish immigrant population and two that formed that were of African descent and known as the "Colored Regiments" including free black men, escaped enslaved, and members of local Native American tribes. The 29th and 30th were the Colored Regiments of Connecticut and the 30th regiment was a combination of four companies and consolidated with what was also the 31st United States Colored Infantry. The regiments from across the Northeast filled with the new Irish immigrants having just been arriving since the Great Famine were often referred to as the Irish Brigade and given special battle flags. With an abundance of Irish in the Northeast from the ports of New York and Boston, Irish were in every regiment, but Connecticut's Irish Regiment known as the "Irish Volunteers," was the 9th Regiment. In addition to the 30 regiments, there were also two Cavalries and five Artilleries (two considered Heavy Artillery and three considered Light Artillery Battery. Some would go on to earn nicknames showing their propensity for death and catastrophe as the war years blazed furiously. One such regiment was the one where the brothers Brooks were enlisted, the 16th Regiment, known as the "Bad Luck Regiment" or the "Unlucky Regiment." The 14th Connecticut Infantry became known as the "Nutmeg Regiment," and their bravery at Pickett's Charge in Gettysburg was highly commended.

Connecticut received a great deal of acclaim for their military, specifically from President Abraham Lincoln. Connecticut, proving true to its provision state heritage, was notably one of the best at providing food and clothing for their soldiers. But, perhaps, even more importantly the soldiers from Connecticut were ensured payment even if it was at Governor Buckingham's personal expense and he had to take out loans to pay them at different points during the war. The Honorable William Buckingham would be lauded as Connecticut's "War Governor." According to David Lucian of Connecticut Historical Society, the Governor, "invested his own capital to help fund the war. On several occasions he took out personal loans to pay soldiers for the service and during the war, the governor kept in close contact with Union leaders including, President Lincoln." Buckingham believed in quality weapons, uniforms and acknowledgement of all that was being done and President Lincoln would go on to say, "The Connecticut regiments give me no trouble; Governor Buckingham always sends them full equipped for an emergency." Buckingham, the War Governor, continues to be honored for all his work in supporting and organizing the Connecticut troops and

Portrait War Governor Buckingham

Connecticut enacted a "Buckingham Day," starting in 1884 on June 18th. It's first holiday even had a parade through Hartford around the Connecticut State Capitol and the life-sized statue of Connecticut's Governor in the Capitol was unveiled. Buckingham was much appreciated for his service to Connecticut for some time and in fact the William Buckingham House was built in Norwich, CT, in 1847. not far from his native home of Lebanon and where he attended school in Colchester. Buckingham had served as the mayor of Norwich prior to being the Governor and the Buckingham house would serve as his residence and the building where he hosted both Abraham Lincoln and Ulysses S. Grant as guests. The house is known today as a Buckingham Memorial Hall, was used for some years as a meeting place for Sons of the Union Veterans of the Civil War. Governor Buckingham passed away about one decade after the war's conclusion and though he passed in Norwich where he is interred at Yantic Cemetery from likely natural causes, it is not Norwich that is most well-known to be haunted by the supportive Governor's spirit. The statue of the former Governor that was put into the state Capitol on Buckingham Day sometime after his death was put into a relatively new Victorian Gothic State Capitol. Since the completion of the bronze statue, a spirit has been seen near to the statue and cold spots are felt around it. The spirit, that locals believe to be the Governor loiters in or near room 324. In fact, it was a Lieutenant Governor in the 1920's who claimed to have seen Governor Buckingham's ghost standing directly in the room which is most recently the Republican caucus room. The Capitol Security staff claims to hear Buckingham walking around in the quiet nights. It's said, however, that he must be a good ghost, haunting the building he never got to work in though he worked until death on a variety of Connecticut and war issues and he worked tirelessly on the right for black men to vote during his final years. He still wants to serve the Connecticut constituents and is doing our work at the State Capitol and the children of our state encourage his spirit, rubbing the feet of the statue for good luck at behest of their teachers and guides as they say, he will bring them good luck.

With a supportive Governor, an impressed President and motivated men, Connecticut was ready to bring her brave men to the frontlines.

Many regiments were formed and mustered out of the New Haven or Hartford areas of Connecticut – of course, the major cities being able to respond to Lincoln's request by gathering men from all over the vicinity. As the years went on, smaller cities like Norwich, Bridgeport and Litchfield provided their own regiments or artilleries. The original response for Lincoln from the Nutmeg State included 13 regiments with 13,037 to fill a quota. There was then acceptance of another training type regiment before more started to merge, muster out and more and more men or regiments were required as the war raged on with no end in sight and men being lost in such a high number to injury or disease.

Seventh Connecticut Infantry Regiment

Varied regiments seemed to acquire varying reputations over the course of the war, be it for their bravery, their tragedy, their country of birth, or the color of their skin. One regiment became known for the number of substitutes and draftees they had acquired as well as the almost disjointed ensemble that overcame the regiment that had suffered hundreds of deaths by 1863. The 7th Connecticut Infantry is just that such regiment though you may not often hear them referred to in this way. They were originally mustered out of New Haven in September of 1861 and were not discharged until August of 1865 though exactly who made up the regiment would change. The 7th trained in South Carolina and totaled 1,000 men over their service. In total 364 of the 1,000 would be killed or lost to disease over the service, making up just over a third of their force which is also hard on morale. During their training and introduction to the Southern States, Private Walkley detailed their feelings of homesickness that overcame them at the stark difference to the life and people they were used to as new soldiers. In the History of the Seventh Connecticut, Walkley features a poem from the early winter of 1861 expressing his and his comrade's sentiments.

A HOME SICK SOLDIER TO HIS WIFE.
I stand alone on the moonlit shore,
When the soldier's work is done, And I think the thoughts often felt before, As I've seen the surf with its dashing roar
Leap up 'neath a southern sun.
I think of a land where the glistening snow,
Twinkles clear 'neath the moon to-night, Of a cheerful home where full well I know, Shines a mellow lamp with its cheerful glow,

And a fireside's genial light.

I think of a mother who's sitting there,

With a dear little boy on her knee; And she tickles his neck so soft and fair, Till I seem to hear through this misty air, That child laugh ringing and free.

Then she kisses good night to the lips so red.

And pillows the sunny hair. In a neat and snug little cradle bed; It may be she presses her weary head,

And wishes that I was there.

Now the pearly eyelids sleepily close,

Shutting the blue orbs in; And a motherly hand smooths down the clothes, Tucks them around the uneasy toes,

And under the dimpled chin.

How the days grow short which were long before,

When I think what a wealth of joy, Will be mine when my country's need is o'er And I look into those hazel eyes once more, And clasp our own bright-haired boy.

Then I pray that if here I am called to die, We may meet with the spirits who roam.

Through the beautiful worlds in the starry sky;

And on shining pinions where're they fly, They are never away from home.

According to the Olustee Battlefield Site and Reenactment, the 7th spent its entire enlistment prior to Olustee in the Department of the South fighting in the siege of Fort Pulaski and the battles of Secessionville and Battery Wagner. In 1863, the regiment formed part of a garrison in Florida in the same brigade as the Seventh New Hampshire, whom they served alongside for the duration of the remainder of the war. In 1863, the regiment status was changed to "boat infantry," for the purpose of leading a night assault as Fort Sumter, not far from where they'd trained, but the project filled with impracticalities did not go through. They would go on to

Olustee, Drewry's Bluff where some would be imprisoned, Bermuda Hundred, Deep Bottom and more.

Fort Fisher, North Carolina (Courtney McInvale photo)

At the conclusion of the war, they would find themselves at Fort Fisher for first and second battles, ending the war there at this placement just outside Wilmington. Still at Fort Fisher with their companions, the 7th New Hampshire, they would become acquainted with Cape Fear and meet their end of the war here. Upon visiting Wilmington, North Carolina and speaking with the Park Ranger regarding the battle site, I asked him, if there was anything, he could tell me that he thought notable about the Connecticut men at Fort Fisher. He chuckled to himself and said,

"Well, since they were always with the 7th New Hampshire in the same brigade, the rebels decided to call them the "77th New Englanders," and that's funny right there."

His southern drawl and laughter showed the years of the story being passed down as a clever verbiage from the Confederates and, he was right. That nickname stuck and many both in the North and South still refer to them as the 77th New Englanders. It was in 1863 – early 1864, though, as mentioned that this noted disassembly had happened to the 7th. In the fall of 1863, there were new additions to the regiment to comprised of 112 substitutes and draftees; draftees, of course, not being there by choice and substitutes being men who had received compensation from a draftee that had elected not to serve. In January of 1864, three hundred of the seasoned enlisted veterans of the regiment were furloughed. The morale was dropping, and they were considered "quite forlorn with depleted ranks," by the time they had reached Florida in 1864, they were only four companies and just short of three-hundred men with nearly half of those being the draftees and substitutes. The draftees and substitutes were oftentimes immigrants or people impoverished and would have quarrels with another that often escalated. Captain Benjamin Skinner was exhausted of the "scuttlebutt," so he often ignored it, even when it came to murder among his own. It was only the ghost story that would convince the Captain and the rest of the men of the story's validity. It was during the battle of Olustee in February of 1864 that the true crime among the 7th's own ranks transpired. Private Jerome Dupoy of Redding, CT had enlisted as a substitute in November of 1863 and during the battle had been shot in the back of the head and killed.

It became clear, rather quickly that it was someone in their own ranks, namely a man, who had been a substitute for a drafted man, at least once in his enlistment. That man, Private John Rowley of Ridgefield, of the same Company D as Dupoy had been heard quarreling with him prior to the event. Rowley had even been stabbed by Dupoy prior to the incident. Sergeant Broes was ready to charge Rowley with the death of Dupoy, that was clearly him trying to end some sort of feud, but Rowley was all too ready to confess. He had been haunted by the ghost of Rowley and could stand it no longer. He even described in detail how this was not his first murder, or even second for that matter. Rowley confessed as follows in his statement,

"Well, Sergeant, I did kill Dupoy; he stabbed me on St. Helena; I swore if ever I got a chance, I'd kill him; I had one at Olustee, and I killed him. Nor is he the only man I have killed or caused to die. I cut out the entrails of a sailor on a gunboat, since the war began, and I killed by a stabbing, a man in New York which caused me to leave my family and go a substitute for a drafted man last fall. But the ghost of Dupoy is the only one that even troubled me. Since the battle, I have dreaded the nights, for they are horrible nights. When on picket, I always see Dupoy stand a little way in front, his face all blood, and the bullet hole in his forehead. At night, when in my dreams he stands at the entrance, I awake, he is there pale and bloody but vanishes as soon as I see him. I could not keep this horrible crime a secret any longer."

Both men, substitutes for another, both said to be of poor character, met gruesome ends. Rowley was arrested after his confession, found guilty of murder by General Court Martial and hanged on September 3rd, 1864 in Petersburg, Virginia. The news would be printed in varying spots across the nation and detailed in full in the article, *A Soldier's Murder Remorse*, in the *Dayton Daily Empire* in May of 1864 while Rowley was still alive. According to the history of the 7th, Rowley was so plagued by the sight of ghosts that the other men almost felt uncomfortable around him for that and the murder they were certain he committed and had him placed in the guardhouse which is the entrance where he first saw the ghost of Dupoy.

The six months or so between murder and execution was not without even more colorful stories of the tale. Rowley knew that before he could be executed, a warrant had to be signed for Lincoln and the Connecticut man begged for his life and for mercy, however Lincoln, who was often merciful, knew the crime of murder was not one such crime to extend mercy to and signed the warrant. Rowley still attempted to find sympathy and love even after the warrant was signed. A somewhat handsome men of dark hair, eyes and complexion, he was known to be charming with the ladies. A woman named Harriet Hawley sent her "love," and a Bible to Rowley prior to his execution though she was the wife of Rowley's commander, Joseph R. Hawley. She had become acquainted with the man when she served as nurse in South Carolina and his situation broke her heart. She insisted he was remorseful and felt that he was a bad man, but she could not condemn him. Mrs. Hawley believed he suffered a tough life with no education or training and bad family influences. It was said that neither Rowley or Dupoy were fluent in the English language and could not speak it very well, though it's unclear what language they did speak. Dupoy is a French name implying that he may have indeed been a Frenchman or French Canadian. Rowley, however, is an English name.

The matter was brought to the Smithsonian regarding Rowley, the vengeful murder's background because in the middle of Main Street in Ridgefield at the head of Branchville Road is the Ridgefield War Memorial and Rowley's name is inscribed upon the others. The only story told of him was that he was a substitute who sought vengeance, murdered Dupoy and continually saw his ghost. Who was he to the town of Ridgefield? What the Smithsonian Institution historian, Silvio a. Bendini could find, however, about the man from his native town was that there was no record of residence of the man in Ridgefield in the 1800's, however, the National Archives suggest that an English-born man named Rowley who mustered out of Bridgeport at the same time was named John Rowley and he took the lace of Charles B.

Woodhouse for three years. Likely one and the same, which begs the question, why did no one think he spoke English? Perhaps due to his lack of education, he just spoke it poorly. And where was this Ridgefield connection? Perhaps, Rowley stole the identity of one of the previous victims he had coldly murdered or a name he picked up along the way. That could account for the lack of property records in the town he stated. To be sure, some mysteries remain but one may think that perhaps Mrs. Hawley still

7th Connecticut Color Bearer (Library of Congress)

wanted the man she felt sorrowful for to be commemorated with the rest of the 7th.

Would the scuttlebutt have become proof if the ghost of Mr. Dupoy did not haunt Rowley? Any why the sudden guilt over this murder rather than the others? Dupoy, if the spirit story is true, continued to show his wounds, his sorrow and to make appearances everywhere Rowley went until the end of the day. One must wonder, what happened when the two spirits encountered each other on the "other," side.

Tenth Connecticut Infantry Regiment

Not all regiments have as well documented ghost stories as the 7th happened upon, that's not to say there weren't ghost stories told among the men. Some of the regiments seemed increasingly more ill-fated than others due to no fault of their own, as if their destiny were carved out before their enlistment and some regiments were doomed for loss of life and devastation where others were put on a path to victory and accolades. The 10th Connecticut had a destiny of success. The men came from all over Connecticut, towns and cities when they mustered in 1861 having all registered as volunteers. They were able to spend time training at Camp Buckingham and continue training in Annapolis Maryland before joining the North Carolina Expedition. Over 2,000 men served with the 10th over twenty-three battles and over twenty skirmishes. Of the 2,124, they lost fifty-seven in battle, fifty-nine to wounds and 152 to disease for a total of 268 deaths, about twelve percent of their total forces. They were considered one of the top Union regiments, gained acclaim from General Ulysses S. Grant and even accompanied Grant for the surrender of Lee in Appomattox having successfully teamed up with the First Connecticut Calvary and blocking Lee's escape.

Sixteenth Connecticut Infantry Regiment

The 16th Connecticut, the "Unlucky Regiment," would have a different destiny. According to the Hartford Courant and regimental history, only 130 enlisted men returned home in the summer of 1865 – 130 desperate, hungry, tired and disheartened men. There was an honorable march through Hartford welcoming them home as the Governor and Honorable Ezra Hall of Marlborough, State Senator and lawyer spoke of the 16th's bravery and of their devastation at Antietam, Plymouth and the hundreds lost at Andersonville Prison. Hall stated,

"They fell away from home and friends, and most of them rest in Southern graves, but though they fell thus, they died at their posts.

History will keep fresh their memories, and write their names on more than granite shaft or marble column...After an eventful life and a noble death, they rest well. The friends of the dead of your regiment are more than of the living, and my heart was sad as I saw the tears start in the eyes of the little child, the tender maiden and the mother with her little ones, as they looked in vain among your passing ranks for their friends. But they will never again watch their returning footsteps, or hear the sweet sound of their voices. No words of mine can heal their wounded hearts. I can only say they have the highest claim upon the nations' gratitude. The noble deeds of their martyred dead will ever live in the archives of the State, and their memories will be embalmed forever in the feelings of the American people."

To understand Hall, we must understand the 16th, what brought them to this terrible point? Numbering over 1,000 men in August of 1862 when they mustered out from Hartford under command of Colonel Frank Beach, the men would see a total 1,087 members, 130 who would come home in 1865, 386 who would be discharged prior to being mustered out and the rest lost to the cause of the Union. That is over half of the regiment. In 1862, the men of the 16th were incredibly young and starting in the sweltering summer hear as they carried thirty-to-fifty-pound sacks on their way down South was a shock enough though not as shocking as the fact that they were not provided muskets during their preparation. Except for the 27th Connecticut whose average age was 27, the average age of the 16th and most other regiments was 21 with many being just a year or two older or younger than this, many still teenagers. The 16th was notably young – most eighteen and nineteen, untrained, unarmed and ill experienced. Some were saving for university such as nineteen-year-old, Ira Forbes, others were apprentices such as George Brooks who was only eighteen or so and Robert H. Kellogg, who was just 18 and apprenticing as a druggist. Survivor, George Whitney, as a teenage machinist when he enlisted in the 16th. When the statue of the "Andersonville Boy," was placed in Hartford, a copy of the boy at the Connecticut monument in Andersonville, Whitney spoke of his comrades, whom he had also written about to ensure their memory and recollected their doomed path. Their story begins just a couple weeks after their having mustered out of Connecticut, when there would be baptism by fire on the fields of Antietam, on the fields of one of the single deadliest days in American history. They confess feeling ill prepared for the devastation that awaited them as they made their way into Sharpsburg, Maryland and saw dead soldiers on the side of the road, a sign of what was to come. Fighting began at dawn on September 17th. The sounds of gunshots came, and Private Marx Neisener likened the fire's quickness to coming down like rain. Some ran into the woods to hide and others fell flat on to the cornfield for two hours. They waited to fight anxiously, getting sick to their stomach and overcome with anxiety. Private Lamphere said,

"One of the most trying positions troops can be put into is to be lying around inactive and yet be under fire. It requires courage and it is a great consumer of nerve power."

The men were armed, having just been equipped in the day or two prior to battle with no training. As the day continued, they walked in water up to their shoulders, holding their weapons over their heads on their way to support a Union battery and outflank Confederates. Immediately upon arrival, cannons fired upon them. They joined other regiments when their commanding officer Beach, put them into formation. The color guard forgot their flag and they could only wave a black flag they were equipped with. Author Lesley Gordon, documents this as an omen of what was to come. Volleys of musket fire descended upon them, vision was obstructed by cornstalks, and they were in crossfire with limited vision. Scared, ill-equipped and following their flight or fight instincts some men became wounded and died in those fields while the rest ran to hide, many panicking and retreating. They knew nothing of war or the world, let alone guerilla warfare.

Former Director, Dean Nelson and Librarian Kelly Nolin of the Connecticut Historical Society spoke to the *Hartford Courant* in 1997 about the battle and explained to journalist Jesse Leavenworth detail of the 16th's lack of experience and the graphic and traumatic nature of precisely what they endured at Antietam. Kelly Nolin wrote of the 16th's experience at an anniversary gathering and stated

16th CT Monument Antietam (Courtney McInvale photo)

"Five days before the battle of Antietam, many of the men had not been schooled in loading and firing their rifles, Nolin wrote. On Sept. 17, the 16th Connecticut entered a wide, sloping cornfield. They were hit by volleys from two South Carolina regiments posted behind a stone wall 10 feet in front of their right wing and from the 1st South Carolina behind another stone wall to the left, Mayhem ensued, and the regiment retreated in disorder. Pvt. William Relyea of Company D passed Cpl. Michael Grace, who was on his hands and knees as if searching for something, Nolin wrote. Grace, Relyea discovered, was dead, "telescoped" from end to end by a cannon shot. The Confederates were firing not only regular projectiles, but all

161

kinds of junk, including horseshoes, twisted telegraph wire, doorknobs and hammer heads."

The 16th lost 238 to Antietam and buried forty of their dead over a day after the battle's end near to a large tree and stone wall where the hardest of battle was fought. They gathered their wounded as best they could and mourned the loss of Newton Spaulding Manross who had helped to form the corps of Volunteers. A Bristol native, Doctor of Philosophy and scientist and engineer was much beloved by the men and fell at Antietam. A monument sits for him at the Forestville Cemetery in Bristol and was placed by survivors of the 16th, Company K in 1887.

Just three months after Antietam, the 16th would be present at the Battle of Fredericksburg and throughout their service see several skirmishes, sieges and campaigns, losing men to conditions, disease, injury and action. It was during this year-and-a-half period that the 16th would suffer desertion in great numbers, officers returning home and resigning, refusing to come back, months without pay due to errors and a drunk man who took their money and vanished. They suffered hunger, lack of leadership and feared having to have draftees and substitutes. One man slit his own throat in the demoralized atmosphere. They turned against each other – some not liking the Irish, or those with money not liking those who didn't come from money and vice versa. They would find excuses to go home, not wanting to face another day of hunger. Their guns were recorded to be ragged, in terrible condition, their lack of training haunted them. They felt a lack of justice, a lack of training, a sadness and a bitterness. It is recorded that some, feeling as if there was not enough support for the Union and the Constitution in their own army, deflected to the other side. They differed on the virtues and morals of fighting for abolition versus fighting for the country. Author, Lesley Gordon, states

"Different soldiers told different stories, with some more willing than others to admit the unit's failures and foibles. The strands of the story they were trying to create never really came together."

There was also judgment for years about their reaction at Antietam, other regiments and those who did not flee mocking those who did for their lack of courage and their fear. As the regiment went back and forth through the harsh travels, lack of food and combat, their engagements caused more death and there was also a series of accidental drownings when their boat collided with the Black Diamond losing seven lives before the end of the war.

16th CT Young Men (Connecticut State Library)

Prior to Plymouth, one was lost at Fredericksburg, eight on Edenton Road in Suffolk, Virginia, ten to Providence Church Road in Suffolk, Virginia and the worst was yet to come. The worst, believe it or not, was to come for the 16th in April of 1864 at the Battle of Plymouth. It was not just the Brooks who see the terror of that day, but the entirety of the regiment would be scarred or lost to the circumstances at Plymouth, North Carolina. They were seasoned now, braver, knew what to expect. They would not flee; they'd joke far less, and they would face what the rebels would unexpectedly bring their way with courage and perseverance. Their losses that day would number 436.

As detailed with the Brooks, The Confederate assault at Plymouth lasted over nearly four days. After having just marched on the parade ground, Private Lamphere reported around 5 PM on the evening of the 16th that there was an enemy attack. The fire in both ways began suddenly and the 16th fell back. The Confederate rebels were attacking in full force. The 16th of over 400 men were trying to hold Fort Williams. Some of the privates started sensing that something was more than just a rebel attempt, that they were greatly outnumbered by thousands to their hundreds and began to scribble notes to their parents that they were praying, that God would keep and protect them. They knew they had howitzers and abundant ammunition which gave them hope in the beginning, but they didn't expect the number of rebels and the consistency of attack. By the late evening of the 16th of April, Company H escorted women, children and civilians aboard a steamer for Roanoke Island. Little did they know, they'd be the lucky ones. The Confederates coming from every direction started to overwhelm and overpower the 16tgh at the Fort. Through engagements, the 16th and Union minimized casualties and held the fort well. The siege continued into the morning of the 19th and hope was dwindling. The Confederates used the power of the water and rammed the Albemarle ship into the region, sinking Union ships. The impromptu earthworks didn't protect the 16th, the reinforcements didn't help, and fun fire assault continued. Men started being captured, Private Lamphere suffered an amputation from being shot, the Confederates took the town, demanded surrender and were relentless. They had a choice upon them on

April 20th. Company G had a clear shot at a Confederate general. They could kill him and fall victim to retaliation, or they could succumb to the inevitable capture and try to survive prison. The 16th had only lost about a dozen to the attack, prison, at first seemed a better bet though it would turn to be the deadliest decision they'd ever made. Many residents of Plymouth, North Carolina still feel haunted by the events that transpired there, having always been a Southern town in support of the Union and against slavery, this was a sad event for many residents.

The local Windley-Ausbon house that saw the battle still stands and bullet holes can be seen all round the second story window where Union men from the 16th Connecticut took out a Confederate sharpshooter who was in the window and who would die of his wounds in the home. Legend states that rebel still haunts the house and will always try to fulfill his role as a sniper, even in the afterlife. After the capture of the 16th on the 20th of April, the non-commissioned officers and enlisted were brought to Andersonville Prison for the next five months. In September of 1864, the survivors of Andersonville which were limited were moved to other prisons, many staying in Charleston or Richmond and officers in Libby Prison in Virginia until late February of 1865 when they were exchanged in Wilmington, NC, where they were exchanged in such poor condition that 18 more died just after release.

Of the 400 in prison, 177 would die of conditions, dozens more of disease surrounding the conditions and two were shot by rebels – one in prison, as so often happened when rebels used them as target practice and another when trying to escape and getting too close to the deadline. William Drake of Company A was shot in the prison in Charleston. The regimental history estimates that including those captured at Antietam, the regiment lost at "least two hundred and twenty, by death from rebel cruelties and starvation." The devastation was palpable with the women becoming widows and their parents losing their children and learning of this in 1865 was painful even for survivors to recollect. The Regimental History recollects,

"Those who had husbands, brothers, or relatives in the regiment, watched us eagerly and looked strangely into the ranks, hardly believing that any could be missing. One lady, the wife of an officer, was told for the first time of her husband's death. So great was her grief, that friends who accompanied her could hardly get her into a carriage to convey her home."

One may wonder was the 16th "Bad Luck," or "Broken?" It was a combination perhaps of terrible luck, broken morale and a group of men neglected by their peers and many of their leaders left to fight for a Union and feeling deserted in their effort to so.

One of the places where the 16th can be felt the most, where their horrors and collapse of all dreams into nightmare still sits over the cornfields and in the trees and rocks that bore witness to unimaginable death is Antietam Battlefield in Sharpsburg, Maryland. It still feels as they described. The cries and groans of the wounded that lay on the battle-field could be heard distinctly, and the occasional report of artillery sounded solemn and death-like." The monument to the 16th Connecticut, placed where many of them waited and encamped, where some may still be buried is at the South end of the battlefield about 150 yards east of Branch avenue on the Otto Farm, the monument having been dedicated over three decades later in 1894. You can look upon the directions that the rebels came from and fired from and hear the screams of terror in reaction. It is set apart from some of the bloodiest parts of the battlefield, perhaps for the best of the ill-equipped 16th but their taste of loss and vulnerability still haunts the ground. You are keenly aware when you stand there that is the moment that young men realized they too could die and it could be at any day, or even hour. When conducting a small paranormal investigation on a cold winter day at the monument, we utilized the EMF detector, the SB-7 Spirit Box and an audio recorder to try to communicate with the fallen in that spot. We introduced ourselves to any spirits present – Courtney, Marty and Andrew. We told them how we hailed from Connecticut. After a few moments of silence on the white noise, a male voice, said clearly, "William." "Did you say, yes?" "Yes, he replied. A different voice, said "John." There were two of them. We asked a few more questions and the deafening silence came back over. Were they scared? A voice tried to answer where they were from. "When were you handed your muskets?" "Night," someone replied. A few more minutes transpired, and I asked, "Can I help you?" The desperation sat in the air. "A voice that sounded as if speaking through tears came through, "My mother," he asked for. We took a moment to decide how to talk to this man who perhaps reliving this moment hoping for his family to be by his side. We assured him that he was loved, and we would pass on his message back home to Connecticut. We reviewed later to see a record of who died at Antietam of the 16th. Noted was Lieutenant William Horton and Captain John Drake and they were buried near to each other on the field. When returned home, John Drake was sent home with the body of William Nichols almost a month later. William Nichols was in the same company as the brothers Brooks. William Nichols was nineteen years old when he took his last breath and was re-interred back home to Zion Hill Cemetery in Hartford with few records of his life before the war. John Drake has no official record of age but was estimated to be around age 32 when he passed and had worked at the Colt Arms Factory in Hartford. He was recorded to be a remarkable gentleman and one of the most well-mannered and kindest members of the 16th. William Horton was married with small children and as just 31 when he died at Antietam. Were these some of the young men that spoke to us that day? Are their souls still there? Drake's body was re-interred from the field to Spring Grove Cemetery in Hartford and Horton was re-interred in Stafford, Connecticut at Stafford Street Cemetery. Instinctually, we might say Nichols would be the one to call out for his mom, his youth, his fear and we can only hope he knows that he can now come home at any time. Nichols much like Tarbox, who was in the suffering 11th regiment, also youthful and ill-experienced was barely more than a boy, scared and completely unknowing as all men were of the violence that would lay ahead and the brevity of the human condition.

I will never forget the sound of that young man asking for his mother. Listening to the recording even brings tears to my eyes and it reminds me of the story of another young man from New York who died in battle in 1863. Legend states that the young man named George Roberts fell on Sunday, June 14th, 1863. That morning miles away from where his son was in battle in the deep south his mother getting ready for church heard her son's voice echo, "Mother, Mother," in the house. She was so upset by the clarity of his voice and him not being there that she became ill over the matter and shortly thereafter was informed of his death at the exact moment she had heard his cries. The connectedness of the soul to those they love, the child ever looking for their parent for their comfort as they take their final breath, could be heard at battlefields across the southeast for four, long years. Boys who would never get to become men and mothers who would outlive the children they bore and raised to near adulthood. The country would never be the same.

Fourteenth Connecticut Infantry Regiment

The 14th Connecticut Regiment was perhaps one of the most remarkable of the Constitution State's history. Known by many as the "Fighting Fourteenth," they fought for the entire war and endured the most battles. The 14th was organized in Hartford,

Connecticut in August of 1862 and initially 1,015 men mustered out under the command of Colonel Dwight Morris. Many of these men were from the shoreline, Connecticut region. The regiment was formed to answer the Governor's call for more men, and though enlistment was slow, when they were filled by August 22nd, they mustered out on August 23rd. Two companies were assigned Sharp's rifles and the rest were assigned Springfield's rifles. After mustering out, as they made their way to Maryland, casualties already started taking place due to exhaustion and accidents, but nevertheless they made it to the area where they like the 16th would have baptism under fire. The 14th was another regiment that saw a high casualty toll at Antietam and other large battles. The 14th had a pseudo miraculous come-back at Gettysburg fighting bravely on the frontlines, but the incredible achievements came amid yet more tragic losses. A Madison, Connecticut minister wrote of the 14th,

"I have at last turned over a new and bloody leaf in my experience, and seen a battle, and am now writing you, sitting in a newly plowed field all strewn with the dead of our gallant Union soldiers, still unburied, lying as they fell."

After more loss at Fredericksburg, after Antietam, amid enduring heartbreak 14th Connecticut Lieutenant Fiske wrote,

"Oh! My heart is sick and sad. Blood and wounds and death are before my eyes; of those who are my friends, comrades, brothers.... Another tremendous, terrible, murderous butchery of brave men."

By the following summer of 1863, the men of the 14th were armed with courage and had nothing left to lose in their eyes. They stood bravely upon Pickett's Charge at the angle of Gettysburg and jumped over a stone wall to capture six enemy battle flags and three of the men received a Medal of Honor for this action. Fiske had new comments.

"I have at last had the desired opportunity of seeing a battle in which there was real fighting; hard, persistent, desperate fighting; a fighting worthy of a noble cause and the confidence of a gallant people.... Hurrah for the gallant old 14th!"

14th CT Monument Antietam (Martin Reardon Jr. photo)

The bravery at Gettysburg will be detailed in the chapter on battles. And while the 14th was proud of their acts there – it was after Gettysburg that they had deserters who could bear the struggle no longer and the two deserters were found and executed. Ultimately, the heroic deeds of the 14th would spare them from the titles of "broken" or "unlucky," an unfortunate entrance to the war at Antietam.

The 14th participated "gallantly" in five of the top ten deadliest battles of the war – Gettysburg and Antietam being just two; the other three being the Battle of Chancellorsville just two months prior to Gettysburg and occurring in April to May of 1863. and the Battle of the Wilderness and the Battle at Spotsylvania Courthouse both back-to-back and occurring nearly a year after Chancellorsville in May of 1864. They would also endure the vicious Battle of Cold Harbor. The 14th would also be present at the Bristoe Campaign, Overland Campaign, the Siege of Petersburg and the Appomattox Campaign and, of course, there remains the fact that the regiment participated in more battles than any other Connecticut regiment. The 14th was commendable in many aspects not the least of which being that despite their high casualty count, they did not replace the dead or wounded. The company initially totaling 1,014 men, many from shoreline Connecticut was down to just 165 officers and men by Gettysburg after which they were down to 100. Author, Dr. Ira Spar described a story from a nineteen-year-old of the 14th, entitled "My Chum," as follows,

"He was the best wrestler and hardest worker, carried the most firewood, participated in every battle, was always helpful to his fellow soldiers and was out there doing his duty while his friend was home on medical leave... We tented together, slept together and ate together, share dangers of campaign together. We shared all."

The friend would die alone however, showing the intimate nature of life and death that coursed through the veins of all in the 14th. It was after this severe depletion, that if they were going to carry on in the war, new men would have to be recruited and they were. The prominent 14th regiment was notably named after its home state that it so bravely represented throughout the war and was known as the "Nutmeg Regiment." They had a saying at the 14th, however,

"You would meet death or promotion within a year."

More would meet death, but the promotions and honors were immeasurable and well deserved.

Ninth Connecticut Infantry Regiment (Irish Regiment)

As time goes on, regiments leave an impact in history for who was part of them, it's the men that make the stories.

Connecticut is known for many infantries with nick-names but also for regiments that were made up of men almost all Irish descent or all African descent. The all-Irish Brigades were relevant on both sides of the war and from many states. In the Nutmeg State, Connecticut's Ninth Regiment Volunteer Infantry were uniquely patriotic, having come as so many Irish did from a destitute position in their home country. Many of the Irish came over after the potato famine of 1847 wreaked havoc and caused them to desperately flee in search of a better life. Irish weren't welcome right away but Connecticut was filled with them. Having previously been a Protestant state, many did not welcome the starving Catholics with open arms, and they took manual labor jobs on railroads and in quarries. Others opened their own businesses or became policemen and firemen. Irish women took work too and it was common in Connecticut for them to work at the Connecticut Hospital for the Insane in Middletown. In just over a decade, the Irish population in Connecticut was estimated to be greater than 50,000. Irishmen wanted to support their new home despite discrimination they may have faced and enlisted in infantries as soon as volunteers were sought however for the beginning months, Connecticut was hesitant to allow an Irish regiment. Governor Buckingham, however, was pro-Irish and saw their patriotism and decided they could help.

The bulk of the Irish population was in Middletown and Portland, Connecticut or New Haven, Connecticut and this is where the Irish regiment, the 9th would recruit and muster from as well. The state went on to say of New Haven and Middletown

"The Irish population of this city and vicinity are unanimous in their wish and determination to support the Government. In spite of the prophecies of many to the contrary, we have not heard of a single Irishman who has shown a disposition to prove false to the stars and stripes. They have shown a great readiness to volunteer, and several are enrolled in the company that has just been formed. In addition to this, there is a prospect that a large company will be formed composed mostly of Irish volunteers."

Battle Flags of CT's 9th

The 9th was deemed as "destined to be gallant and had a special battle flag overlapping the stars and stripes with an Irish harp. Recruitment efforts were most successful at Camp English in New Haven though it took some time to supply everyone appropriately. The regiment numbered 845 men by the time they mustered out in November for Camp Chase in Massachusetts and participated as members of the "New England Brigade," under General Benjamin Butler to assist in the capture of New Orleans. Recruitment continued until their numbers totaled about 1,200 men strong.

Many Irish folks would tell stories of their heroes which were several and were immensely proud of James T. Mullen of the 9th who would be the first Supreme Knight o the Knights of Columbus as well as John C. Curtis, the regiment's 17-year-old Sergeant Major who received the Medal of Honor. Colonel Thomas Cahill would lead the men with his military experience from the antebellum state militia and Captain of the Emmet Guards while fellow Irishmen Lieutenant Colonel Richard Fitzgibbons and Major Frederick Frye who had served at the First Battle of Bull Run would join the ranks as well. IT was perhaps, in part, due to the experienced leadership in combination with the training that kept the Irish regiment well intact and safe in combat situations. The regiment in total would lose less in combat or imprisonment than almost any other Connecticut regiment. Colonel Cahill and others would describe the regiment as also being large, stalwart, handsome men, who were able to withstand more than the average and who were grateful to be among their kin. Cahill wrote to his wife,

"My Dear Wife,
...I am taking in a large number of recruits and they were verry [sic] stalwart men much Larger than the overage [sic] of our men: They are natives of Ireland Germany and some of the Northern and

Western States. They represent themselves as having suffered terribly during the Last year and seem glad to Come among us. our regt has such a tremendous name here somehow or other that they walk out here about 8 miles to join us. While I write I heard 6 have Come into Camp."

Ten were killed in the war and 230 lost to disease some from exposure – most of these during their station on the canal opposite Vicksburg on the Mississippi River. 150 would die of diseases such as malaria during this work just one year after their enlistment and muster. The 9th saw engagement eleven times in Virginia and Louisiana. Working on the canal, a project that was eventually abandoned was the deadliest time for the regiment. The canal was to be known as "Grant's Canal," so the Navy forces could capture Vicksburg. The 9th supplied over a thousand of the 3,2000 men assigned with building this. Due to the disease and falling river levels, the canal was abandoned until Grant took interest and helped to solve some of the problems but again, they were met with difficulties that were too large to overcome. The Irishmen were not accustomed to the summer heat and exposure plus the dehydration that would accompany this, and it was a rough start to the war. They kept their morale high despite dysentery, heat stroke and malaria. They were moved down to Baton Rouge excepting the sick who were left on a boat for several months, many of them succumbing to their afflictions. The General Thomas Williams they had been reporting under fell in a Confederate charge in August of 1862 and Colonel Cahill took command of his troops. Some compared the Irish in 1862's Battle of Baton Rouge to the equivalent of Fredericksburg or Gettysburg for other regiments, "the most important battle to proving their manhood and capabilities as soldiers," according to Professor Ryan Keating, author of a book about the 9th. It was in Baton Rouge that the young teenager Curtis, earned his Medal of Honor "having sought the line of battle and alone and unaided captured two prisoners, driving them before him to regiment headquarters at the point of a bayonet," as documented in his citation in 1896. That, is perhaps, one of the bravest accounts that could come out of war, to act alone with such confidence that you can capture your enemy. After their time in Louisiana in 1863, they would make it home by spring of 1864 amid great-praise prior to re-enlistment and the 9th heading to Bermuda Hundred, Virginia and participating in battle at Deep Bottom, and continuing in action throughout Virginia before mustering out in August of 1865. The Irish had fought oppression and starvation before, they'd been pushed out of their home before and they banded together in their new home to ensure that they would not have to do that again and their bravery is commended to this day. Monuments to Irish brigades are on most battlefields and Connecticut's Ninth is honored with a large monument in New Haven, Connecticut.

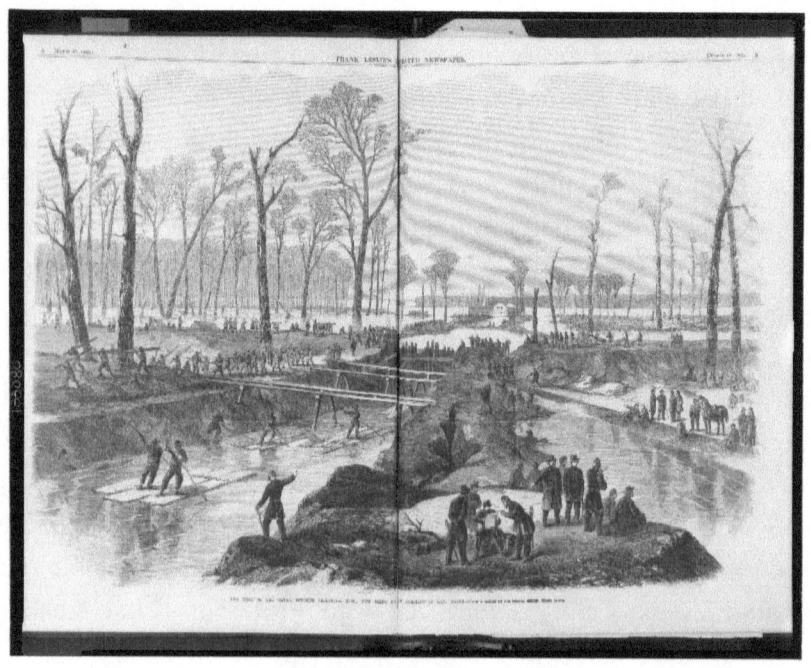

Grant's Canal near Vicksburg 1863 (Courtesy of the Library of Congress)

There are several hauntings linked to the attempted development of the Grant Canal and the surrounding regions of Mississippi and Louisiana as well as with the Battle of Baton Rouge, many of the stories being down South, focus on spirits of the Confederates the believe seem to be trying to make it home or who perished there when the 27th Connecticut came during the Siege of Port Hudson just across the way. One theory, that we have asserted when looking for historic ghost stories and finding that so many sightings report what is a man in a Confederate rather than a Union uniform, is that perhaps the Confederate men have rested less easily as historically speaking, more of them were left on battlefields and in hospitals, their bodies not being returned home oftentimes for a final resting place. It could be that this disturbs their eternal rest more than those of the Union. In Baton Rouge, along a road near Louisiana State University, there have been tales that around the anniversary of the Battle of Baton Rouge, men in Confederate Uniforms can be seen walking across the road near the campus however recently, rather than seeing the rebel forces, a dying man has been seen covered in blood, possibly in Union uniform, staggering across the street. He appears so vividly and clearly injured that the police have been called to aid him, however whenever the police arrive, they find no one. One of the 9th Connecticut? Perhaps. In nearby Port Hudson, the site of the 1863 battle lasting 48 days with the 27th Connecticut and not far from where the 9th had worked on the canal is a National Cemetery where many of the Union dead are buried. The Confederates are buried in a town cemetery that has often been overtaken by flooding however one peculiar burial story stands out for its ghostly nature. The nearby area is no stranger to cold spots in the summer and chilling feeling of nearby ghosts are often reported by visitors however it was in 1990, while looking for a better burial for the Confederates and dedicating a local peace monument that the remains of an unidentified Union soldier and unidentified

Confederate soldier recently found on a nearby buried together side by side. Now there are cases even at the Gettysburg National Cemetery where men were erroneously marked as Union and buried in the wrong manner, but this seemed purposeful. A local historian suggested it would be of great significance showing a healing of old wounds and a path forward to bury the two together in a coffin called a 'toe-pincher' pine box. It would be significant, showing that it was a healing of old wounds and final bonding – a sign of peace. After the two men were buried together, a sudden strong storm appeared out of nowhere despite having not been in the forecast. Winds and rain hit the monument furiously and the coffin was immediately flooded out of its place by rapidly rising water. They took the backhoe and quickly forced the coffin back. As everyone focused on the horrific re-burial, an oak tree on the other side of the nearby museum split down it's middle through the trunk sending off an explosive sound and damaging fragments. At the same time, a Confederate portrait of a deceased soldier from the day fell off the wall. Union or Confederate, the divided area of Port Hudson and Grant's Canal was not ready for a path forward just yet, at least not according to their ghost.

9th CT San Rock Reunion 1903 (Courtesy of the Library of Congress)

At home, the family members of the Irish mourned their beloved family members who had just survived the trying emigration only to make their way on to a deadly battlefield. One family from the small town of Colchester, Connecticut was particularly deflated to hear of the lost of their family member, an Irishman who had recently moved to the region. Word was brought to them in early 1865 and they paid the large sum of one-hundred-and-fifty dollars to retrieve his body and have proper burial and funeral. It was some days after the burial that an Irishman walked into his home and greeted the woman and children as his wife and his offspring. They were shocked – it was the man they had just buried. His ghost had returned and the news of the ghost returned home made local and national news. It was weeks before they realized that he had indeed returned home and that the man they had mourned and buried was someone else who remains unidentified and buried somewhere in Colchester 'till this day. Poor fellow could be stuck haunting a town he never knew. As the Irish would say, "Ar dheis Dé go raibh a anam dílis." (May his noble/faithful soul be at the right hand of God.)

The ghosts of men on both sides of such a deadly war are felt throughout the East Coast and you can be sure that some of them are the Irishmen, the fighting Irish who knew, many of them, nothing but struggle their whole life and gave all to a new beginning for them and their loved ones. And the Irish, you see, believe more than most that a soul lives separately from the body and that a spirit world exists. And if you ask battlefield experts, it's the Irish who still speak in Gaelic on the Bloody Lane in Antietam. The 9th are a pride and joy for Nutmeggers today, with a large population claiming Irish descent.

Twenty-Ninth Connecticut Infantry Regiment (Colored Regiment)

Nutmeggers have another great source of pride and joy in their Civil War Regiments too. The 29th, Connecticut's African regiment. Talk about changing history and the face of the U.S. Military. This was Connecticut's first African-American regiment. The 29th can be followed throughout Connecticut cemeteries and the like on the local Freedom Trail and are specifically featured on the "Concept of Freedom Trail."

The 29th Connecticut was not formed until about halfway through the Civil War, seeing most of their action in the final year of the war. The reason for this is that it wasn't anything to do with choice. The Union army had been feeling desperate. The first two years of the war had an unprecedented number of deaths and they were running out of able-bodied men willing to fight. They had to enact a draft which did not go over well (as one can see by the 7th Regiment.) The African-American population was eager to fight but was not allowed to serve at the beginning of the war. At the end of 1862, the government allowed the enlistment of black men but only if they had their own regiment. Regiments consisted of, usually, at least a thousand men and ten companies. It was in November of 1863 during the formation of the 29th, that it was decided it would be a black regiment. Not everyone supported this, however the men of the 29th were more than ready to prove themselves worthy of the title of soldier. The stigma regarding a black regiment had started to be released by many who held views against it due to the successful and heroic acts of the 54th from Massachusetts during their assault on Fort Wagner. Some Connecticut men had indeed enlisted in the 54th and assisted in this. This motivated Governor William Buckingham of Connecticut to approve of black infantry units, however, he was met with much debate. Buckingham, like Lincoln, was a

Republican and the support of many in his party. However, notable Democrats of the time such as William Eaton, believed that black men should not be allowed to enlist. He stated, in fact, that he "would rather let loose the wild Comanchees than the ferocious negro. He is both ferocious and cowardly...you will let loose upon every household south of the Mason and Dixon's line a band of ferocious men who will spread lust and rapine all over that land." Connecticut residents and journalists were furious at this statement and the *Hartford Courant* responded to this verbal assault when they published,

"The armed negro is not a brutal and ferocious being, let loose to ravage and plunder. He has shown himself to be docile, humane and generous. He fights bravely, meeting dangers and death with alacrity, not merely for himself, but with the ennobling purpose of striking the manacles from the hands of his race."

The *Courant* shows the personal motivation that in a way would give the black men more heart in battle than their white comrades.

By January of 1864, the regiment of volunteers out of Fair Haven and New Haven, CT and the surrounding regions was full and by March of 1864, the company would muster out. Half of the regiment was men from Connecticut, the other half men were Mashantucket Pequots, fugitive enslaved people, and residents of neighboring states such New York, New Jersey and Massachusetts. The enlisted included Alexander Newton, an active abolitionist who felt that he was helping to liberate his race by continuing to the battlefield and who wanted to play the part of Moses for the people still enslaved as his father before him was. There was a man named Orrin Hawley, an enlisted private who was the father of seventeen children who became so wounded in service that he lost his farm. The men were laborers, farmers, mechanics, shoemakers, servants and men who loved their family. They knew what this service would mean for their families and for those hoping for the freedom that many of them had. They were under the command of Colonel William B. Wooster Of Derby, Lieutenant Colonel Henry C. Ward of Hartford and Major David Torrance of Norwich. The regiment totaled over 1,200 in strength and first assembled on the New Haven Green.

It is told that the formation and enlistment was truly a grass roots movement, started by two local families who spread the word and helped to motivate their friends and neighbors to join the cause. Due to the excessive size of the force, 400 men would serve to form the 30th Connecticut which would later merge with the 31st. The average age of the newly enlisted was 25. However, entire families, would enlist. One family, the Percy's out of

29th Colored from Connecticut in SC 1864

Granby had a father enlist in the 30th Connecticut Infantry and three of his sons enlisted in the 29th. Mr. Leonard Percy, the patriarch would perish from wounds suffered in battle at age 57 – his sons, however, it is believed made it home. Before their muster date in March, it was in late January that Frederick Douglass himself addressed the men of the 29th and 30th in New Haven. He had been active in recruiting them to form the regiment and gave them a motivational speech. Frederick Douglass gave many talks in Connecticut, even on the topic of Connecticut native, John Brown but some may so this was the talk that would directly impact the hearts of every man who heard it. When he addressed the men of the 29th and 30th he reminded them of the inherent goodness of both them and their cause,

"You are the pioneers of the liberty of your race. With the United States cap on your head, the United States eagle on your belt, the United States musket on your shoulder, not all the powers of darkness can prevent you from becoming American citizens. And not for yourselves alone are you marshaled — you are pioneers — on you depends the destiny of four millions of the colored race in this country.If you rise and flourish, we shall rise and flourish. If you win freedom and citizenship, we shall share your freedom and citizenship."

The men were trained in New Haven and when they took a parade in the streets just before their muster, one soldier noted that people of all colors were touched by the sight of them, were sick of the loss of lives and were praying for their safe return. Private J.J. Hill stated,

"White and colored ladies and gentlemen grasped me by the hand, with tears streaming down their cheeks...expressing the hope that we might have a safe return."

They boarded a steamship that March to make it to the South Carolina coast where they were attached to the District of Beaufort from April to August of that year and handed their new Springfield muskets. It was during this attachment that a law was passed ensuring equal pay for the African-American regiments as the other regiments. It was in August, now receiving equal pay for equal work that the regiment made their way to Bermuda Hundred, Virginia and then further up to Petersburg and Richmond where they would see violence escalating. The 29th engaged in many small battles between Richmond and Petersburg and by September helped to take Fort Harrison just ten miles from Richmond, still the Confederate capital.

Through a scouting expedition, they then then made it the Battle of Darbytown Road where Major Camp would lose his life in October and just weeks later engage in the Battle of Kell House which was incredibly deadly for the unit and lead to over 150 casualties and several imprisonments. The Battle at Kell House was a reconnaissance of Darbytown and a forward movement of the Army of the Potomac just outside Richmond. The 29th formed the skirmish line and drove the rebels into the Confederate works and participated in this throughout the entire late October night. The 29th were the only regiment to have loss of life during this battle and soon after, the survivors were placed in the First Brigade and assigned with garrisoning the line of forts on Newmarket Road. "We took delight in hitting them," recalled Captain Edward Bacon of the 29th. The fighting was so intense that men of the 29th forgot to remove their ramrods from their rifles, and these hurtled

29th Colored from Connecticut in SC 1864 (courtesy of the Library of Congress)

184

through the air like missiles. The Confederates were driven back to their main line of defense, and the 29th took up a position only 200 yards from the rebels.

One of the casualties of Kell House, as seen with so many other battles, was just a teenager, whose parents would have had to sign permission for him to go and that was Private Joseph Porter. Joseph was just seventeen when he enlisted and had been working as a farmhand. He was killed in the engagement and within his pension record sits a letter he wrote to his mother just five days prior to his death. During the fall of 1864, the National Park Service lists the 29th as engaged in Deep Bottom, Chaffin's Farm and the Battle of Fair Oaks in the Darbytown Road area. The following spring, still close to Richmond, two companies of the 29th were the first Union troops to enter the Confederate capital. The 30th / 31st Connecticut was present until the end and served in the Richmond -Petersburg theater and witnessed Lee's surrender at Appomattox. Both colored infantry regiments were mustered out honorably in November of 1865. In sum the 29th lost 198 men during service including one officer and forty-four men killed and one officer and 152 men suffering from disease. The 31st lost 57 to battle whether killed on the field or through mortal wounds including three officers and lost another 101 men including an officer to disease. The 31st also had casualties of accidents, drownings, sunstroke and murder totaling another seven and 20 who died as prisoners or of unknown causes for a total of approximately 185. Henry Ward who had served as their Lieutenant Colonel after having served with white troops for the previous two years, wrote about his time with the 29th at the conclusion of their service and stated,

"Before closing this report, I beg leave to speak freely as to the character of the troops I have had the honor to serve with. I entered the colored service in January 1864 and have commanded a battalion or larger body of colored troops for most of the time since that date, and — am convinced that, in all the essential qualities of good soldiers, they fully meet all requirements and are equal to the standard of any service I ever saw."

Sadly, it was just one month prior to their arrival home that the state had voted against the right for blacks to vote, and it would be another five years until the adoption of the 15th amendment. Their arrival home was deemed to be warm and welcoming, however, that must have been a disheartening and disappointing fact to come home to after risking your life and losing your comrades in the name of the Union who was meant to be advocating the rights of free men including free black men.

Today, the 29th and the 30th – 31st holds a special place in the hearts of Nutmeggers as a group of strong, capable men who risked it all to help those whose suffering they not only sympathized with but often empathized with. For them, it was personal and their hearts pure. They gave all and we honor them. The 29th Colored Regiment Monument sits in Criscuolo Park in New Haven where they were once trained. The memorial is a black stone obelisk encircled by smaller stones with the names of the participating members. Are the spirits of the 29th around? Much like with so many regiments, some were left on the battlefield or buried in southern cemeteries and others were brought home. Old North Cemetery in Hartford boasts a Freedom Trail stop with the burials of 26 of the members though currently only two markers remain. Here they are not far from the famous Commander Ward. Or you may see several at Indian Hill Cemetery in Middletown, not far from General Mansfield – men they would never know except on the other side. The men of the 29th or 30th/31st aren't specifically mentioned though some may believe them and their comrades to be present just outside Richmond where Union soldiers are reported to be seen marching or at Appomattox, where the 31st saw the end of the war and one of their comrades in NY was killed in action and now a spirit of a Union man is seemed walking around hastily, angrily, cranky with the visitors and his footsteps are heard walking around the park town in the night. The 54th Massachusetts who dispelled so may rumors and misgivings about what it meant to have a black regiment with their demonstration of courage are believed to haunt the site of their bloody battle. Many of the deceased that fought at Fort Wagner are buried on Morris Island where people still hear the sounds of battle and on Folly Beach where a Union soldier of the 54th, perhaps left behind is seen looking to Morris Island in the distance. There are tales of washed-up bodies and orb like lights surrounding the area believed to be them. The area of Kell House where the 29th fought is not often talked about or honored in battle histories or legend. Some have even referred it to as a minor event or skirmish but if, like the 54th, they are there still buried and still spreading their tales of courage, perhaps as you drive in the rural landscape around Richmond, you too can see the orbs or a lone soldier looking for his men and know that they too made history and remind them that YOU will share their story.

The Regiments of Connecticut infantry were filled with youthful boys and young men, sons, husbands, fathers who worked as laborers, farmers, shopkeepers and men who believed in a united country and such, came together to make up some of the most successful units in the Union Army, receiving accolades from Meade, Grant, Sherman and Lincoln and sharing remarkable stories of triumph. They, too, had their share of tragedy, fear, deflection and chaos in the face of unwarranted danger and a war that no one expected to escalate to such a violent degree. They, like every one of us, were human, not perfect nor imperfect but people who fought for what they believed in and together they aided each other and took up arms together. They persevered. Each regiment has a unique story filled with their assignments, trainings (or lack thereof), battles they participated in and people they fought alongside, and this chapter dove into the stories of just a few of these regiments who changed the face of American history, though their stories and the legacy are without end. As we go through the stories of battle, I encourage you to also look to the stories of the 14th, the 20th, and the 27th who became some of the most battle-hardened and experienced regiments the Union would ever see and who would experience casualties no one could expect. The spirits of Connecticut have been seen on battlefields, at burial sites and at forts, they've been seen by each other and by visitors to notable spots even a century later and their spirits let us know, that their story, the story of Connecticut in the Civil War still must be told.

Deadly Combat: Courageous Connecticut Men on the Bloody Battlefields
Stories of Courage, Death and the Residual Phantoms of Warfare

"Those who say they would like to visit a battlefield seldom know what they are talking about. After darkness has put an end to the struggle, a hush settles over the field. Such a contrast to the roar of the fight. Never is silence more oppressive, more eloquent. You hear the cries of the wounded, which is never distinguished in the roar of battle…. You see the outlines of forms gliding through the gloom carrying on litters pale, bloody men. Or perhaps your friend with his hair matted with blood over his white face and his dead eyes staring blindly up to the sky." – Private Erskine Church

The reasons there is so much documentation on the Civil War is that it was a war with an immense amount of action. There were an estimated 8,000 to 10,500 occasions including battles and skirmishes where "hostilities" occurred. When one thinks of conflict and violence in any location, that location is often deemed as a place that is haunted, whether by history, spirits or both. According to the Civil War Sites Advisory Commission (CWSAC), 1993 reports, of the occasions of hostilities in the war, there are 384 that can be classified as battles in one of four classes or categories including: Decisive, Major, Formative or limited. 47 battles are deemed in the highest category of decisive and just over a hundred classified as major. The ten deadliest battles include: Gettysburg, Chickamauga, Spotsylvania, The Wilderness, Chancellorsville, Shiloh, Stones River, Antietam, Second Manassas and Vicksburg. Cold Harbor comes in close with casualty count as well for the Union. Of the top ten, Connecticut men participated in seven of the highest casualty count engagements and hundreds of smaller engagements. Of renowned horror at, Cold Harbor, five Connecticut regiments and artillery were present at the battle that would forever change Union General and future President, Ulysses S. Grant. And at the final Siege with the Petersburg Campaign, depending on with tens of thousands of casualties between 1864 and 1865 over a series of skirmishes and battles, Connecticut had a regular presence. Of the top ten, deadliest battles as classified by the American Battlefield Trust, Connecticut participated in six of them firsthand and in nearby campaigns on one other. Connecticut was present throughout the Campaign at Petersburg in a variety of the hostilities and battles including the conclusion. Most of the boys from the Nutmeg state would be involved in what is called the Eastern Theatre. Battlefields are often thought of as being the most haunted places that one may encounter in their journey around the United States and may battlefields are preserved today by the National Park Service and American Battlefield Trust so that people may walk the roads and paths and encampments of their ancestors and the beloved dead. In these visits that started with family commemorating their loved one's loss and survivors visiting sites to establish monuments and then as visitors descended upon these fields to honor the past, to learn the art of war, and to reflect upon where we came from, more and more ghost sightings and occurrences started being reported. The number of casualties associated with the war was and remains incomparable.

There were more deaths in the Civil War for Americans than there were in every other major war, America was involved in combined. The death toll is staggering, coming in at roughly 620,000 – 644,000 men. 644,000 men fighting their countrymen, their brothers, their friends over four bloody and brutal years leaves a stain literally and figuratively on the soil of these grounds where the most was lost, where the souls of thousands would depart their bodies or become in a way, stuck in time, forced to relive the worst or most terrifying moment of their lives. Battlefields have stories of residual and active hauntings and our investigations prove that both are quite real and prevalent at these battlefields. With thousands of deaths, it's sometimes hard to figure out which side you're communicating with, let alone which state or regiment they may have been and their name, which is always remarkable evidence to help in an investigation. Oftentimes battle ghost stories of the Civil War differentiate only between a Union or Confederate uniform that is witnessed.

Second Battle of Bull Run/Second Manassas

Just over a year into the war, Connecticut participated in what would become one of the top ten deadliest battles, coming in at number nine on the list, is the Second Battle of Bull Run or the Second Manassas as it was also known taking place from August 29th through August 30th of 1862. Connecticut had participated in the First Battle of Bull Run about thirteen months earlier, but this would result in more casualties and just like the first would end in Confederate victory. Present at the Second Battle of Bull Run is the First Connecticut Battalion aka Connecticut's Volunteer Cavalry. The Volunteer Cavalry served on Provost Duty for the Bull Run battles. Provost in the Civil War would serve as the Union's military police and look for deserters and spies as well as assisting nearby civilians. The four companies of the Cavalry were there making up the 1st Connecticut Battalion of the Cavalry Brigade under Col. John Beardsley of New York. The Second Battle of Bull Run was led by Union Major General John Pope and Confederate Major General Thomas "Stonewall" Jackson, Stonewall being the nickname he acquired in the first battle of Manassas due to his techniques on the battlefield. Stonewall Jackson and his flanking march had captured the Union supply depot at Manassas Junction. Of notable mention here, is that Stonewall Jackson's horse, "Little Sorrel" was a Connecticut native from Somers on a farm owned by Noah Collins and became one of the most famous Connecticut residents and war legends. Little Sorrel earned a place of honor at the Virginia Military Institute and Somers even has a street named after him. Little Sorrel was supposed to be Union horse and was purchased for use in the government for the war but was captured with other horses by the South in Harper's Ferry in 1861. Jackson, at the time, took two of the horses and Little Sorrel was going to be the horse he gave to his wife until he found out that Big Sorrel was no battle

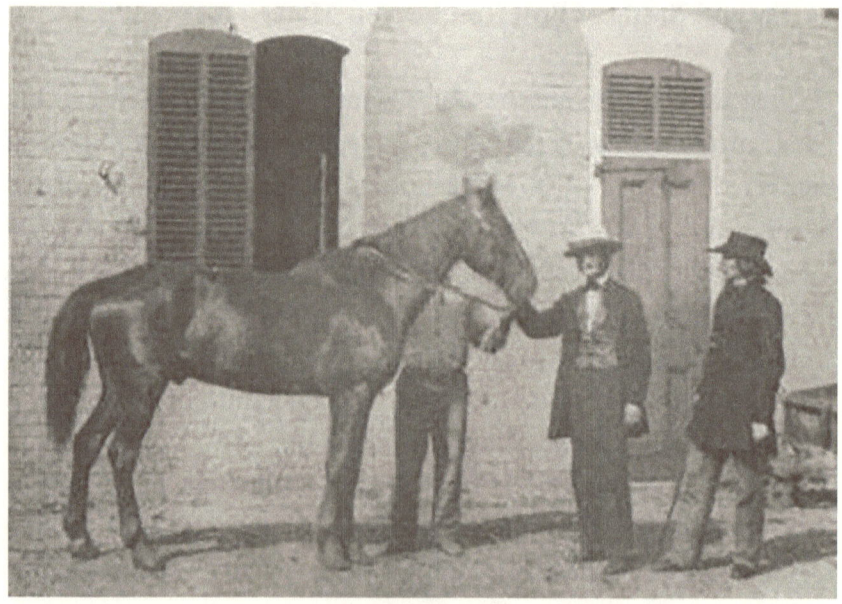

Little Sorrel before 1865 (Wiki Commons)

suitable horse and the horse he had named Fancy was perfect for the job. So Fancy was renamed Little Sorrel and became his companion and well-known Confederate. Sorrel refers to the chestnut-colored hair of the Morgan horse.

But we'll get back to Connecticut's famous horse shortly. Jackson had Little Sorrel when the Second Battle of Bull Run took place. This concerned Pope who would need this for his life of communications with Washington, D.C. After the capture Jackson was able to set up positions of strength in the defense on the Stony Ridge while more back-up arrived from Confederate Major General James Longstreet. Today, you can still visit the unfinished railroad where Stonewall Jackson placed his Confederate troops. The two groups of Confederate rebels had the upper hand and on August 28th, the night before the battle, Jackson attacked a Union column resulting in a stalemate and Longstreet broke through the Union coming to the battlefield. Although this looked bleak for the Union, Pope thought things would end up alright, that the Confederates had been trapped with Jackson and as the battle begins on August 29th, it's the Union Army launching assaults against Jackson at the unfinished railroad Lee had under construction. The fighting was repulsed quickly and strongly, and the casualty count built up swiftly that morning. By the afternoon, Longstreet became the right flank of Jackson and Pope, thinking it was just Jackson, began another assault of renewed attacks but the now amassed Confederate artillery devastated the Union taking out an entire Corps.

In fact, this assault in the counterattack from Longstreet in tandem with Pope's assault made history as the longest simultaneous mass assault of the Civil War. The Union was driven back, with their only win, being an effective rear guard. This Confederate victory put Lee in a good position and began the Maryland Campaigns that will lead to one of the deadliest days in American history. In all, there were 22,180 casualties at the battle of First Manassas though any casualties for the 1st Connecticut Battalion were minimal here and throughout the war, they did still lose some to death and injury here and throughout the South. When one thinks of haunted battlefields, admittedly, Manassas may not be the first one that comes to mind, however, they have no shortage of paranormal activity and being one of the deadliest battle sites that was the site of not just one, but two battles of enormous proportion would lead to several ghostly accounts. In 1989, Park Range James Burgess, a self-identified skeptic by all accounts, had himself encountered many concerned and frightened visitors who had an experience on the battlefield in Prince William County. Common reports included sudden drops in temperature on humid summer days, strange noises from the Battlefield Stone House that maintains floorboards where gravely injured soldiers carved their names, house lights in areas where there are no house being seen and the strange aromas of black powder and odors of burning flesh. Perhaps those that sense that are less concerned with the vision of lights or strange smells as they are with the full-bodied apparitions that some say can be nightly at sunset near to the woods on the end of the park. The men are believed to be from the union and their red pantaloons and white leggings suggest nighttime attire to the present-day observer and can be seen on the men and often attributed to a regiment from New York who may have had Connecticut residents as well and they were referred to Zouave for the distinctive uniform. On a field trip to the site, a teacher asked the children if they knew what a Zouave uniform looked like and one girl answered in detail. The teacher, surprised, asked how she knew and casually, the young girl pointed to a cannon on a hill and said she saw someone wearing it standing right there. Investigations took place over the years but left those who participated refusing to go back, claiming that the men in uniform were beckoning the living into the woods and that there was a surreal out-of-body experience upon seeing them. The

National Park Service Supervisor in 2012 would state that the Battlefield is called the "Vortex of Manassas" because of all the inexplicable activity both good and frightening but always without explanation. So perhaps on your next journey to Northern Virginia, you may find yourself following in the footsteps of Connecticut's men on horseback, the military police, the cavalry who fought bravely against Jackson's cavalry and just perhaps you'll see them beckoning you from beyond into the woods with them. What do they want to show you? If you're not feeling quite brave enough to make the journey you can visit the Soldier's Monument in Danbury, Connecticut with a special honor for those who went to Manassas both the first and second time.

Battle of Antietam/Battle of Sharpsburg

As the war rages on and Manassas leaves Lee with the ability to start the Maryland Campaign, it's only a matter of weeks before all these briefly trained or completely untrained young men would descend upon the regions of Frederick and Sharpsburg, Maryland where they would convene by the Antietam Creek for a horrific battle. The date was September 17th, 1862 and present in Union General George B. McClellan's Army of the Potomac were the 8th, 11th, 14th, and 16th Connecticut infantries. Antietam was considered the first "field army level engagement," in the Eastern Theater of the Civil War and the bloodiest day in American History totaling 22,717 casualties in just one day and the eighth highest casualty count of the decisive battles. Of the 12,400 Union Casualties, it is estimated that over 600 of the men were from Connecticut. Historians have determined there was no clear victor at Antietam and that the result was a stalemate however, in 1862, the Union claimed victory. What happened that day? What went wrong? What went right? Can anything go right when that many men die in one day? McClellan had followed Lee into Maryland

and launched attacks near to the Creek. It was at dawn that Major General Joseph Hooker of the Union assaulted Lee's left flank. Though Hooker begins attack, the Union undercame artillery fire near to the Nicodemus Hill by Dunker Church and made their way near to the cornfield by Dunker Church. By this time General Lee had ordered the troops from General D.H. Hill's command to move to the cornfield and Connecticut's son, Mansfield's Twelfth Corp had crushed some of these troops as they numbered over 7,000. It was here that General Mansfield received his mortal wound. It was by seven AM that morning, that the Confederates counterattacked in the Cornfield as immediately as the Union set foot upon it. According to the National Park Service, the 24-acre cornfield saw some of the country's most horrific fighting as General Hooker and Connecticut General Mansfield's forces fought Jackson's confederates.

Cornfield Antietam (Martin Reardon Jr. photo)

The Cornfield changed hands several times during the attacks and counterattacks. The cornfield was the center of the storm with over 25,000 soldiers engaging in that field and that even continuing for nearly four hours. It was by 9:30 AM, about halfway through the cornfield fighting that thousands lay upon the earth where they fell as they continued to move southward toward the Sunken road. "Fighting Joe," aka General Hooker remarked, every stalk of corn in the northern and greater part of the field was cut as closely as could have been done with a knife, and the slain lay in rows precisely as they stood in their ranks a few moments before. It was never my fortune to witness a more bloody, dismal battlefield." It was the 16th CT and the 4th RI of Col. Edward Harland's Brigade that took much of the onslaught of the Maj. General A P. Hill's Confederate counterattack in the 40-Acre Cornfield As the battle was moving Union troops came out of the East Woods under orders to move into the West Woods and hit Confederates driving them to Sharpsburg. Over 5,000 Union troops took on this task however the Confederate forces shored up their left side and when the Union moved in, it was a blood bath for the boys in blue. One Private said that the Union was "mowed down," as soon as they were seen and within 20 minutes had to fall back. General Stonewall Jackson brigades slept through the cornfields as they continued to come back time after time.

By late morning, the Union soldiers started to make their way even closer to the Sunken Road that today is better known by the name Bloody Lane. The farm lane was a breastwork for the

Bloody Lane/Sunken Road Bodies 1862 (Courtesy of the Library of Congress)

Confederates and for three hours over two-thousand Confederate troops would hold off the Union force of 10,000 until the early afternoon when they fell back. For over three hours, the thousands of men were firing at each other point blank and in those few hours, over 5,500 men would become casualties and lay in the sunken road. The survivors called is the "road of death," and "ghastly flooring," as there were just heaps of men slumped in the road and upon the fence rails. One witness would go on to state,

"They were lying in rows like the ties of a railroad, in heaps like cordwood mingled with the splintered and shattered fence rails."

Confederate General Longstreet even said to his men of the terribly scourge at the lane, "This is a hard fight, and we had best all die than lose it." The outcome was clear and no matter the side, you would be a martyr for your cause. Words are inadequate to portray the scene.

Burnside Bridge Antietam (Martin Reardon Jr.)

As if that wasn't enough, the afternoon was still young and the battle not over. And our Connecticut boys were still on the field, though those that had survived thus far may not make it through

Dead near 16th Otto Farm Antietam (Courtesy of the Library of Congress)

the afternoon. The "Lower Bridge" or "Rohrbach Bridge," that had been built by local Dunker farmers sets the stage for the next events. The bridge today is called Burnside Bridge, named for the Major General Ambrose Burnside of the Union who tried to take the bridge repeatedly. The 11th Connecticut including young Private Daniel Tarbox would meet their foe at this site. Some of the events had been overlapping with the other morning attacks and hostilities. Somewhat near to the bridge where General Lee's soldiers numbering about three-thousand under the command of General David Jones however the ones closes and responsible for the action at the bridge numbered just under 500 and were commanded by General Robert Toombs. They were placed to as to guard the bridge and had nearby breastworks tucked at the site. They were to hold it and guard it however just as fighting reached a peak in the nearby Cornfield, the Union army assaulted the bridge at 9:30 Am. The fighting was deadly for the ninth corps, but the Confederates held the bridge at the cost of running low on ammunition. When Union General Isaac P. Rodman, once a banker from Rhode Island, attempted with his troops to cross Snavely Ford on their flank, they got closer, but the Confederates used almost the remainder of their ammunition to keep them away. The Union outnumbered the Confederates at the bridge by thousands, but they held them off fiercely until the third assault would force them away toward the Harper's Ferry Road. The survivors strapped in for the next and final attack of the Battle of Sharpsburg.

There were over two-thousand remaining Confederate troops and forty cannons remaining on the road from Sharpsburg to Millers Sawmill Road. There were over 8,000 Union men commanded by General Burnside on an eastern ridge. Union General Rodman had assumed the high ground and was able to push them back down the hill toward the village of Sharpsburg. It seemed Union victory was imminent until Confederate General Hill arrived from Harpers Ferry and struck the Union left flank driving them back under destructive volleys. Burnside and his men fell back and that evening the death toll went up into the tens of thousands. Ultimately, since the rebels had fallen back south, when Lee arrived and retreated on September 19th, the Union were able to declare victory. This gave Lincoln the opportunity, after claiming this victory at Sharpsburg amid great bloodshed, just days after its conclusion to make a great announcement. On September 22nd, Lincoln released the Emancipation Proclamation and gave Confederate states 100 days to rejoin the Union or by January 1st, 1863, the slaves would be declared "thenceforward, and forever free." The violence and horror cannot be overstated at Antietam so perhaps it's no strange thing that the bloodiest day in American history became the height of many ghostly tales. Most ghostly documentation centers upon the Sunken Road aka the Bloody Lane

8th CT Monument Antietam (Martin Reardon Jr. photo)

with some ghostly anecdotes relating to Burnside Bridge but as an investigator and medium as well as a historian, I find that the most haunting piece of land at Antietam may indeed be the Cornfield. It is from the Cornfield where you can hear the whispers of men convening in the woods, where you can hear the rebel yells and the Confederate rally cries as they charge forth, where you can hear in the distance the agonizing cries of the wounded and dying that linger in the air just over the ground of the battlefield.

There are stories from local schools and students who visit the battlefield on field trips. Teachers admit, it's not uncommon for students to look for ghosts or even talk about wanting to see them on such field trips. In 1982, a group of students from a local school were doing just that one morning but as the field trip progressed through the day and events transpired, the kids grew a bit more quiet and after a meeting with the Bloody Lane, the children, in their early teen years, were told by their teachers to lay in the Bloody Lane and listen for the sounds of horses, rustling in the corn and to smell for gunpowder – to really immerse themselves in understanding what had happened. One of the teachers who had run into a barbed wire fence was experiencing a heck of a lot of pain for a scrape that his belt took the brunt of and as the teacher focused on his minor scrape he and one of his colleagues heard a scream from a different part of the nearby cornfield where they found two students huddled on the ground, curled up in fear. Other visitors had tried to help the boys, but they asked them to step back, leave them alone and it wasn't until their teachers arrived that the students confessed seeing a Union soldier coming through the field quickly, his feet almost not touching the ground and heading towards them. Their classmates said at the same time, some of them witnessed a riderless horse. The field trip took place on the 120nd anniversary of the battle, but it would not be the only field trip to report activity. Many of the kid's sensations and connectedness to the other side overcame them at the Bloody Lane, a site where people consistently report strange sensations upon being close in proximity – a sense of doom, a pit in their stomach, the uncontrollable urge to throw up due to overwhelming nausea, the smell of blood and feeling of death. Even those who survived could not go back near the spot on the Sunken road and many visitors have ended their battle trip early.

Sunken Road Bloody Lane Antietam (Martin Reardon Jr. photo)

The most notable ghost story from Bloody Lane refers to some of the Irishmen present. While Connecticut's 9th was not there, Connecticut men were likely involved with Richardson's command Meagher's Irish Brigade at the Bloody Lane. They were a brigade of men who still had their battle cry in the Irish language. During a field trip from a boy's school in Baltimore, the boys were finishing up their field trip at the Bloody Lane. The boys had some free time and were asked to be do a writing assignment about the day during this time. The boys started commenting aloud and in their writing about the strange noises they heard near the observation tower on the Bloody Lane. The observation tower is where the Irish Brigade under Meagher from New York had charged the Confederates. They heard a chant that reminded them of a familiar Christmas carol, "Deck the Halls," as they recognized the tune and sounds of "Fa-la-la-la." Wait, why would they hear a holiday tune? Historians say, they, of course, did not, the boys heard the Irish men chant "Faugh-a-Balaugh," as they would yell

11th CT Monument Antietam (Courtney McInvale photo)

when they "Clear the way." The men from Ireland still charging strong on that Bloody Lane, almost as if maybe this time they will change history. Another Antietam hot spot that was known to have a great loss of Connecticut life was of course the Burnside Bridge. As mentioned, it was at this bridge that Daniel Tarbox communicated during investigation. It turns out park rangers and Civil War re-enactors have had more strange things happen at that bridge after dark than almost anywhere else. At the bridge, a phantom drum beats in cadence as calling out for battle as it quietly fades away and blue balls of light move around the area as if each one represents a person still at the site. Some believe they represent those who were hastily buried by the bridge and bodies not brought home. Is it possible some of the men of the 11th didn't get brought back home? Could they be the reported blue orbs?

On a recent visit, our team member, Andrew and I were crossing the bridge when he remarked about the flag he saw in the water and pointed at it for me to see. I looked and saw no flag or anything like a flag and we assumed it was the water movement playing tricks on his eyes. After visiting the 11th monument and crossing the bridge, once more, Andrew swore he could see it there, perhaps residual, perhaps the flag taken in one of the three assaults on the rebels. For me, I will undoubtedly say, that the Cornfield is the place where I felt the souls of the restless and the fighting the most. I could see them almost in a haze and in fact, with all the artillery and gunpowder, the survivors remarked that the men looked almost ghost like themselves making it a surreal target to aim at one another. But at the roads of the Cornfield, you can feel them running through you and around you, charging forward. I walked in for a few moments one early evening, just after sunset and as I saw the shadows moving all around me, some even caught on camera, I confess that I ran out to my car on the main road as fast as my legs would take me. With such a haunting and saga like Antietam, it's hard to imagine carnage getting worse for our New England lads, to lose over 600 from Connecticut in just one day was nothing short of traumatizing and sadly, it would be just the beginning.

Burying Dead at Antietam 1862 (Courtesy of the Library of Congress)

Battle of Chancellorsville

Alas, it wasn't long before most of them would see violence in other skirmishes and battles. The next deadliest of the major battles that Connecticut men would participate in is the Battle of Chancellorsville, just a bit further south than Maryland in northern Virginia. Once more, we would see here the leadership of Union Army Major General Joseph Hooker's Army of the Potomac pitted against General Lee's Confederate Army of Northern Virginia. Chancellorsville was a great success for Lee, a victory for his army and one he would dub the "perfect battle." Historians would refer to the event as Lee's most significant "tactical victory." Lee would curse and mourn the engagement that he lost one of his favorite and most intelligent Generals, General Stonewall Jackson who became mortally wounded in that Virginia town. Chancellorsville would also see the return of Union General Joseph Hooker and the Army of the Potomac whose forces were twice that in number of the rebel forces – Hooker with approximately 115,000 and Jackson with 60,000. Joseph Hooker was there to replace General Ambrose Burnside who had been promoted to Commander in November of 1862 but due to hasty decisions made in December and the loss of the Battle at Fredericksburg with 13,000 Union casualties, Burnside was replaced by Hooker. The Battle at Chancellorsville lasted a full week and would result in 24,000 casualties as the fifth most deadly engagement in the Civil War. Taking place in the spring, April 30th through May 6th, 1863, New England had a heavy presence. Engaged at Chancellorsville from Connecticut were the 5th, 14th, 17th, 20th and 27th Connecticut infantries as well as the 1st Heavy Artillery. in the head were documented. The men fell with sword in hand and were noted for their courage. The 5th Connecticut was described to have "moderate," losses received 21 casualties to being killed or wounded and another 35 who were captured and imprisoned including Colonel Warren W. Packer. The 14th suffered approximately 56 casualties.

The 17th Connecticut documented being pushed back from the field with a flank attack by Stonewall Jackson in the Wilderness and were caught unprepared. The 17th Connecticut received much criticism as they were surprised and a large loss of 106 at the battle. The 20th was also taken back by General Stonewall Jackson's surprised assault and this their first battle, despite good leadership from Lieutenant Colonel, William Wooster, they would receive a baptism under fire like the 16th did at Antietam. Their losses at Chancellorsville totaled 197. Bravery of men such as Sergeant Major John S. Root of West Hartford who was killed by a shell at the barricades and Second Lieutenant David Griffith of New Haven who was killed by a musket shot to the head. The men fell with sword in hand, a great display of courage. The 27th had a great deal of suffering and was cut down to just three companies strong at Chancellorsville due to 37 casualties (killed and wounded) and eight companies out of the ten present being captured during the event. There was the Heavy Artillery, who were present at the defeat of Fredericksburg as well made their way to Chancellorsville with two companies, though their losses were minimal compared to the infantry losses, they were eager to see victory after all the harsh defeats. Chancellorsville remains one of the most arguably haunted battles of all in Civil War history because the grounds that saw the unimaginable death in 1863 would see even more death on the same grounds almost exactly a year to the following date. The region of Chancellorsville, Spotsylvania Court House and the Wilderness would account for three of the top ten deadly battles between 1863 and 1864 and be in the same exact small region of Virginia. It was in 1864, the men would find themselves fighting among literal corpses from the year before which haunted each of them. And the men would document the ghosts that were with them upon that return. Connecticut would be at all three battles with her living and her dead. At Chancellorsville, Hooker thought with his numerical advantage, that it would be best to put two-thirds of his force at Fredericksburg to feign a front assault and then brought the rest of the men across the Rappahannock River attempting to come behind the Confederate Army, but Lee was ready for offense. Lee sent only one-sixth of his men to Fredericksburg in hopes to deter the Union Major General (and Connecticut native who rises to even more prominent in future battles) John Sedgwick. Lee marched forward to meet Hooker leading to the open field battle just outside the Wilderness on May 1st, 1863. Hooker, ignoring the objections from his lower ranking officers, withdrew his men to the defense around Chancellorsville, giving initiative to Lee. Come May 2nd, Lee was ready and decided to split his army again, this time sending half with his right-hand man, Stonewall Jackson.

Jackson and his army of 28,000 men strong carried out the surprise assault on the right flank and caved in the Union XI Corps line. Leaving the Union flank exposed caused the death of half of Hooker's forces. It was on May 2nd, that Confederate General and right-hand man to Stonewall Jackson would receive a mortal wound being fired upon by his own men after dark between his own lines. Jackson's bone above his left shoulder was shattered and his arm amputated and buried on site, marked today by a gravestone. Confederate General J.E.B. Stuart took over the command but told Jackson, he would have traded places with him if he could. It was just one week later at age 39, that Jackson passed away from pneumonia. Meanwhile, while Jackson was on-site trying to recover the evening of the 2nd   thought he was ultimately losing a battle with what is believed to be pneumonia that he caught from being dropped too many times upon being carried for care and fluid build-up in the lungs. Chancellorsville continued for the men and May 3rd was the bloodiest day of the engagement. Multiple attacks were launched at the Union men. Both sides had exponential losses and Hooker's Army pulled away. The same day, the Union had a small victory at the Second battle of Fredericksburg and then later the Confederates had victory at the nearby Battle of Salem Church. By May 4th, Lee was focused on Sedgwick's forces and when Sedgwick retreated on the 5th, he went back to Hooker on May 5th through 6th. The campaign ended on the 7th as the men readied themselves for Gettysburg. The men were left on the field, many of them to remain there for some time including when the Army would return to the spot in 1864. That is when the ghost stories would begin, and body retrieval in some instances would take decades. The ghosts of Chancellorsville, Wilderness and Spotsylvania will be discussed in detail as we follow the men's return to the site in the deadly engagements but first, we will venture to Gettysburg which takes place just a month after this catastrophe.

Now, you may be wondering if Stonewall Jackson's ghost haunts the grounds of Chancellorsville. While he is just one of many documented ghosts, many of the ghosts at Chancellorsville being recorded as Union soldiers, the Confederate General is said to haunt the site where he lost his arm, ever fighting, ever trying to evade that fateful shot that would lead to his ultimate demise. And legend states, his ghost, while not wandering the battlefield makes it way to Gettysburg, where he has changed sides in his ghostly form to be anti-slavery and pro-Union. Union veteran and war author, Morris Schaff, documented that Stonewall's ghost appears nearby Chancellorsville while "the Spirit of the Wilderness," stalks him in the brush.

Stonewall Jackson on Little Sorrel (Courtesy of the Library of Congress)

Stonewall passed away on May 10th, 1863 after having been shot off his Connecticut horse, Little Sorrel by one of his own North Carolina regiments. Little Sorrel went on to live an exceptionally long life, spending some years with his widow and then living the rest of his years at the Virginia Military Institute/Confederate Soldiers Home. He lived to be 36, his hide was taxidermized. The horses cremated bones were buried in front of the institute and can be visited today where they rest by Jackson's statue. But it would seem the spirit of Little Sorrel sleeps better than his famous General. When the "Spirit of the Wilderness", finds the good General in his spirit form, he is seen as a gaunt, hollow-breasted, wicked eye, sunken cheeked being," Stonewall's ghost is then beseeched.

"Stonewall, I am Slavery and sorely wounded. Can you do nothing to stay the Spirit of the Wilderness that, in striking at me, struck you down?"

Does his soul hear the spirit of the field? According to the *New York Times* and the *Muscatine Weekly Journal* out of Iowa, just weeks after the battle of Gettysburg,

"The rebels say that since his death, his ghost is still seen hovering near the scenes of the battle, if they are sure of this, the issue of the late campaign would seem to give color to the assertion of a spiritual medium who has lately been en rapport with Jackson and who averts that since his death, he has turned Abolitionist and fights for the cause of the North."

So, let's travel with Stonewall and the Union to Gettysburg before we come back to the ghosts of the Wilderness. The area around Chancellorsville, the Wilderness and Spotsylvania became known as the bloodiest ground in North America. But the bloodiest battle and highest casualty count was right on the heels of Chancellorsville in July of 1863 – the Battle of Gettysburg.

Battle of Gettysburg

Gettysburg took place just two months after the Battle at Chancellorsville and though the Confederate General Lee felt he had a strong success from Chancellorsville to give him the upper hand, the loss of his right-hand man would forever change him and ultimately would change the face of the war. The Union would change, as well. General Hooker, Fighting Joe had been one of the major leaders for the Army of the Potomac to this point but his defeat at Chancellorsville was unforgivable and the men refused to fight under him. He was thought to be more concerned with drink and women in his spare time than military tactics and when he did not deliver on his promises at Chancellorsville to make Lee and the rebels regret confronting the Union, Lincoln was at an impasse. Hooker was not the man for the job in the Eastern Theater any longer and just days before the Battle at Gettysburg, he resigned from the Army of the Potomac and Major General George Meade would take over on June 28th, 1863, three days before the blood bath would begin. General Hooker continued to express his upset as he had moved the army, on orders, in search for Lee north toward Pennsylvania, and it was during his dispute about defensive forces in Harpers Ferry that he impulsively resigned. Congress would then thank Meade for some of his early work at Gettysburg with a "Thanks of Congress," even though some of that work was Hooker's. When Hooker moved to the Western Theater and earned promotions for the victory under Grant at the Battle of Chattanooga, it was General William Tecumseh Sherman who would be credited rather than him, not helping him impetuous temper. But at Gettysburg, our Union was under the command of Meade now, for better or for worse, which made Lee feel more secure in victory. Connecticut had the same exact infantries it had at Chancellorsville present at Gettysburg – Connecticut's 5th, 14th, 17th, 20th and 27th infantries and the 2nd Light Artillery. Of the approximately 1,270 men from Connecticut at the Battle of Gettysburg, nearly one-third would become casualties with the number at an estimated 340 men. One of the most prominent Connecticut men that would come to Gettysburg from having survived Chancellorsville is Major General John Sedgwick of Cornwall, Connecticut who holds a monument at Gettysburg today. Her was in command of the Sixth Corps Army of the Potomac. His monument calls him "Loyal Citizen, Illustrious soldier, Beloved Commander," and he is depicted on his horse named Handsome Joe on Sedgwick Avenue. In 1863, the Sixth Corps he commanded had just arrived from a thirty-mile night and day march and Sedgwick was found having to command units on both the extreme right and left flanks of the Army. Sedgwick would lead bravely in Gettysburg, but we will come to see his end near the Wilderness at the Battle at Spotsylvania in less than a year from this time.

The Union Army and the Confederate Army met at Gettysburg on July 1st, 1863 where the three-day battle would begin.

The Pennsylvania Campaign had begun in June of 1863 and it was Robert E. Lee's goal to get to the North, after viewing his victories and seeing heavy loss, to pull themselves out of the war and elect a new leader that would deal with the Confederacy. By the end of June, Lee had Confederates in the tens of thousands spread throughout Pennsylvania gathering food and supplies while causing panic to residents. Hooker (and then Meade) and the Union men had followed them North and when news reaches Lee that they were close, Lee brings his men to converge around the Gettysburg, PA area as they had roads that were desirable heading in every direction. 75,000 Confederates move toward the town and the Union with many of our Connecticut regiments including the 5th who had been stationed at Frederick, Maryland previously after going to make their way to this convergence. June 30th, 1863, 2,700 Union Cavalrymen under John Buford's leadership arrive.

Buford took the Confederate infantry by surprise and that brings in more Confederate troops. Buford wants to delay the Confederate troops that are there in great numbers until the Union infantry can arrive. By eight in the morning on July 1st, against all odds, Buford's Cavalry confront the Union infantry on McPherson ridge as forces on both sides increased their numbers. Buford's 1st Corps of Calvary and a unit called the Iron Brigade were able to attack the Confederate infantrymen that morning in a lethal, hour-long battle, but still they pushed back. Support started to arrive by 10 AM with brigades from New York, Pennsylvania and Indiana. Major John Reynolds took control with the Union First Corps Infantry however was shot in the head and killed instantly near the eastern edge of the woods. The Iron Brigade, however, was able to push back the Confederates and capture prisoners including officers.

Shortly, thereafter more reinforcements came including the 11th Corps whose 2nd Brigade included the 17th CT Volunteers. Private Justus Silliman of the 17th wrote of their arrival,

"The roads were muddy and the march very tiresome as we were pushed forward in great haste. On arriving to within about three miles of the town, we heard cannonading, and, for the first time, it entered our minds that we might soon have some fighting to do."

They came into Gettysburg with Barlow's 1st Division. One of the first moves from the 17th, suggested by Lieutenant Charles Doty of Norwalk was to secure a small wooden bridge near to a brick house, and a small detachment went forward to do that. The rest of the men under command of Major Allen Brady led the call for volunteers from Norwalk, Darien, Fairfield and the surrounding region's companies. They formed the extreme right of the Union line and were the only organized units engaging the rebels on the far side of Rock Creek. Close to Rock Cree, Bayard Wilkeson, a

19-year-old boy, whose story would resonate through the Civil War and beyond, had made the decision to bring four of his Napoleon cannons as he was part of the 4th U.S. Artillery, and put them about 500 yards northeast of the Rock Cree border near the

Lieutenant Col. Douglass Fowler 17th

Alms House. It was decided that he would need infantry to support his position there and six companies of the 17th Connecticut would serve on the left at that regiment. They had zeroes in on two Southern batteries near an area known as Oak Hill. At the highest point of the assembly of the infantrymen, Wilkeson's weapons fired and the rebels returned fire in kind. The 17th's Lieutenant Colonel Fowler cried out,

"Dodge the big ones, boys!"

The Connecticut men on the opposite side of Rock Creek continued to fight off the Confederates, with two companies of the 17th deployed as skirmishers and two held reserve and advancing in line near the Benner Farm where they stated the enemy poured in firing. The Connecticut Major Brady led his men to the buildings for protection, but it didn't take long for the Confederates who saw this to set the house on fire with their weapons. Then, Brady and the 17th were called to return to town. Of the 386 men brought by the 17th to Gettysburg, 20 were killed, 81 wounded and 96 recorded as missing, most on July 1st. The survivors from the July 1st engagement near to Barlow's Knoll formed in line of battle on East Cemetery Hill the next night and engaged in repulsing assault. Barlow needed help on the knoll as Confederate General Ewell and his men pressed forward. When Southern fire on the knoll worsened, the young Wilkeson was knocked from his horse and mortally wounded. His leg was tore through by a Confederate shell. He amputated what remained of it with a pocketknife and was taken to a nearby poor house where he would die hours later. His father, a local journalist from New York, who'd arrived as a correspondent was able to visit his son under a flag of truce on July 1st right before he died. The boys of the 17th CT, the six companies of them that had been caught up fighting got caught up in fire from General Gordon of the Confederates. Gordon turned loose a brigade from Georgia who broke into open area at the foot of the knoll. Some men ran away first thing they could do. Lieutenant Colonel Fowler was fearless as he had been before. The Nutmeg State native was no stranger to danger, he had left the hospital at Chancellorsville to lead his company and was one of the most successful there in the regard he was one of the last to retreat. Lieutenant Doty said of Fowler's bravery at Gettysburg, he commanded the men with enthusiasm, "Colonel Fowler at once rode to the front and gave the command to deploy columns, and swinging his sword, said,

"Now, Seventeenth, do your duty! Forward, double-quick! Charge bayonets!" And with a yell, which our boys knew how to give, they charged."

Unfortunately, those would be Fowler's last words, as a prominent target sitting upon his horse, he was struck right away, some say a cannonball completely decapitating the poor man.

To be sure one of the 17th's biggest losses was Lieutenant Colonel Douglas Fowler of Guilford, who was a locksmith prior to being a soldier. He had previously served in Connecticut's 3rd and 8th, he was Captain of the 17th until the day he died, when he was promoted to Lieutenant Colonel. His name and the name of the others who died at battle are listed on the monument on Barlow's Knoll near to where they were during the battle. Officers who died at the same as him included Captain James Moore, Captain Wilson French and Lieutenant Henry Quien. Sergeant Major Frederick Betts of Norwalk had tried to recover Fowler's body onto his horse but was unable to lift his weight and had to leave him. More Confederates descended upon Barlow's Union soldiers. Some were able to reform their division near the Alms House. Major Brady took control of the isolated companies and pulled back from Rock Creek under fire. The Confederates were coming for the Connecticut companies. Major Brady, being resourceful got four of his companies beyond reach by tricking them on where they would go, and they continued to attempt to slow the Southern men. Brady stated,

"Any attempt to make a stand in this bewildered and frantic mob was attended with the greatest difficulty and peril, yet many fragments of both Corps did their level best to brave the storm and repulse the Rebels. Amidst all the excitement, I could see the 17th Connecticut deployed in the streets, firing several rounds before it was compelled to fall back."

When the companies collected in town, they fired volleys at the enemy with success.

Members of the 17th went to gather their Lieutenant Colonel after the battle but found that the Rebels had stripped the bodies of Union dead and stripped of all their valuables before tossing the men into mass graves. Fowler's body was never found, leaving him anonymously buried somewhere at Gettysburg, perhaps restless in spirit. Of note, while writing this book, a photograph

17th Connecticut Gettysburg Monument (Martin Reardon Jr. photo)

came to my attention of some Union officers held prisoner in South Carolina. The photograph dated Fall 1864 displayed men that had escaped the prison and as such had been executed. Some of the men were merely partially identified and one of those men was identified as Fowler. There is a striking likeness between the Fowler at Gettysburg and the one in the photo. Is it possible, that it was not he decapitated by the cannon but rather someone else and that he had been captured? With 19th century photography and partial records, it's hard to say but adds some mystery to our Connecticut hero's tragedy.

The first day at Gettysburg was hard for the Union, especially the 17th and when Major Brady mustered the 17th Connecticut on the morning of July 2nd, only 241 men answered the roll call. The regiment had lost 145 of its 386 men: 17 killed, 73 wounded, and 55 missing or captured.

And Day 2 of Gettysburg would see more carnage and Connecticut men would be even more present. General Meade ordered all Union forces in Gettysburg that night, more than 90,000 troops. One of the regiments arriving that evening was the

Escaped Union Prisoners Fowler (Courtesy of the Library of Congress)

14th Connecticut who held a position called the Angle for the remainder of the battle including the fateful Pickett's Charge on the 3rd day. The 14th Connecticut would engage with Confederate Skirmishers on the 3rd of July on Bliss Farm between Seminary Ridge and Cemetery Hill trying to thwart Confederate sharpshooters as well. The 20th would come and would form a line on Culp's Hill by the morning of the 2nd. The 27th would come and exchange deadly fire in the Wheatfield on the 2nd. The 5th Connecticut arrived late on the 1st clearing the Confederates from Wolf Hill and by the next day formed a line on Culp's Hill until they were moved to support the 3rd Corps and lost their position. They regained position and lost it again when they assisted the Corps during Pickett's Charge but suffered the least of all Connecticut regiments at Gettysburg. The Connecticut Light Artillery led by John Sterling of Bridgeport brought 106 men and four fourteen-pound James Rifles and two twelve-pound howitzers, the only battery with such arms thus protecting their men as well. The Union was gathering in number from all states.

They had time to do this because Ewell hesitated on Lee's orders to attack Cemetery Hill and as such Meade had time for people and more artillery. Lee had arrived the afternoon of the 1st of July, Meade arrived in the overnight orders going into the 2nd. On July 2nd, Lee ordered two of his Generals, Longstreet and Ewell to attack the Union flanks on Culp's Hill, but Longstreet did what Ewell had done and delayed, which was strengthening the Union even more. After delay, Confederate General James Longstreet attacked with his First Corps against the Union left flank and Hood's Division attacked Little Round Top and Devil's Den. As the day settled into evening, nearby, Confederate General Lafayette McLaws attacked the Wheatfield and the Peach Orchard where the 27th Connecticut would be the leading regiment of the Union and Confederate General Ewell turned full scale attacks on to Culp's Hill and East Cemetery Hill where the 20th Connecticut was present. The attack in the Wheatfield was not the 27th's first confrontation with war. They had served in the 2nd Corps of the

View from Little Round Top Gettysburg (Martin Reardon Jr. photo)

1st Division of the Army of the Potomac in the Battle at Fredericksburg and were trapped on what was considered the killing grounds for most of the afternoon. The 27th were then at Chancellorsville where most of their companies were cut off during the retreat. A Georgia infantry had offered them the opportunity to unit. They wanted to push through but knew it wasn't possible and a great number of them were sent to Richmond where they treated horribly and spoken to horribly.

They were distributed between prisons and warehouses converted to prisons. Though some were exchanged in June of 1863, few made it back to their unit for Gettysburg and the encounter that would take place. About 75 men were present for the 27th on that haunting Wheatfield.

The Wheatfield assault began as Longstreet had opened assault on the Union left and the Union 3rd Corps Line in the Wheatfield who had only been reinforced by the 5th Corps for a brief time took the brunt. General Meade came in to reinforce as best he could just after six o'clock PM. In early July, sun still sat in the sky with the hints of evening starting in the sky. The reinforcements of Hancock's old first division arrived and brought what was considered a woeful amount of 3,211 men. By their arrival, Confederates had controlled the woods, the Devil's Den was going to the rebels. Brigades of Patrick Kelly and Edward Cross came into the field and flanked it east to west and a third brigade went to Stony Hill. Perhaps the Union could the Wheatfield, they did for a short time. It was only a half-hour later as the open field fell into gunfire that Division Commander called in the reserve of Col. John R. Brooke including the 27th Connecticut. You may remember their 75 men filled out barely three units and one of the units was under the command of Jedediah Chapman and was filled with survivors from all the other broken regiments. The 27th took a position on a minor incline in the middle of the field. Brookes realized the poor placement and swept forward in a counterattack across the field.

"As the regiment enters the wheat-field...A few steps.... bring the men under the full sweep of the enemy's fire. Lieutenant-Colonel Henry Merwin falls while leading the command with his accustomed bravery...the line still presses forward at the double-quick, through the wheat-field and woods beyond, driving the rebels a quarter of a mile, across a ravine...The men with much difficulty clambered up the rocky steep, but as they appeared upon the crest of the hill, the enemy [was] drawn up in readiness..."

The Georgia men were in front of them just like at Chancellorsville but this time the woods were filled with them. The 27th and their comrades were able to make the Georgians fall back but they had back-up and the new brigade were at was considered "pistol-range," with the 27th Connecticut. Like Chancellorsville, the 27th rescued their colors and put them on a crest of a ridge as they squared off against the 51st and 10th

Bodies Wheatfield Gettysburg 1863 (Courtesy of the Library of Congress)

Georgia, the 10th, being the same that they faced at Chancellorsville. This would go on for 30 minutes in a back-and-forth. The outcome was deadly for the 27th. When they did roll-call at Cemetery Ridge at the conclusion, about half were there – 37 men, the other 38 lay dead on the Wheatfield. Those 37 would continue their service until they were mustered out a few weeks later. Three monuments on the Wheatfield are dedicated to the 27th for obvious reasons. In total, the Wheatfield pitted 13 somewhat small Union brigades against six Confederate brigades and engaged 20,444 men back-and-forth for less than an hour total and resulted in a casualty count of nearly 7,000. The Wheatfield would not be the site of any future battles or attacks, but it would remain there covered with the strewn remains of thousands.

Private Erskine Church who had served with the 27th Connecticut at Fredericksburg and the 12th Connecticut in Louisiana painted a picture that would haunt the hearts and minds of all those who came to know the Wheatfield, in particular, and who visit it today,

"Those who say they would like to visit a battlefield seldom know what they are talking about. After darkness has put an end to the struggle, a hush settles over the field. Such a contrast to the roar of the fight. Never is silence more oppressive, more eloquent. You hear the cries of the wounded, which is never distinguished in the roar of battle…. You see the outlines of forms gliding through the gloom carrying on litters pale, bloody men. Or perhaps your friend with his hair matted with blood over his white face and his dead eyes staring blindly up to the sky."

As mentioned, previously, my investigative team and myself conducted an investigation of the Wheatfield at the same time of evening that the battle took place. It is here that we felt the grabs on our legs from the wounded, our clothes visibly tugged. We heard the whispers, the cries and watched the shadows dart back and forth across the field. The Wheatfield is perhaps one of the most sobering places to remark on what happened at the Civil War and one of the saddest. Some have recorded sounds of fifes and drums in the Wheatfield as if they are still playing in the distance. Others have captured photographs depicting apparitions of ghosts in the Wheatfield. If you visit, perhaps you can see the ghostly phantom of the 27th flag flying high, as the Connecticut boys fought with the last survivors they could bring to the brutal attack.

27th CT Monument Wheatfield Gettysburg

And yet, believe it or not, the second day the battle of Gettysburg is home to many ghost stories. The attack of the Confederates on Devil's Den which is an aptly named grouping of large rocks on the field left behind perhaps one of the most frequently reported ghosts. The Devil's Den which a Confederate victory caused at least 1,800 Confederate deaths and 800 Union deaths and was referred to as the "Slaughter Pen." Visitors to the Devil's Den have reported seeing a long-haired hippie man, barefoot, in a floppy hat who seemingly gives visitors directions, "What you're looking for is over there," he says. He appears slightly disheveled and has been reported to park rangers for loitering near the rocks. Park rangers of course have not found the man that they believe to be a dead Texan as they often came without shoes and had the appearance described. One woman heard him shout from the top of the rocks, "First Texas," before he walked out of sight and vanished thus validating the Texan spirit theory. On our investigation of Gettysburg, we went to the Devil's Den before and after sunset. It was after sunset that we captured a male voice telling us, "That way," and we turned ourselves around instinctually to Little Round Top, when he said, "Go back." Is he directing and saving? Did he know where we were from? Nevertheless the "Hippie," ghost at Gettysburg is likely a soldier ghost.

Devil's Den Gettysburg (Martin Reardon Jr. photo)

Another prominent and perhaps even more tragic ghost of July 2nd, 1863 is that of a Southern General's dog. General Barksdale was killed by the sight of Cemetery Ridge and his body was left there for the coming weeks until his wife made it to the site to identify him. When his widow arrived, she brought their trusty dog, who immediately went to the site where his master had perished and had been buried in a shallow grave. When his body was exhumed, the dog let out a heartbreaking and piercing howl and remained by the gravesite. For days, the widow tried to pry him away from the site because even with the body removed, he wouldn't leave. The dog refused. The widow, heartbroken by the whole ordeal returned home and the dog remained at Gettysburg at that site refusing all food and water from residents until he died too. And now on July 2nd at the site, people still hear the heartbreaking howl. But July 2nd, despite the haunts of the Wheatfield, the Devil's Den and Cemetery Ridge is not the end of the bloody assault that stained our nation's history. July 3rd is around the corner.

20th CT Monument Gettysburg (Courtney McInvale photo)

The 20th Connecticut and 14th Connecticut are about to have the most unexpected day imaginable. The 20th Connecticut was furious on the morning of the 3rd. They had formed their position on Culp's Hill and when it moved to support the engagements I the evening, they returned to find their position occupied by Confederate Ewell's Corps. They spent the night in line of battle and at dawn advanced under cover of artillery and fought for five long hours to reoccupy the words. They were relieved by the

123rd New York and later moved to support the Second Corps in Longstreet's Assault/Pickett's Charge. The 20th would lose 5 to death, 22 to wounds and 1 recorded at missing at Gettysburg. Many of the survivors would go on to fight under General William Sherman in the Atlanta Campaign and his March on the Sea. One of the great tragedies of the 20th at Gettysburg was discussed with George Warner, the private from the New Haven area who lost both arms in the attempt to take back Culp's Hill. The 20th had received orders not to dislodge their foes but to relay information to the artillery. The firing commenced and continued however, and William Wooster learned quickly that many Union shells were striking their own men. Commander Archibald L. McDougall described what the 20th endured. "Lieutenant-Colonel Wooster, who was in command of this regiment, had a difficult and responsible duty to perform. He was not only required to keep the enemy in check, but encountered great difficulty, while resisting the enemy, in protecting himself against the fire of our own artillery, aimed partly over his command at the enemy in and near our intrenchments. His greatest embarrassment was, the farther he pushed the enemy the more directly he was placed under the fire of our own guns. Some of his men became severely wounded by our artillery fire." It's important to note that the 5th Connecticut also helped to form the line on Culp's Hill and had to fight to regain position prior to assisting in Pickett's Charge. They lost seven men at Gettysburg. Culp's Hill became a bloody sight, where Confederate men were stacked three deep, pined to trees and whiskey was handed out for funerals.

One night, years, later at a nearby campground a man reported to hear calls for help coming from the Culp Hill area. Despite the park being closed at 11:00 pm, the concerned doctor tried to locate the individual and listened as they heard the cries for help. They felt close when a park ranger stopped them, and they all heard the cry and the park ranger radioed for help. They followed the cries for hours unable to find the source. Others suggest that there's also a phantom soldier seeing wandering on the trail from the summit to the parking lot in Union uniform. One feels the tragedy and wonders if the souls will ever find place or be forever crying out from the Gettysburg fields. But ultimately, the grand finale of the three-day event took place around three o'clock in the afternoon on July 3rd. Though the Connecticut regiments of the 20th and 5th would be back-up at the assault and the artillery would be present it was the hard luck 14th who had suffered greatly at Fredericksburg, Antietam and Chancellorsville who would be at the forefront, at the angle of Pickett's Charge as they held the repulse at the position they had been holding since their arrival at Gettysburg.

5th CT Monument Gettysburg (Courtney McInvale photo)

On July 3rd, General Lee wanted to use the same attack plan as the day before despite his General Longstreet's concern. When the bombardment happened at Culp's Hill and the second fight ended in late morning, the Union was still strong. Longstreet was then set to command Pickett's division and six brigades from Hill's Corp and attack the Union line on Cemetery Ridge. Longstreet strongly objected to this plan as he felt there were more than Lee realized and that they were set to fail, and Lee made one of the biggest errors in judgment for his Confederate army in not listening to Longstreet. Beginning at 1 PM was one of the largest artillery bombardments in the Civil War as nearly 200 Confederate guns fired at the Army of the Potomac. It took almost 15 minutes before the Union including CT's artillery fired back with 80 Union can. The Confederates ran out of ammunition quickly and it was at three o'clock that the 12,500 Confederates began to walk the three-quarters of a mile to the Cemetery Ridge in an event that history would call "Pickett's Charge." The Union was flanked on Cemetery Hill and north of Little Round Top. The 14th was near the center and in the center the commander of artillery had held fire for the moment of assault due to Meade's orders and when the

Pickett's Charge – The Angle 2020 (Courtney McInvale photo)

Confederates got close, they unloaded the fire. The Union line waivered in one place, the Angle, where the 14th was.

The Confederates made it past an area of trees and rushed into the breach but were repulsed and hand-to-hand combat with any weapon available including hands and rocks began. After a half hour of charging and fighting, the Union held the line, they had won at Gettysburg and Lee had to remark on all the men, he had, in essence sent forward to die. The Confederates suffered 6,500 casualties in the charge. The 14th Connecticut was credited with capturing more than 200 prisoners and five battle-flags in the immediate front, and for capturing sharp shooters. They lost the most at Gettysburg. The regiment arrived with somewhere between 160 and 200 men and lost 61, over a quarter of their regiment. The 27th had lost half but had been cut down even more severely than the 14th at Chancellorsville. Corporal Christopher Flynn of the 14th was an Irishman, aged 35 who resided in Sprague, Connecticut near Norwich. He captured the flag of the 52nd North Carolina during the charge and received the Presidential Medal of Honor. He survived the war and is buried now at St. Mary's Cemetery in Baltic, CT. Sergeant Major William Hincks of Bridgeport, at the young age 22, at the time also earned the Medal of Honor for capturing the colors of the 14th Tennessee, outrunning his companions amid a storm of shot, swinging his saber over the Confederates and uttering a terrific yell. He was credited with encouraging the rest of the men with his bravery, his character, and action. Hincks survived the war and rests now in Bridgeport, Ct at the Mountain Grove Cemetery. Private Elijah W. Bacon of Burlington, Connecticut and later Berlin, Connecticut was awarded the Medal of Honor for his capture of the 16th North Carolina Battle flag at Pickett's Charge. He was estimated to be 25 to 26 years old at the time. He survived the battle at Gettysburg but would perish less than a year later at the deadly Battle of the Wilderness by age 28. He is buried in the Maple Cemetery of

Pickett's Charge Portrait 1887 (Courtesy of the Library of Congress)

Berlin, Connecticut and is honored with a plaque at the Kensington Soldier's Monument. His Medal was awarded posthumously.

Who were these brave men of the 14th led by? Major Theodore Ellis, who had been a civil engineer in Harford before the war. He rose to the rank of Brigadier General, U.S. Volunteers two years later and when the war concluded became the surveyor-general of Connecticut. He is buried in the same cemetery as Connecticut hero, Camp, Cedar Hill in Hartford. The air on the grounds by the deadly Angle at Pickett's Charge remains thick and when one visits, there is still a hazy even on a beautiful clear day, a haze no picture can determine but that visitors can see. The screams, the cries, the rebel yells and the Yankee calls, the firing, the dying that happened where you stand is overwhelming for some and on my first visit years ago, without realizing where I was, I had fainted just seeing them all – the only time in my life that happened except for one occurrence giving blood. The energy can push you over.

Some say that the tree by the angle where bodies were propped up is a paranormal hot spot. Others say they whole area is. My third visit to the grounds and investigation of them was filled with EMF readings all along the line of what was called the "High-Water Mark." The EVP's were quiet whispers looking for help and, in a way, it felt wrong to bother them. They were just men who knew they wouldn't make it home. Our guide even shared with us that some of the men walked with their backs facing, just to die with honor as they knew death was inevitable. While some hear the men, others hear the horses, and some hear

14th CT Gettysburg Monument

music. But to stand on Pickett's Charge is to stand between worlds, especially if you stand with the 14th Connecticut monument that marks where they stood. The grounds of Pickett's Charge were deadly for so many that our human bodies can still feel the fear and vulnerability today. Phantom images, smells and sounds abound at the site that park rangers and visitors agree may be one of the most haunted sites on the grounds. Other paranormal hot spots at Gettysburg include Iverson's Brigade Charge. One of Confederate Iverson's commands, under O'Neal advanced too early on a planned assault at an area called Oak Hill and were repulsed by the Union with ease. Shortly after Iverson's men formed into battle lines and stepped off perfectly in sync not seeing the Union officers still in front. When they got close, the Union got up and picked them off one by one in perfect line. Legend states that the first recorded ghost story at this site came from the farm owner a year later.

The dead were buried in formation, blood flowed around them, and it was a haunting scene that recreated itself at sunset as each man would stand back up in formation one, by one and fall back down. They say as you stand by the eternal flame at sunset, you can still see them do just that. Little Round Top boasts a ghost story of a Union man, his regiment unclear, however, during the filming for the 1993 film, *Gettysburg*, one of the extras was approached by a man in a ragged and burned Union uniform and smelled of gunpowder. He spoke to the men of the battle and gave them spare rounds of ammunition. When the extra checked with the producers about the ammunition, if it was from then, they were shocked to find that the strange old man had held and distributed to them, genuine musket rounds from the period. The film focused on the story of General (then Colonel) Joshua Chamberlain and the 20th Maine, who in fact had their own phantom sighting in Gettysburg. The first occurrence occurred on the road in. The Union soldiers watched as the clouds parted and the moon shone upon a man on a horse, tall stature, in an elegant coat and tricorn at on a notably white horse. Chamberlain wrote about the event and thought it was an officer of some kind until the men waved their hats, cheering loudly with exclaim that they recognized the figure and that it was George Washington. "General Washington, himself, come to lead us." The 20th Maine had miraculous victory at Gettysburg as they tried to capture Little Round top. They were charged by 4th Alabama as they made their way up the steep, rocky incline. Told to protect the position at all costs despite the odds and the whirring of gunshots, Chamberlain ordered the charge, and it was there that George Washington was seen plunging down the hill with them. The Confederates fled. To be sure there was a miracle. Later, in life, Chamberlain reflected on the event and wondered if it was a manifestation in the mind of the men or if the one and only, General Washington had made a mystical phantom appearance. On July 4th, it was determined by

Meade, against Washington's wishes not to attack the retreating Confederates. The death toll was too much for everyone. One Union soldier wrote.

"Corpses, swollen to twice their original size [due to summer heat], actually burst asunder...several human, or inhuman, corpses sat upright against a fence, with arms extended in the air and faces hideous with something very like a fixed leer."

Gettysburg totaled 51,000 casualties and neither Meade nor Lee could continue.

It was the turning point in the war in tandem with Vicksburg which ended it's 47-day engagement just a day after Gettysburg under the leadership of General Grant. Currently, some of the Connecticut men who perished at Gettysburg are buried at the Gettysburg National Cemetery where there are notably two misidentified Confederate men who are buried among them and one can't help but wonder if such a misidentification in the Connecticut plot was common throughout the war and if that also impacts the spirit world. But one thing is for certain and that is that Gettysburg was the most violent three-days in American history and that by July 1863 the Civil War was changing but it was far from over.

While Connecticut wasn't involved in all the battles and engagements deemed to be the deadliest in the war, they were involved in the majority, and there was more to come after the conclusion of Gettysburg and in less than a year's time they would be engaging in two of the top ten deadliest engagements of the Civil War back-to-back near Fredericksburg, even closer to Chancellorsville at the Wilderness and Spotsylvania Court House. One of the regiments that we've already seen at Gettysburg, Chancellorsville and Antietam would return to that spot for back-to-back engagements and that is the 14th Connecticut. The 14th By the end of Gettysburg, the 14th had gone from over 1,000 men to 100 and had just had additional enlistments to fill part of the depleted first for the first time since they mustered out. This was also the third time the 14th would find themselves here, as they had also been here for Mine Run in December of 1863 as well. The 1st Connecticut Heavy Artillery was also present at Mine Run which was yet another inconclusive and deadly battle, albeit, smaller than Chancellorsville, Wilderness and nearby Spotsylvania. The sheer number of battles in "The Wilderness," make it one of the most haunted areas associated with the Civil War and the history of Connecticut's 14th.

Battle of the Wilderness

By 1864, we now have Ulysses S. Grant as Commander of the entire Union Army and present in the Union theater. This adds to the changes that we see in favor of the Union since the Battle at Gettysburg. The Battle of the Wilderness was the first battle of General Grant and General Meade's Virginia Overland Campaign. The Wilderness would be recorded as the 4th deadliest battle in Civil War history totaling 29,800 casualties and at least 5,000 killed directly on the field. Present from Connecticut are three regiments including Connecticut's 1st Regiment Volunteer Cavalry, the seasoned and battle-hardened 14th, regiment, and the 30th Colored Regiment who was new to the war. Grant attacked with immense force and his leadership though effective would often result in high casualty counts earning him the title of the "The Butcher." By the Wilderness, Grant was looking for a war of attrition method, to just pressure Lee to stand down and to give up Richmond. Grant was on the offense and was going to follow Lee wherever he went. The bulk of the battle takes place during the overnight period of May 5th through 6th. On May 4th, Lee knew Grants plan and strategies and tried to plan accordingly on his side.

Grant outnumbered Lee with 120,000 men to the rebel's 65,000. The Union also had more artillery. It was then that Lee decided to intercept the arriving Union in the Wilderness. Confederate General Ewell marched east on the Orange Court House Turnpike to Robertson's Tavern and camped only a few miles from Warren's Union Corps unknowingly. Longstreet approached from the south to come against the enemy's flank as Jackson had done in the area a year before. The Union didn't realize how close they were, and misinformation was given to Meade. It was then that he left Union men such as Sedgwick of Connecticut and two others in charge of holding off the Confederate advance, he thought was just a potential. When the 14th Connecticut received their orders to leave their posts and head toward the Stony Mountain, they gathered the necessities and maintained the orders to stay silent. They marched with their Third Brigade and reunited with the Second Division and Second Corps under the command of General Hancock. They marched from Stevensburg and by May 4th began to cross the Rapidan.

As they marched closer and closer to Chancellorsville, the men began to recognize their surroundings and the eerie feeling of deja-vu, except this was no supernatural vision. These men had been there before on these grounds and proof became evident. As they came closer to the region, marching in utter silence, reflecting on their losses the year before, they began to see that they were not marching around on just mere earth, rocks and leaves. They were marching by the bodies, the bones, the uniforms of their comrades who had been left in the Wilderness in 1863. They walked with their heavy sacks and weapons in silence, staring at the blue uniform on the ground, they had a glimpse of what had been and what was to come. The Spirit of the Wilderness was there, and it was ready for more. William Landon of the 14th Indiana, the same brigade as the 14th Connecticut remarked,

"Strange feelings crept over me as we marched along the same road and over the same ground where one year and a day before I had stood up with my comrades in the line of battle, the old white house occupied as headquarters by General Couch during the fight shattered and torn with hostile shot and shell, still standing, a refuge for bats and owls, ghost too for aught I know."

The poor 86th New York of the Third Division was forced to spend a night among the graves of their comrades from the year before. Charles Brewster of the 10th Massachusetts also reflected,

"There were lots of human skulls and bones lying top of the ground and we left plenty more dead bodies to decay and bleach to keep their grim company."

The men looking upon past and future sallied forth that early May day, many of them toward that inevitable graveyard at their feet. It was by the morning of May 5th that the Union saw the Confederate Corps appear in the west and Grant gave the orders to infiltrate at any opportunity.

The Fifth Corps had run into Ewell's entire corps. But Meade, suspicious, that it was not the full corps, halted and in the meantime, the Confederates built earthworks. The mixed signals and delays were problematic. Union generals requested delays so they wouldn't be subject to enfilade fire but General Meade, frustrated by delays by the afternoon of the 5th ordered Union General Warren to attack while Sedgwick approached. The enfilading fire ensued, and Union General Bartlett had to retreat. Sedgwick's men were engaged in the fight under his leadership. The Iron Brigade began to advance through the woods and the Confederates counterattacked forcing the Iron Brigade, who had already suffered a great deal of loss, back further and breaking for the first time ever. Near to the Higgerson farm, Union brigades attacked Confederate brigades and both attacks failed under heavy fire. Finally, Sedgwick's Corps reached the field by 3 PM and the fighting was over. Nevertheless, they attacked Ewell's line in the woods and the attacks went back and forth for an hour. The real climax to the battle was coming and so was the 14th. Hancock knew orders would be coming for the Second Corps and there they were, directly from Grant, summoning them into the fight. The decision was such that if Hill could be destroyed, then the rest of the army could descend upon Ewell. The Fourteenth had been near the front of the Second Corps by Todd's Tavern and when orders came to turn around, they were near the rear. The fighting continued near the Orange Plank Road amid smoke and confusion in close quarters in a roadside thicket. Lee had his headquarters at a local farm and a part of Union soldiers came to their headquarters through a clearing scaring the Union Generals Lee, Stuart and Hill away, but the Union was confused as to how they got there and went back into the woods. That story depicts the confusion, the lack of visibility and the lack of clear lines. Meanwhile, on the Confederate side, Longstreet let his men tired from march rest and Lee allowed Hill's men to rest and no movement was resumed until after midnight.

There needed to be a better plan and awareness on both sides. Though the fighting continued until nightfall, Grant made a plan. He ordered an early morning attack on Hill's Corp on the Orange Plank Road by the II Corps and a resumption of assaults from the V and VI Corps against the Ewell position on the Turnpike. It was by 5 AM that the Second Corps with the 14th Connecticut attacked Hill and the Second Corps overwhelmed their divisions. The 14th was led by Col. Ellis just as they had been at Gettysburg. Ewell's men had tried to attack at quarter to five but had been kept back by attacks from Sedgwick and Warren as Grant planned. The men of neighboring brigades walked into the smoke-laden woods over the breastworks evading heavy fire from Hill and trying to navigate the morning fog. The losses grew as they continued forward and as Confederate lines began to break, hope was given to the 14th. The Confederates were falling back at the exact moment that Longstreet and his column finally arrived. General Lee was excited to see the Texans at the vanguard. The Texans encouraged Lee to get to a safe location feeling relief. Longstreet counterattacked. The Union advance had to stall near Widow Tapp farm and fresh brigades were needed, which meant that the 14th was at the frontlines for Longstreet's attack. Sgt. E.B. Tyler described the moment in the infantry's regimental history.

"There is a feeling of uneasiness in the stoutest heart in facing danger that one cannot see and know. The mystery is doubly intensified by the sudden, silent dropping dead, or fatally wounded, of men on either hand that somehow does not seem to connect itself with the constant roar of musketry that is going on. The zip, zip of the bullets as they pass so closely to your head that you cannot help but think that had the rebel aim been varied ever so little your career had been ended."

The Union lines began to fall, and Gettysburg Medal of Honor recipient William Hincks of Bridgeport described the battle, "There was intense fighting for about half an hour and in this brief space officers and men were falling. Among those seriously wounded during these moments was Captain Samuel Fiske of Company G, who died a few days later (May 22nd).

The men stood like heroes to the work until a regiment at the right gave way, producing something of a panic among several regiments of the brigade, about half of whom fell back to the Brock crossroads and were seen no more that morning." Ammunition was sent, Hancock ordered withdrawals and on their fall back stopped to hide behind trees and bodies, adopting the guerilla warfare they deemed "Indian style," fighting to continue in their efforts. Then the Union breastworks were set ablaze by the Confederates and a fight for the breastworks continued. The 14th would get no rest. A second battle emerged on Plank Road as the Union had to act in defense when the Confederates broke another Union line.

Hincks recalled the event and the hand-to-hand combat and gunfire at point blank range that would be the worst of the battle for Connecticut's 14th.

"The shattered ranks were reformed, and ammunition dealt out. Col. Carroll coming up spoke in warm terms of commendation of the behavior of the regiment. The men were then moved a short distance in the rear of the line of battle and told they would have twenty minutes for rest and to make coffee. Hardly five minutes had passed before the Confederates advanced and the Fourteenth was at once called into action and the fiercest fighting of the day occurred. The men of the Fourteenth charged with fixed bayonets and met the enemy and repelled the charge."

Most of the 14th engaged in this died or was taken prisoner. One major loss for the company was the loss of Captain Samuel Fiske of Madison, Connecticut. He had served as Captain of the Meriden, CT Company G, had been imprisoned after being captured at Chancellorsville. He was held for ransom, and when released was one of the only men from the 14th to make it back to fight at Gettysburg and in the   Longstreet attack on Wilderness he received a fatal gunshot. His family would come to his side and just a couple short weeks later, he passed away. Fiske was famous in his own right as using the name "Dunn Browne," he submitted articles that were published in the *Springfield Republican Newspaper*.

The few survivors that remained from the deadly engagements of the day were met on a nearby road with survivors from other

Battle of Wilderness Portrait 1887 (Courtesy of the Library of Congress)

regiments. Their reprieve was only brief as they would receive little rest or time to mourn before the next battle would be upon them.

Another notable loss was of course Gettysburg Medal of Honor recipient, Elijah Bacon who would not escape the Wilderness. As for our other Connecticut men at the Wilderness, The 1st Connecticut Volunteer Cavalry had arrived from traveling into the Orange County region with the Cavalry Corps under General Wilson from the Stevensburg, Virginia area where they had recently lost Sergeant Fish of Company H. Fish had been shot over 20 times by Confederates with his own revolver and left for dead. He surprisingly lived long enough to tell the tale. With fury in their hearts, they crossed the Rapidan a month after the event and entered the Wilderness Battlefields as an advance guard and would confront Confederate General Longstreet's advance and open the Wilderness battles on their left. Major Marcy of the 1st with about

200 men, reconnoitering (observing) was cut off. In order to escape, the Major ordered sabers drawn and a charge at the rebels. Regimental records state that they were successful in their feat and that it was "gallantly accomplished." Their loss totaled to approximately 40 men. The Union troops, tired from fighting had become disorganized and fell back near to the Widow Tapp Farm. The First Connecticut fell back to Todd's Tavern where they stood and checked the enemy for two days. The Texans were ruthless and lost over 500 of their own men attacking the Union flank. Longstreet led four brigades on a surprise attack against the Union and the lines rolled back. Union General James Wadsworth lost his life. Longstreet became victim of friendly fire by accident later himself but survived his wounds but was not able to return until months later. The friendly fire incident was eerily close to where it happened to his friend Stonewall Jackson. Robert E. Lee believed it was the spirits of Wilderness that would attack Longstreet and said he had not, "reckoned upon a second intervention of Fate: that the spirit of the Wilderness would strike Longstreet just as victory was in his grasp as it had struck Stonewall." At the Orange Turnpike fighting continued and inexperienced Union troops were targeted. Sedgwick's line was extended due to doubts and delays on the Confederate side making this possible. Grant grew concerned when the Union lines were falling. Author, Brooks Simpson documented a conversation that occurred when the concern grew in his book about Grant. "Reports of the collapse of this part of the Union line caused great consternation at Grant's headquarters, leading to an interchange that is widely quoted in Grant biographies.

An officer accosted Grant, proclaiming, "General Grant, this is a crisis that cannot be looked upon too seriously. I know Lee's methods well by past experience; he will throw his whole army between us and the Rapidan and cut us off completely from our communications." Grant seemed to be waiting for such an opportunity and snapped,

"Oh, I am heartily tired of hearing about what Lee is going to do. Some of you always seem to think he is suddenly going to turn a double somersault, and land in our rear and on both of our flanks at the same time. Go back to your command and try to think what we are going to do ourselves, instead of what Lee is going to do."

Despite Grant's attempts, by the next day, the Union troops could not catch up with Lee, there was no clear victor at the Wilderness, casualties neared 30,000 and the stage was set for the Battle of Spotsylvania Courthouse. The First Connecticut led the advance in Grant's move to Spotsylvania Courthouse in early morning hours following the battle. They had successful driven out the enemy and captured 35 infantry prisoners from their opposition. The Regiment was equipped next with Sharp's and Spencer's rifles to replace the "inferior Smith's.' General Wilson told the Connecticut 1st, they "had earned the right to carry them." A battered and defeated 14th, an optimistic 1st Volunteer Cavalry and a 30th Regiment that had not engaged, were on their way to Spotsylvania, the third deadliest of all Civil War battles. Ellis would bring the 14th all the way to Appomattox as a General and many others received promotions for their bravery and survival. The men of the 14th always said, "You would meet death or promotion within a year." But the Spirit of the Wilderness had changed them all. And for those who had revisited the spot, who stepped over the bones of their comrades and slept near their graves, the ghosts of the Wilderness were real and would haunt them the rest of their lives and all those who visit such a site. The Wilderness was a site where, despite government efforts at the war's conclusion, it was nearly impossible to retrieve the remains of so many who had died there over the multitude of engagements. Union soldiers returned for up to twenty years to bury some of their dead and on one such occurrence a Union soldier who had returned to bury some of the casualties who were further than a mile from the hospital, just six weeks after the battle, estimated that at least 15,000 Union men were on the field and an equal amount or more of Confederates remained there. He said, "remain as death found them, with the exception of their clothing," he continued, "Imagination in its wildest fancies cannot begin to paint the spectacle." He deemed it the "wilderness and shadow of death." In June of 1865, a major effort was made to bury some of the remains however a traveler in 1884 stated many bodies still remained and that he would on occasion come "suddenly upon a skeleton with a few tattered threads of blue or gray clinging to the bones – a ghastly reminder of war's grim horrors." Author William Swinton of the period described the Wilderness battlefield as a

"horrid thicket there lurked two hundred thousand men; and, though no array of battle could be seen, there came out of its depths the crackle and roll of musketry like the noisy boiling of some hell-caldron that told the dread story of death."

"So, the question remains, is it haunted in the traditional sense of phantom spirits and unexplained activity? By all accounts, of course, it is.

There, is, naturally the famous ghost of Stonewall Jackson in the area but of the 200,000 men at the Wilderness and nearly 30,000 casualties, many more restless spirits seem to be inhabiting the northern Virginia region.

One of the first ghostly accounts of the grounds is associated with a body itself. A Union soldier, perhaps from the 14th Regiment or a member of his brigade, returned to the battlefield to look for his fallen brother. He found partially exposed bones and tried to pull on one of them and felt a resistance as if something were pulling or retracting on the other end. He felt a hand on his shoulder and commented as it was if he heard a voice say,

"Don't disturb my bones with such rude hands."

The soldier was so scared about the "lifeless bones," and the fact that they made 'resistance as though still animated by an unwilling spirit," that he confessed to be filled with dread and hurried away quickly.

Wilderness Body Recovery (Connecticut Men) (Courtesy of the Library of Congress)

The men on both sides of the war believed that spirits rambled about the "hell-cauldron," with frequency. In more recent times you may notice that the trees still carry marks of cannonballs affixed in the bark and the air remains still. According to a journalist, in the not too distant past a visitor came across a boot with a fully skeletonized foot still inside. And the locals say you can still hear the screams of people burning alive and fighting – the purposeful fire, the guns, the death came for the men of the North and South in every which way. The 14th recorded that the woods were on fire and they couldn't get away quickly enough. It was the belief of some of the men, that in the afterlife, the men from both sides were working together to carry the souls of the lost. Union Veteran, Morris Schaff documented a moment when he found a dying comrade on the field and the spirit of the ghosts. He went on to say, of the moment that he noticed,

"The spirits of dead soldiers, from both armies, rise above the treetops...a great flight of them towards Heaven's gate.... Two by two they lock arms like college boys and pass in together; and so, it may be for all of us at last."

The Wilderness remains haunted by the stains of death and is perhaps one of the most long documented Civil War hauntings for both sides of the war as the documentation of the ghosts of the region began in 1863 from the soldiers themselves.

As you recall, the First Connecticut Cavalry was leading the advance to Spotsylvania and so we arrive at the last of the top ten deadly battles that Connecticut would participate in with Cold Harbor, Petersburg, Plymouth and a series of others still yet to come afterward, but the last of the top ten greatest casualty count according to American Battlefield Trust is Spotsylvania. Joining us along with the 1st, is again the 14th, the 30th and the 2nd Heavy Artillery. For the most part, excepting, artillery reinforcements, we are working with the same Connecticut line-up as the Wilderness.

Battle of Spotsylvania Courthouse

The Battle of Spotsylvania Courthouse was another inconclusive battle that caused just over 30,000 casualties compared to the Wilderness' 29,800 – the difference between them in casualty count just a couple hundred to a couple thousand but the difference in battle length immense. Some records state that the ultimate casualty count was 32,000. Both sides declared victory at Spotsylvania. The Battle of the Wilderness lasted three days in total (most fighting over the duration of two). The Battle of Spotsylvania Court House lasted 13 days – almost two weeks! Certainly, there wouldn't be action the entire time, but it was still

Portrait John Sedgwick

deemed part of the broader Overland Campaign. Grant and the Union's move from the Wilderness slightly to the southeast was an attempt to fight Lee in more favorable conditions. Lee's army, however, beat Grant to the location of Spotsylvania Court house and began entrenching. It was now up to Grant and the Union to break the Confederate lines. New York/Rhode Island Yankee, Governeur K. Warren and Connecticut Yankee, John Sedgwick attempted on May 8th to remove the Confederates from Laurel Hill so that they could remove the block from the Court house. On May 9th, the brave Sedgwick from Cornwall was probing skirmish lines ahead of the Confederate left flank and directing the artillery placements. The Confederate sharpshooters were located about 1,000 yards away and Sedgwick's men started ducking for cover much to his frustration.

He pressed them, asking what they would do when there was open fire on the battle lines if they had to dodge singe, random bullets. The men, feeling, guilty continued to duck. It was then that the General, they affectionately knew as "Uncle John," shouted out.

"What are you dodging like this? They couldn't hit an elephant at this distance.'"

Those would be the Major General's fateful last words as it's reported that at that very moment, he was shot by a sharpshooter equipped with a Whitworth rifle and was struck under the left eye. A native Canadian and New York resident named Martin McMahon heard the noises whirring all around and when he heard the dull, heavy stroke, tried to get Sedgwick's attention not realizing he was shot. "General, they are firing explosive bullets." And Uncle John turned to face McMahon the blood was spurting from his left cheek in a steady stream under his eye and he fell over despite McMahon's efforts to hold him up. Despite the immediate summoning of Corps medical personnel, Sedgwick remained unconscious, and continued to bleed until even his hair turned red. Sedgwick bled out until dead. The General's death shocked Ulysses S. Grant who was stunned and kept asking, "Is he really dead? Is he really dead?" Sedgwick was the highest-ranking Union death in the Civil War. Though he oversaw a corps rather than an army, he had the most senior rank of all major generals killed. It was a shock that ran through Grant and all those in charge. They too were vulnerable, and no battle was safe. Sedgwick had commanded the Sixth Corps through Chancellorsville, Gettysburg and the Wilderness prior to his death on May 9th, 1864. He had commanded another corps at Antietam prior to that and was shot three times there and returned to his post just three months later. He had also been recovering from wounds he gained at the Battle of Frayser's Farm and had continued fighting with. At Chancellorsville, his men had successful stormed Marye's Heights which was defended by a West Point classmate of his on the other side. Though held in reserve at Gettysburg, Sedgwick's men gained much respect for their performance at the Battle of Rappahannock Station the following November, able to cancel several enemy colors and prisoners. The Commander of the 6th Corps, the senior General in the Army of the Potomac, is regarded in memory, in Connecticut legend and in statue as Uncle

John on his horse Handsome Joe at Gettysburg and his statue and memory are also regarded as aforementioned at his alma mater. There is also a large monument in which McMahon spoke at the dedication at the Spotsylvania Courthouse and recalled the last moments. The most senior General, a beloved man is lost, Grant is shocked and it's only within the first 24 hours of Spotsylvania. Connecticut men are spread out and their records tell us about their movements and actions from their specific view.

Death of General John Sedgwick (Courtesy of Crossroads Blog)

Notably, the 1st Connecticut Volunteer Cavalry on a detachment order led by Major General Phillip H. Sheridan recorded that over the period that the Union is mostly battling in Spotsylvania, they engaged in the Battle of Yellow Tavern on May 11th, part of the same Overland Campaign and it is referred to as Sheridan's Raid. This is a Union victory with the fatal wounding of Confederate Major General J.E.B. Stuart, which was the greatest success of that battle. The Union suffered 625 casualties total at Yellow Tavern, including some from Connecticut. However, in the event they were able to recover 400 Union prisoners.

The 1st Connecticut had fought all day against Stuart's men on the 10th and 11th and on May 12th, the 1st Connecticut were in the extreme advance near Richmond and fought all day within the defense of Richmond, later withdrawing across Meadow Bridge at night. On May 15th, the 1st met with supply steamers and rejoined part of the army on May 25th at the Hanover Court House for the next event after the conclusion of Spotsylvania. This was meeting up with the disengaged from Spotsylvania for the Battle of North Anna from May 23rd through 26th, leading later to Cold Harbor. The 1st Connecticut Cavalry documented that they lost 150 horses in Hanover, Virginia and the previous raids and some of the riders as well, with the rest being sent to Dismount Camp. The 14th Connecticut, still engaged in Hancock's Second Corps, in the Second Division, Third Brigade, still with their leader, then Col. Theodore Ellis would have been closer to the Spotsylvania action. According to Regimental historian, it was after the Wilderness and enroute to Spotsylvania, in the beginning of the battle, that the 14th Connecticut and the rest of the Second Division assisted the Fifth Corps. On the nights of May 7th through 9th, they were formed in battle lines and met up with the 5th after that. Their skirmishes had already begun. During their march they were exposed to heavy shell fire as they marched in the rear and then suddenly, the brigade was in the line of battle. "We advanced over the line of breastworks, behind which lay part of the corps we were supporting and charged forward against the enemy." The 14th was engaged in dangerous terrain on a difficult road and had to constantly reform their line. The woods, being on fire, made it difficult for them to breathe and the fire coming at them from the rebels prevented their advance from going further. They were forced to maintain their position in the woods and fire at the enemy. After six hours, they were relieved and lay in the second line by the breastworks. The 14th had 11 officers and 220 enlisted present and in the middle of the night, they marched east and an assault was made on the rebel earthworks.

The 14th was second in line directly after First Division venturing into enemy territory on the morning of May 12th. Here, they were successful in gathering many prisoners. When some rebels ran, the regiment became scattered in the advance and chase, looking to the colors for guidance. They captured enemy cannon and were able to utilize it as well. They spent the next two days in the same area and marched westward on the 14th, remaining "in the works in line of battle." They formed a skirmish line on the 17th with other regiments and advanced on the Confederates again, leading to a skirmish on the 18th and consistent shell fire, yet surprisingly, no casualties for the 14th. After fighting for some hours and being relieved again, on May 22nd, after Spotsylvania had concluded, they engaged once more in a skirmish with Confederate Cavalry and on the 24th they moved across the North Anna River to where we would see the 1st Connecticut. Their line advanced and drove the rebels half a mile away across a wheatfield before they were once again relieved with no more ammunition. On the 25th, they engaged in ridding of Confederate entrenchments and on the evening of the 26th of May resumed driving the enemy from the earthworks and advancing.

They continued marching and skirmishing until the end of the engagement. Connecticut's 30th, which was being merged in with the 31st at this time is documented as having been there in the 11th Corps, 4th Division, 2nd Brigade, but seems they may, if present, may once again have been in reserve despite being on the order of battle. The 2nd Connecticut Heavy Artillery engaged with the First Division of the Sixth Corps in the 2nd Brigade. The Artillery participated in their first skirmish in duty along the North Anna River close to the 1st Cavalry and 14th Regiment and it was their first loss. They would then have a terrible first battle at Cold Harbor beginning just weeks later. They were under Colonel

Kellogg's command and had just reorganized as an artillery in late 1863 after having previously been an infantry. So, we know the 14th, the 1st Volunteers and the 2nd Heavy Artillery are engaging in fierce and violent skirmishes and going between offense and defense to maintain lines of their own and their own earthworks while capturing the enemy, the 14th, arguably with the most success in this venture, but what ultimately was happening at Spotsylvania? In all, the fighting was sporadic as it occurred between May 8th and May 21st because Ulysses S. Grant was trying a variety of schemes to break Confederate lines.

The differing schemes and outcomes are why this was "tactically inconclusive." The Confederates held defense, but the Union never stopped the offense as can be seen by the 14th's continual advance and caused a great deal of casualties and most deadly of the Overland campaign. The day after Sedgwick's death, Grant ordered attacks. He was aggressive and motivated. He ordered attacks on the entire line of Confederate earthworks spanning four miles as evidenced by the 14th's positions. The Confederate lines or salient were known as the "Mule shoe," and because of this were able to keep their lines. There were failures and successes and on May 11th, Grant planned for the grand assault on May 12th. Hancock's Corp was directed to assault the Mule Shoe due to some promise from the previous day's events on breaking through. However, attacks by Horatio Wright on the western edge of the Mule Shoe led to hand-to-hand fighting, described as some of the most lethal and deadly in the entire War and the area became known as the Bloody Angle. The 14th participated in the Mule Shoe Assault as did, at least in rear lines, perhaps part of the 30th by record. On May 13th through 16th, we can read that the 14th moved their position and attacked different lines and that was the process of Grant reorienting the lines. It was May 17th through 18th that Grant orders final attacks. Part of the delay was due to bad weather. The 2nd Corps and 6th Corps attacked the Confederates on Fredericksburg Road, away from the Mule Shoe, with the 2nd Corps in front as described prior. But Ewell had improved his earthworks, had prepared and the efforts were to no avail. The 14th made out remarkably well at this particular event.

But overall, the Union, did not have the decisive victory Grant had hoped for. The determined Union Commander tried one more time on May 19th by abandoning his battlefield and ordering the Hancock Corps to march the railroad line toward Richmond and turn South to bait the Confederates and make them vulnerable. Lee, did not follow, however and sent Ewell and his Second Corps. The fighting lasted some time into the dark and night and was a large casualty loss for the South. As we see the 1st and 14th as well as the artillery arrived at the Battle of North Anna because of that last event setting a delay on southward movement. Battle of North Anna was a major engagement, but perhaps not one whose legacy was as long lasting as Cold Harbor and the subsequent Petersburg Campaign. Spotsylvania marks the end of the top ten deadly campaigns, at least statistically speaking, for the Connecticut boys and men. Perhaps, the most haunted area for the Union and Confederate ghost at Spotsylvania is the Bloody Angle.

Legend states and accounts of modern-day paranormal investigators record accounts of frequent, thick fog rolling in over the battlefield in which you can see phantom soldiers. Reenactors claim that when they spend time on the field, they can hear disembodied cries, screams and gunfire from the trenches when all reenactors are resting. The Spotsylvania Courthouse Battlefield, part of the Spotsylvania National Military Park made the Washington Post news in 2006 when determined ghost hunters investigated the site. Legend stated that souls walked the grounds, and they were certain if spirits would appear anywhere, it would be on the side of that Bloody Angle, located on a nearby farm. The fields had run red with blood and bodies. The most remarkable incident of their investigation was the sound of wailing moan of agony, likened to a mix of a human and animal sound coming from the woods. They summoned a park ranger who investigated for the sound he too had heard. The cause of sound was not heard but the ranger concluded, it was not uncommon, to hear the agonizing cries of soldiers passed away. Battles such as Spotsylvania haunted the few survivors of regiments like the 14th.

One man, Private Dwight Davis from Canterbury and participated in 34 battles and skirmishes including: Antietam, Fredericksburg, Chancellorsville, Gettysburg, Mine Run, The Wilderness and Cold Harbor. He had the fast-shooting muzzle loader Sharp's Rifle in his company which perhaps, aided in his survival. He was wounded in the Wilderness, shot or otherwise injured in the knee and lower right ribs. He laid in the field for 10 days and made his way back to his company engaging in the ongoing fight before he took a small break until August of 1864. He stayed until the end of the war when his company was mustered out on May 31st, 1865. When he returned home to Canterbury, he took care of the family farm but had what his wife could only describe as "episodes," of terrible head pain and he would get confused as to where he was oftentimes. They thought then it was because of his prolonged exposure to the sun but in reality, it was the trauma, the ghosts of his comrades and the past he had witnessed and could never forget. Life was never normal for these survivors again. While I cannot detail in one book or even several the accounts of each man from Connecticut in each battle that was not remarked as one of the top ten deadly battles, nor is there enough space to document all the ghost stories from Civil War battle sites, I do want to touch briefly upon Cold Harbor and Petersburg regarding Connecticut.

Battle of Cold Harbor

Cold Harbor took place just over a week after Spotsylvania Courthouse and occurred near the town of Mechanicsville, Virginia just about ten miles from Richmond from May 31st to June 12, 1864 and resulted in the casualties of an estimated 18,000 men. Cold Harbor marked the near end of the Overland Campaign and was particularly tragic for the Union who launched an unsuccessful frontal assault against the Confederate Army. Cold Harbor was labeled one of "American history's bloodiest, most lopsided battles." General Ulysses S. Grant would remark on Cold Harbor as one of his greatest regrets and wrote about it in his personal memoirs, stating,

"I have always regretted that the last assault at Cold Harbor was ever made. ... No advantage whatever was gained to compensate for the heavy loss we sustained."

Cold Harbor was a big win for the Confederate Army who also sustained a great deal of casualties, but it was a game changer for Grant and thus would put Grant and the Union on the path for victory. Present from Connecticut at Cold Harbor was once more Connecticut's 14th Infantry, the 1st Volunteer Cavalry, the 8th, 21st and 11th Infantries and notably the Connecticut's 2nd Heavy Artillery. The 2nd Connecticut Artillery was formed originally as Connecticut's 19th Volunteer Infantry, with most of the men coming from Litchfield County and trained under the guidance of Major Elisha S. Kellogg of Derby. After training in Washington and guard duty, in November of 1863, the War Department ordered the regiment to be re-organized as the Second Connecticut Volunteer Heavy Artillery Regiment. Officers recruited more members in Connecticut. By of 1864 they traveled to Cold Harbor, Virginia. Grant wanted to maintain an aggressive strategy by this point and the artillery was necessary. And the 2nd Connecticut Heavies were the on the frontlines by June 1st for, what would amount to their first time seeing action in the entire war to date. It may have been 1864 but Cold Harbor was the 2nd Heavies Baptism under fire.

The Second Connecticut Heavies operated as an infantry in the thick of the fight. Colonel Elisha Kellogg was described as "physically imposing," and he commanded the unit across open ground toward the Confederates. Kellogg was a native of Glastonbury, Connecticut, a merchant-sailor and toolmaker by trade who had moved to the quiet area of Winsted when he married and settled after an excursion prospecting for gold in California (just like Captain Thomas Wolfe had dabbled in prior to the war!) Kellogg had answered the call in 1862 and enlisted with the 19th and upon being mustered out he was the regiments Lieutenant Colonel. He was considered to be red-faced and some thought a bit of a bully on parade grounds, but he commanded respect and he respected all the men around him. There was a noted closeness between Kellogg and his men. Though the then Lieutenant Colonel was ill in 1863 when the regiment changed to the Heavies and he was unable to do much, he was promoted to the rank of Colonel. The work of the 2nd heavies in Washington was garrison duty for Kellogg and the rest leaving them quite inexperienced by Cold Harbor and in a dangerous position. The other soldiers were not nice to the 2nd Heavies, not appreciating their lack of experience and called them "paper-collar," and "band-box soldiers." Cold Harbor changed their perspective of Kellogg and the 1,800 2nd Heavies who were fearless on the frontlines lead in the charge. Kellogg readied his men at Cold Harbor, "Now men, go in steady, keep cool and until I order you to charge, then go in arms a-port with a yell. Not a man of you fires until we are within the enemy's breastworks. I shall be with you." Shortly after the first valley of shots fired over their heads as they made their way to the entrenchments. By the second volley set-up, Kellogg had ordered his men to lie down thus saving them a second time. After this, still intact, Kellogg and the men scattered the men in the first line of entrenchments, made it to within 20 feet of the Confederate Earthworks when the rebels stood up and fired directly and purposefully at the 2nd Connecticut Heavies. Kellogg continued to encourage his men throughout the brutal assault and being under fire from the front and the flank.

Much like Camp, Kellogg described as knight, wanted to get his men covered and cried out the order, "About-face," which was his last order and last words. Moments later he took two bullets to the head and his body fell atop the rebel parapet immediately, the 39-year-old Colonel was dead. Nearly three-quarters (75%) of the 2nd Connecticut Heavies fell dead or wounded at the same time just behind their brave General. It's estimated that of all that fell 323 were killed or wounded with inability to serve. The survivors had just lost the title of "paper-collar," and continued to serve and eventually rejoined Grant in Petersburg after some time under Philip Sheridan in the Shenandoah Valley. Kellogg's body is now buried at the Forest View Cemetery in Winsted, Connecticut. A monument at the Cold Harbor Battlefield sits for the 2nd Connecticut Volunteer Heavy Artillery next to the "Bloody Baptism of Fire," wayside marker and the base states, "Connecticut Remembers Her Fallen Sons." As for the men that I like to call the Frontline Fourteenth – at Cold Harbor, the regiment recorded that they first were left on picket when they arrived on June 1st. When the bulk of fighting occurred on June 3rd, their line was moved forward toward the Confederates, but not being at the front, they engaged in "sharp skirmishing but no general engagement," in their vicinity. They entrenched themselves in front of the Confederate earthworks and remained quiet with some shots between pickets. They were protected by their earthworks from the heavy fire near them and assisted in repulsing

Confederates on June 4th. The 14th reported being under fire every day of Cold Harbor but that they endured as hey always had. The men were described to "not complain." By then, of course, they were seasoned and just trying to survive. Ellis commended the bravery of William Hincks again at Cold Harbor. The 14th was attacked often at Cold Harbor, repulsed successfully and captured three privates and an officer from the 42nd North Carolina. One of the 14th sharpshooters took out a Confederate sniper and some others were injured. They thanked their Sharp's rifles for getting them through.

Theodore Ellis left a full description of the Battle at Cold Harbor in letters to Brigadier General Morse in the 14th Connecticut Regimental History. The 1st Connecticut Cavalry was again under Sheridan's Division who was tasked with to secure Old Cold Harbor and the crossroads. Fighting took place near to the crossroads but Sheridan and his men held them off, left briefly and returned before dawn June 1st to be victorious when Lee's Confederates tried to attack for the crossroads and came after a dismounted cavalry. Well-armed, the Cavalry was able to fire intensely. The Cavalry remembers them being scared and trying to hide quickly. The intersection would remain under control of the Union and the Cavalry including Connecticut's 1st would be part of this charge. The 8th Connecticut was under the First Division, 2nd Brigade, as part of the XVIII Corps under General William Smith. Smith and his men including the 8th Connecticut were part of an attack on June 9th that had failed, and he and the men were ordered to advance on June 15th, however Smith delayed the assault against better judgment and attacked too late, which permitted Confederate reinforcements to arrive. Smith lost a great deal of men in his corps at cold harbor. Between June 1st and 10th including the first assault the 8th Connecticut had 40 casualties. They lost an additional 29 between the 15th and 17th of June though it's unclear if that was still part of Smith's delayed assault, it likely was and is described as "near Petersburg." The 11th Connecticut who was part of the Second Division of Smith's Corps as opposed to the First Division with the 8th would have participated similarly with Smith's Corps and deadly assaults. The details of their post like the 8th are not described except in regimental letters or histories, and this was not as deadly for the 11th as Antietam but nevertheless, one of the worst battles they had participated in. The 21st Company was in the same Corps as the 8th and 11th, and in the same division as the 8th. The 21st Connecticut was led by Col. Arthur Dutton of Wallingford at Cold Harbor who met his end shortly after arrival. Second in command, Col. Thomas Burpee of Rockville took over and in the failed attack on June 9th was shot twice in the chest and died just days later. Before joining the 21st in September of 1862, he had served as a Captain in the 14th. The area of the battlefield on which Burpee died is named after him as "Battery Burpee." Burpee is buried in Vernon, Connecticut at Grove Hill Cemetery and in the GAR Room at the Town Hall in Vernon they keep his blood-stained sash, the bullet that killed him and other items relating to him. One member of the Sons of the Union Veterans of the Civil War told the *Hartford Courant* in 1994,

"Burpee doesn't belong to Rockville, he belongs to the State of Connecticut."

Connecticut sits still at Battery Burpee, at the crossroads and on the frontlines that marked the battlefield at Cold Harbor and the losses sustained by the 2nd Connecticut Heavies became known as one of the greatest death tolls for an artillery regiment in the entire war. Cold Harbor started off with failed attacks on June 1st and by June 2nd the men were pinning their names on papers on their uniforms so their bodies could be identified.

One diary even had an account that ended on June 3rd and read. "June 3. Cold Harbor. I as killed." June 3rd was the deadly assault ordered by Grant and as the men advanced through thick fog, they entered heavy fire and either died or got pinned down. Even Gettysburg's Meade, who had successfully led at Gettysburg, was not thinking correctly and making decisions that didn't help at Cold Harbor with delays. After the enormous death toll on the 3rd, the 4th through 12th of June was filled with nine days of trench warfare and sharpshooters. The 4th through 12th would result in more casualties than June 3rd by double. And the assaults near Petersburg were the follow up. The 2nd Heavies and the 14th help bring us to Petersburg in the assault which will be the Campaign that ends the war. What was left behind at Cold Harbor was more than bodies but ghost stories aplenty including reports from locals

Collecting Remains at Cold Harbor 1865 (Courtesy of the Library of Congress)

that they often feel the booms of artillery fire shaking their house, smell burned gunpowder and hear shouts and cries in the woods accompanied by the sound of horse's hooves.

In 2008, a paranormal investigator and author received permission to investigate the grounds of Cold Harbor at night and to further investigate the claims. The park service sent a law enforcement officer and self-proclaimed skeptic to accompany their group on the investigation. They reported strange photos that shocked even the Park Rangers but most shocking was that they kept hearing footsteps walking behind them on the path and with their night scopes and flashlights never saw the culprit be it a person or an animal. They also continued to smell sassafras throughout the battlefield and detected thick fog over the field as if it still sat there in perpetuity just like the soldiers had seen. As for Connecticut, if anyone haunts Cold Harbor, I imagine it would be someone from the 2nd Connecticut Heavies or even leaders such as Kellogg of the 2nd Heavies or Burpee from the 21st who met notable ends at Cold Harbor. Or perhaps, the ghosts of all those lost by June of 1864, came to the ultimate conclusion at Petersburg and Appomattox in 1865. And for this chapter, we will conclude Connecticut's prominent battle involvements with the Siege of Petersburg.

Siege at Petersburg

The Skirmishes that Smith's men engaged in directly after Cold Harbor were considered the Second Battle of Petersburg, however the Siege of Petersburg from June 15, 1864 to April 2nd, 1865 is considered the entire Siege of Petersburg. The siege was a total of 9 months of more trench warfare in which General Grant assaulted Petersburg (to no success) and constructed 30 miles of trench lines around the outskirts of Petersburg to cut off the supply line that was crucial to Lee and his Confederate capital at

Richmond. Several battles took place over the 9 months and Lee finally being squeezed out of all ability to get provisions and ultimately, survive, had to give in to the pressure and abandon Richmond where he retreated and surrendered at Appomattox Courthouse.

The Siege of Petersburg had a great deal of battles with the new "Colored Troops," of African descent including the 29th Connecticut who helped take Fort Harrison less than 10 miles from Richmond in September of 1864 and participated in the scouting mission that led to the Battle of Darbytown. They helped push the Confederates back at Kell House during this siege as well. In April of 1865, the 29th took place in the last attacks emptying Confederate defensive trenches. Connecticut's involvement at Petersburg was immense. The 6th and 7th Infantries participated in the June 9th, 1864 Battle of the Old Men and Young Boys. The 8th Infantry fought in the Petersburg siege from June 15th through 18th in the Second Battle of Petersburg as mentioned. The 10th Connecticut, 11th Connecticut, 21st Connecticut, 29th Connecticut infantries as well as the 14th engaged in the same Second Battle of Petersburg from the 15th through the 18th of June. The 14th Connecticut Regiment would also engage in the June 22nd Battle at Jerusalem Plan Road, the August 25th Battle at Ream's Station, the October 27th Battle at Burgess Mill and the February 5th Battle at Hatcher's Run. The 1st Light Artillery had their presence at Gettysburg and the 1st Heavy Siege Artillery present at the Second Battle of Petersburg in June with the several aforementioned infantries also participated in the July 30th Battle at the Crater and the March 25th engagement at Fort Stedman. The Second Connecticut Heavies participated in the June 22 Battle at Jerusalem Plank Road, the February 5th Battle at Hatcher's Run and March 25th, 1865 Battle at Fort Stedman engaging with of course the 14th infantry and the 1st Heavies.

The 1st Cavalry continued their service in the Siege at

Petersburg with their participation at the April 1st, 1865 Battle at Five Forks. (Notably, the 10th Connecticut went with Grant to Appomattox for Lee's surrender.) It is estimated that 70,000 casualties resulted from the Siege at Petersburg, the "Longest Military Event of the Civil War." Union casualties outnumbered Confederate casualties with an estimated 42,000 Union casualties and 28,000 Confederate casualties. The Petersburg National Battlefield has several sites and at the Eastern Front Unit with the Crater and Fort Stedman Battlefields. At the Chesterfield Battery on the site sits a mortar representing the exact one used by Company G of the 1st Connecticut Heavy Artillery in the same spot that it was used during battle. The mortar, which sits at the same spot as it was during the Siege was called "The Dictator," and weights over 17,000 pounds. It was a rare 13-inch mortar and the railroad flatcar it was reinforced on is what it sat upon. The Dictator used gunpowder charges of 14 to 20 pounds to fire a 200-pound shell at a range of 4,235 yards. The regimental historian of the 1st Connecticut Heavies believed that it was the mortar that held the battery in check. On July 11th, 1864, the mortar broke the flatcar it was on during recoil. After it's reinforcement, it participated in the Battle of the Crater and fired 19 rounds and even took out a cannon and eight to ten rebels in one shot. The Dictator remained in use through September. In Connecticut, at the state Capitol the First Connecticut Heavy Artillery monument honors the Dictator and the First Heavies profound impact in the war and in particular, at the Siege at Petersburg.

Visiting the Petersburg National Battlefield is a profound experience and to see the size of the mortar and the positioning of the Connecticut Heavies is an astonishment. The trails around Petersburg with signs telling you where encampments and skirmishes occurred is in many ways a trip through time and while my husband and I did not investigate on our visit, we walked the trails and paths of the Union. As we came close to the battery in a quiet wooded area, we heard footsteps behind us. Now, at our arrival to the site, the only other folks there were some new enlisted members of the Army who had been training. Their bus had left as we started our stroll and when we heard footsteps halfway through, we both thought, "Oh no, the bus left without someone." We turned toward the hurried boot clomps and saw no one. We investigated the woods where we could hear them coming from but still no one appeared. We even hurried our footsteps as the wind picked up and we could feel the men running around us for the smallest second until the field went back to quiet. The ghost stories of Petersburg, Richmond and Appomattox are several and especially around Petersburg with so many Union casualties are tales of ghostly Yankees. At Fort Stedman on the Petersburg Battlefield, a visitor reported a sighting to his friend, a park ranger that he just couldn't wrap his mind around, especially as skeptic. He had seen a ridge, where the Union soldiers had once formed a battle line facing Fort Stedman and was shocked when he looked upon the ridge and saw the line of them clear as if they were alive. He figured they had to be re-enactors, part of a living history demonstration and just as he was going to turn away from his stare at them, they vanished, the way no living person could. He didn't know if he should approach to find them or call for help on the radio but when he could see they were truly gone, he waited to tell his friend. This didn't surprise a park supervisor who nearby to the Fort Stedman he would hear several mornings around five-thirty a military band playing "*John Brown's Body*," or the "*Star-Spangled Banner*." He said it happened with such frequency it was like an alarm clock. The Confederates left their ghosts near the old Capital City as well and in fact Confederate President Jefferson Davis was reported often but appearing rather as a young boy crying out, "He's Gone, He's gone," as he would wander back and forth. It's told that when Davis' body was finally buried in Richmond, the little boy ghost vanished. Connecticut's present at Petersburg was so profound and our loss in the Petersburg Campaign included the Knightly Soldier Henry Ward Camp and so many others. Connecticut's ghosts perhaps are still there, running on the fields valiantly, their footsteps heard coming through the woods, manning "The Dictator," playing their marching tunes and standing in formation. Ultimately, Petersburg would be the grand finale and on April 9th, 1865 Lee surrendered to Grant and the Union at Appomattox, and you can still visit the historic site of the surrender today and envision the village as it was when the Union emerged victorious over the Confederacy and freedom had a whole new meaning in our united country.

Connecticut counted nearly 5,500 to 6,000 killed and thousands of others wounded, missing, or dead from disease and/or imprisonment by the war's conclusion. Death on the battlefield was preferable for many. Disease and disease from imprisonment being one of the deadliest causes in the Civil War and killing more men than any battlefield. In fact, prisons became the ultimate tragedy and ghost story of the American Civil War and next we will explore Andersonville, Georgia and additional prisons that brought suffering and torture to the Union men in the war.

Connecticut's POWs: Life and Death in Southern Prisons: Torture of the Body and Spirit

Tales of the Dead, the Scarred Survivors and the Angel of Andersonville

"By no such considerations were our imprisoned comrades cheered. Not in the glorious rush and shock of battle; not in hope of victory or fadeless laurels; no angel charities or parting kiss, or sympathetic voice bidding the soul look heaven war while the eye was growing dim; no dear star-spangled banner for a winding sheet. But wrapped in rags, unseen, unnoticed, dying by inches in the cold, in the darkness, often in rain or sleet, houseless, homeless, friendless, on the hard floor or the bare ground, starving, freezing, broken-hearted." – Lt. Col. Homer Sprague, 13th CT

Can one imagine something more haunting than an open field where 45,000 men were tortured, starved, ravaged by disease? A field where 13,000 innocents would lose their life and are buried in the red clay where you stand? A field where the young and healthy endured the worst and most inhumane treatment until they no longer felt like a person and crossed to the other side feeling undignified and unfulfilled is what the field of Andersonville Prison in Georgia is. The Southern Prisons caused more than just death for the men from Connecticut and the other Union states, but caused torment and arguably, there is nowhere, that speaks more loudly to the complete sadness and loss of the Civil War than the grounds of the prisons and the grounds where the prisoners were laid to rest unceremoniously in shallow graves. The spirits of each one stand there are forever connected with the loathsome experience as it was not just their physical bodies ravaged by the experience but their souls and spirit that were broken by the trauma. For this reason, unlike any other ghost story, at the prisons, the haunting is felt with the depths of trauma and depression and visitors feel the need to bring each spirit peace as they feel them gather. Upon my first visit to Andersonville, as I could envision the sunken faces, the filth, the horror, the struggle to communicate as the souls stood around seeking help, I tried to envision each of them as they were most proud, faces full, half smiles, clean uniforms, muscles for strength and I said to the spirits with assurance that that is how they were remembered, and their death

Andersonville Stockade Full View (Courtney McInvale photo)

was filled with dignity and grace. To let them know, that what happened at prison, perhaps, must not haunt their soul forever.

There is no doubt that perhaps the most heart-wrenching, horrific and haunting stories of the Civil War come not from battlefields but from prisons and prison camps where pain and death was long and slowly, by way of neglect, mistreatment, exposure and disease. Death by dysentery, starvation, infections, hepatitis, diphtheria, smallpox, typhoid, scurvy, suicide and, of course, cold-blooded murder were daily occurrences in the Southern prisons. By 1901, the estimate of the War Record and Pension Office was that 211,000 Union men were captured in the duration of the war. In the earlier part of the war, between 1861-1863, it was common for men to briefly be imprisoned and then paroled. However, the parole exchange system broken down in late 1863 and between the end of 1863 and the end of the war 195,000 Union men found themselves in prison camps with little to no chance of escape. Over 30,000 Union men died in prison camps surpassing the approximate 26,000 death toll of Confederate prison camps held by the North; Nearly 16% of all Union men imprisoned would die. 29% of all imprisoned at Andersonville would die while in prison. That does not count those who would die in just days or weeks after their release because of the conditions as we saw was the case with George S. Brooks of Haddam, Connecticut, Connecticut' 16th Regiment.

There were several prisons throughout the North and South. In general, commissioned officers and non-commissioned officers and enlisted men would see different prisons with the latter being placed into the prison camps. The major prison camps for enlisted Union soldiers included: Salisbury Prison in Salisbury, North Carolina, Libby Prison in Richmond, Virginia, Fort Pulaski in Savannah, Georgia, Florence Stockade in Florence, South Carolina, Danville Prison in Danville, Virginia, Castle Thunder in Richmond, Virginia, Castle Sorghum in Columbia, South Carolina,

Castle Pinckney in Charleston, South Carolina, Camp Ford in Tyler, Texas, Castle Morgan in Selma, Alabama, Blackshear Prison in Blackshear, Georgia, Belle Isle in Richmond, Virginia, Camp Lawton in Millen, Georgia and the worst of all prison sites at Andersonville in Andersonville, Georgia which is now the site of the National POW Museum.

The ones that live in most infamy are Andersonville, Salisbury and Libby Prison, the three of which saw a great deal of Connecticut prisoners and an enormous death toll. Andersonville was the site of 13,000 prisoner deaths, Salisbury at least 4,000 and Libby Prison coming in at somewhere between the two. Libby Prison sent many of their prisoners to Georgia in 1864 to Andersonville and became a detention center for former Confederate officers in 1865. Libby and Salisbury Prison often share the title for "second worst," next to Andersonville. In fact, the three prisons can be held accountable for most Union prison deaths in the entirety of the war. Some prisoners were in for weeks, but many saw months and some even years in conditions where overcrowding was an understatement. Andersonville was built for 10,000 prison but at times it held 35,000 to 45,000 prisoners. Andersonville was a rectangular stockade constructed of embedded pine logs. At first the facility stood at 16 acres but was increased to 26.5 acres when the population surpassed 31,000 in July of 1864. There was a small brook that bisected the stockade and was where the men both bathed and relived themselves and where many drank water that would contribute to their deadly disease. They were not provided food or provisions that the Confederate army did not have an abundance of and were left exposed to the elements.

"And if any sight would make a man's heart sink, the middle of this pen would. Twelve thousand men turned into this place just like so many cattle not a tree or shelter of any kind to protect from the sun or rain or cold ... it was the hardest trial of my life." – First Sgt.

Oliver Gates 16th CT

Prisons records state that men were imprisoned and died at Andersonville from Connecticut's 6th, 7th, 11th, 13th, 14th, 16th, 17th, 18th, 20th and 21st infantry regiments for a total of 11 regiments. Salisbury Prison had prisoners and deaths from the 1st, 2nd, 5th, 6th, 8th, 9th, 11th, 12th, 13th, 14th, 18th and 19th Connecticut infantry regiments as well as Connecticut's 1st Volunteer Cavalry and 2nd Heavy Artillery. The 16th Connecticut was perhaps one of the most well-known regiments for their particularly harsh conditions and death toll at Andersonville and the smaller prisons in South Carolina and North Carolina prior to their release nearly a year later if they had survived Georgia. The 16th Connecticut arrived at Andersonville in late April and early of 1864 after the battle of Plymouth, they arrived at the gates of Andersonville alongside their fellow Union captured from the 101st PA, 103rd PA, 2nd MA Heavy Artillery, 24th NY Battery. The officers were taken to Camp Oglethorpe in nearby Macon, Georgia as the rest were divided into detachments of 90 with Sergeants in charge who would divide rations among the men. Outside the 16th Connecticut who had had their fair share of trauma and battle, as well as a lack of all necessary provisions, the others captured appeared to be well-to-do and not battle hardened making them stand out at the prison to the rest. Prisoner, John McElroy wrote that his friend gazed upon them and said, "Hulloa, I'm blanked if the Jonnies haven't caught a regiment of Brigadier Generals, somewhere." And the group of new arrivals, just meeting the grounds known as the "hell-hole," were deemed the Plymouth Pilgrims. With the provisions provided, trade and agreements could be made in the prison but the soon to be executed Raiders had their eyes on them. The Raiders were rogue soldiers who stole and murdered their fellow prisoners for their provisions. Other soldiers formed the "Regulators," to counteract them and by June of 1864 the Raider's leaders were hanged. Some believe that the ghostly occurrences at Andersonville are the Raiders and they are often blamed for the strange sounds and sights, however, others say they are blamed because of their legendary cruelty. Apparitions are seen around the prison camp amid sounds of groans echoing voices as well as marching footsteps.

Andersonville Handing out Rations 1864 (Courtesy of the Library of Congress)

The imprisoned men survived on corn meal as it was available for the most part however to make the cornmeal last the cob was ground along with the corn which was terrible for the men's stomach and contributed along with the filthy water to the disease. The lack of fresh fruit and vegetable led to men hunting rats for food and catching scurvy and still sometimes fighting one another in prison gangs just to get any sustenance. In 1906, the Hartford Courant described the conditions in the summer and fall of 1864 when the 16th and so many other Connecticut men were entering and residing in the prison camp as "indescribable," and states the death toll for the 16th alone at 85 in Andersonville. This does not include the deaths due to the treatment that occurred at other prisons. Of the 400 captured members of the 16th Volunteers, nearly a third would die from the Confederate prison system. By August of 1864, when William Brooks passed away, the death toll was estimated to be every one out of eleven men dead in the humid summer heat.

As the men at Andersonville watched their brethren die, they did their best to have some sort of funeral service before the body was taken to the "dead house." They conducted a funeral service as best they could, explained 16th soldier, Ira Forbes. No one lacked a reverent burial. "Catholics and Protestants alike were given the simple but tender service in the midst of scenes and surroundings that cannot be described by men or speech at the present time." After the men held a tender service, the bodies would be brought by the Confederates in a wagon to the "burying ground," and each man was thrown to the shallow ditch or grave.

Sergeant Major Robert Kellogg of Connecticut's 16th was just 18 when he joined the Regiment in August of 1862 and fought with Antietam until the Plymouth Capture in 1864. Unlike many of his comrades Kellogg survived the ordeal and wrote the all-inclusive book, *Life and Death in Rebel Prisons; Giving a Complete History of the Inhuman and Barbarous Treatment of our Brace Soldiers by Rebel Authorities Inflicting Terrible Suffering and Frightful Mortality, Principally at Andersonville, Ga and Florence, SC*. The title alone, reflects just a small fraction of what life was like at Andersonville but depicts the gravity. When survivors returned home from prison, if they were able, graphic accounts started being printed in local papers to move the military and politicians to act accordingly, the stories were exposed with horror to the public. Kellogg made the recollections personal and wrote of the death of his friend from the 16th, a man named John Damery, also from Wethersfield. On July 18th, 1864 at Andersonville he recollected, "At about 5 M, I went to see him and found him in a dying state, unconscious, and breathing very hard. I spoke to him, but there came no response. He had spoken his last words on earth. He tented next to me and when he came in here, he was a strong well man, but he could not stand the fare we get here. Damery had a bit of money when he entered the prison, but when he became sick rather than buying rice and flour and such things to nourish him, he bought eggs, gingerbread and such things, and in my opining, hastened his death by doing so. It makes one feel as though life is more and more uncertain each day that we have to stay in here." Other men remained hopeful writing letters to their loved ones, assuring them they would be okay, believing they would go home and dying days later. Corporal Joseph Flower Jr. of Hartford kept a diary at Andersonville and spoke to his friend Kellogg of how often he thought of his wife and children, how he longed to just speak with his wife and have breakfast with her. He died on August 9th, 1864 after an ability to eat due to dysentery. Private Horace Steele of Company F, the same company as the Brooks, wrote to his wife Julia, but not wanting to increase her anxiety, he told her he was in "good spirits hoping the time will come soon when there will be an exchange." He was admitted to the hospital at Andersonville in late August of 1864 and died October 7th, 1864 of acute dysentery.

As the prisoners watched the dying take their last breath in the quiet night while the men slept near to them, or watching them cross the dead line by accident or near to it and get picked off for target practice, as they watched once young, healthy men walk with sticks, their gums swell up losing their teeth to scurvy and their bones protruding from starvation, they were growing not to know who to hate more -- the Confederates who watched them die and buried them heartlessly or the Federal Government who did not step in despite their pleas and who knew the cruel mistreatment they endured. As the weeks settled into months, morale was non-existent and some of the men felt that Grant was to blame for not conducting the prisoner exchange they had expected, and they blamed the black prisoners. In reality, Grant was in the western theater rather than eastern theater when the prisoner exchange system was changed, primarily linking to the Emancipation Proclamation and the inclusion of black soldiers. Jefferson Davis, Confederate Prisoner, refused to abide by the laws of the Federal Government and proclaimed that any captured black soldiers and their white officers wouldn't be subject to exchange. This was dictated in the spring of 1863. All this would have been politics that Grant wouldn't have had an impact on as an army officer. Grant spoke to his hesitancy to resume the agreement of the Dix-Hill Cartel in 1864 which in the early years of the war was a soldier-for-soldier exchange with any additional men being paroled to go home while the exchanged could resume their post. Grant did not necessarily favor resuming this because there were more Confederate than Union prisoners and he believed they would not parole to go home but rather support the Confederacy and nearly all paroled Union prisoners exchanged or not went home for rest or to finish out their enlistment. Sherman and Grant both understood that the sick and dying could not return to the forces but were wary to risk some arrangements knowing that the Confederate prisoners would return to the ranks no matter what. While Grant is often blamed for pointing this out, the laws dictated by Federal and Confederate governments would have kept his hands tied and Grant was aware of the inconceivable suffering of his men that he could do nothing to stop.

Some prisoners would become galvanized rebels, albeit an exceedingly small proportion of them. On both sides of the conflict, the Army's would recruit from able-bodied prisoners promising them money, clothing, food and even sometimes property to join their side. While most Union men were hesitant to become "traitors," a small percentage usually four to six percent would take the offers of the Confederate Army. The consent would come out of desperation and knowing that continued life in the prison was inevitable painful death that they saw as death without dignity. While this didn't happen much at Andersonville, there were accounts of galvanization in Millen, GA and Florence, SC.

With death tolls escalating into the fall of 1864 as well as the population number getting beyond control at Andersonville, there was no motivation for the Confederates to better the treatment of prisoners nor was there any perceived ability to care for them. Motivation came when Sherman advanced toward Atlanta, closer to Andersonville and with General Sherman being close came the real fear that he would liberate the prisoners. The men from Connecticut were anxious and excited, had the degree of certainty that finally their release was coming from Sherman, who they called "Uncle Billy." As new prisoners arrived, their hopes escalated that "Uncle Billy," would be there with the army for their liberation at any moment. Sherman did make one large effort during his Atlanta campaign in 1864. He sent a detachment of Cavalry under General George Stoneman to destroy Confederate General Hood's supply lines and communications between Macon and Atlanta and in this mission, Stoneman would proceed to Andersonville Prison and liberate the prisoners of war. Stoneman and 700 of his men on the mission were captured after a series of skirmishes and held for months, making the mission a failure. The Confederates could not let this stand and had to devise a plan to escape the possibility of Sherman's liberation. The Confederates made the decision that many prisoners including Plymouth Pilgrims like William Brooks would be transferred to other southern prisons. All the prisoners were assured that they would be paroled, which was a lie to keep them from escaping. It's hard to imagine the moment where the starving, sick, dying, grieving and frightened would receive such relief at the prospect of rescue and becoming homeward bound only to find out that it was a lie, would take whatever hope and optimism remained in their heart and shatter it completely. The effect would be devastating. They were transferred to Charleston, South Carolina and some to Savannah, Georgia. You would only be allowed to switch prisons, however, if you could walk without a cane which many could not due to the debilitating conditions. Some prisoners were transferred to Florence, South Carolina as well. The prisons by all accounts were close to equal in their deplorable conditions. It is estimated that less than one percent of prisoners was able to escape from Andersonville during it's time as a prison camp.

After the transfers to the Carolina prisons, from Camp Sumter aka Andersonville, survival was far from promised and your life was just as vulnerable with its soul ever ready to leave its body. Chaplain Jacob Eaton of Connecticut's 7th Connecticut was stationed in Wilmington, North Carolina when in the late winter of 1865, the men of Connecticut's 16th and so many others were finally paroled. Wilmington became overrun with typhoid fever which Chaplain Eaton himself contracted. Eaton was a Congregational minister from Meriden, Connecticut and had bravely treated many officers of the 7th bringing them peace in their final moments during the war. Before joining the 7th, he was a private in the 8th Connecticut and after his wounds at Antietam was promoted to Lieutenant and took time to recover before joining the 7th in 1864. Eaton was sick in Wilmington but continued to treat the sick prisoners leaving Andersonville and Charleston of which there were estimated to be 8,000 in Wilmington, emaciated and on death's door. His friends told him not to die trying to save them and he stated,

"They ought to be and must be cared for by someone, and I will do all that lies in my power for the poor, emaciated and helpless creatures."

He wrote of the men,

"Early and late we stand, ministering to once healthy, hopeful men, now mere skeletons, their eyes sunken, glassy, vacant, and wild in expression-men literally covered with reeking filth and crawling vermin – men with long matted locks – with deep lines furrowing their every feature – men reduced to almost idiocy or second childhood by protracted hunger, neglect of body and mind, night and day we pass amid the dying or burying the dead."

After ministering to the men, Eaton lost his life, "joyfully in exchange for the life of the republic."

Certainly, not all would die in the prison walls or immediately after though they would be forever changed physically, mentally and emotionally for the remainder of their lives. It is felt even by the descendants of those who endured the hardships. Matt Reardon, Director of the New England Civil War Museum in Vernon, Connecticut and author, is a descendant of an Andersonville Survivor, Michael Farley who was captured from Drewry's Bluff and served in Company G of the 8th, Connecticut. Michael was a native Irishman from Country Leitrim who was living in Stonington, CT and went up to Hartford to enlist. The 8th Connecticut mustered out in October 1861 for instruction at Long Island, sailed with the Burnside Expedition to North Carolina and engaged in New Bern in early 1862 before participating in the siege of Fort Macon. Farley joined just a few months before they joined the Battle at Fredericksburg and the subsequent Maryland Campaign where Farley and his new comrades fought bravely at Antietam. The 8th was in several engagements throughout the war where Farley would participate until his capture in May of 1864. Farley endured Andersonville and three other prisons before being paroled in November of 1864, but his life was forever changed and when he applied for a pension, he did his best to describe the effects. Farley described that his life before the war was in the village of Pawcatuck for five years where he worked as an outdoor farm laborer and that for three years prior to the war he took on a job as a mill operator. After the war, he returned to Pawcatuck and then later moved to neighboring Westerly, RI for about five years before returning to Pawcatuck and had a variety of occupations that proved quite difficult due to his time at prison. Farley explained that for his first three months home after discharge that he was unable to work at all due to his physical condition and when he could work, he got a job at a woolen factory. He was approximately 24 to 25 years old at this time having entered the service when he was 21. His body was not that of a healthy man in his mid-twenties anymore. The prison camps, Andersonville, had changed that. He reflected on his leg's inability to stand and his eyesight being defected because of his service. He didn't give up and tried to learn carpentry, but once again his legs, namely his knees and eyes failed him. Not wanting to give up working, he returned to the woolen mill. He had a family, he needed to work, he wanted to work but his body ravaged by scurvy at the prison camps was permanently affected. Once more due to his legs and eyes, he had to leave the woolen mill again. Farley's pension records reflects on the causes of his ill health as such,

"Consequence of ill treatment, exposures to storms and many other hardships being without any covering to protect me from storms or sunshine, being all the time when in stockade prisons in the open air with the ground for a back. I was taken with contraction of the cords of my legs, more severely in the right leg which was drawn up that I could not put my foot on the ground, which events as is herein after named: When I had been in the army about one year and eleven months, not having been absent from duty a single day, in perfect health on the 16th of May, 1'864, in the battle of Drewry's Bluff, I was taken a prisoner and sent to Libby, where I remained eight days., while there my shelter, tent, blanket and overcoat were taken from me and never returned. About the 30th of May 1864, I was taken to Andersonville, Ga, a stockade prison, where I remained until the latter part of September 1864, in the early part of September while in this prison, I began to suffer from the disease in my legs which were so contracted, that I was compelled to crawl on my hands and knees. I suffered severe pain and have frequently ever since. On the last day of September 1864, I was sent to Savannah Ga, a stockade prison, where I remained about two weeks, was then to Millen, GA, a stockade prison. I was unable to walk at any time while in this prison. I remained in this prison until exchanged on the 19th of October 1864. I was taken to the Military Hospital, Baltimore."

Farley witnessed the death of his friend, a Corporal of Company passed away on September 1st at Andersonville Prison. He stated that they were together throughout their imprisonment and that he like so many others died of chronic diarrhea, "occasioned by severe exposure, improper food, and a very scanty supply of food. I helped carry the said Charles J. Edwards to the dead house on the day of his death." Farley was candid in his writing about the death of people he came to know and love and about the conditions that were caused by scurvy and ravaged his body. Farley found love after the war, married Anne Gilmartin in 1866 and together they had ten children, nine daughters and one son. His wife died a couple years before their 30th anniversary having suffered tuberculosis and Farley, eventually migrated south with his daughter and their family for the final years of his life in Alabama where he died at age 76. He was buried in Connecticut at Old Saint Michael's Cemetery in Pawcatuck with his wife and three of his daughters. Matt Reardon is descended from his fifth daughter, who married Michael Reardon. Two of her sisters even married Michael's brothers.

Matt has felt a deep connection to his Civil War ancestry and the story of his three-times great-grandfather. His harrowing ordeal, survival of battle and imprisonment is one of resilience and courage. It is common for many of us to visit the sites that impacted our ancestor's life and Matt shared that often he can feel deep connections to places of note where his ancestor, Michael was during the war. Many of you may be familiar with the feeling in your body and your mind as you envision them there and feel their energy. For Matt, he said the connection was particularly powerful at Andersonville. He had visited the attack route at Antietam, the capture site at Drewry's Bluff but it was Andersonville that was the game changer. Matt wrote,

"If things had gone differently, and he died, I wouldn't exist. In a way, my fate was almost decided at Andersonville before I was even a thought. He was so sick when he got out of Andersonville, according to a newspaper, they sent him home to die. But he pulled through it."

Matt continued,

"When I visited Andersonville with my dad back in 2014, I tried to walk through it as if I were my grandfather or at least trying to see it through his eyes. was lucky to have a personal account of his when he was there so I knew some places he had been back in 1864. I walked slowly, imagining I was arriving at the prison. I walked slowly as if I was in a group of prisoners, looked up at the guards, thought I may never get home. When his friend died, he said he went through the south gate and carried his body to the dead house. I searched out both locations, though not labeled at the park and walked the same distance. Then I searched amongst the 13,000 graves for all the members of his unit he was captured with at Drewry's Bluff including his friend."

As he pictured them and walked the grounds, he felt tears come to his eyes, the emotions of Farley, of Edwards, of Company G, of the 8th Connecticut, all Connecticut, all the Union who had died where his feet walked. The spirit of Andersonville is no small feeling and when you walk the grounds where they tried to survive and where their bodies were so hastily buried, you can feel them walking with you and showing you how hard they tried.

Side Profile Dorence Atwater

In many ways, Andersonville National Park and National Cemetery would not exist in the way it exists today, without Connecticut native Dorence Atwater and Red Cross Founder, Clara Baron. Dorence Atwater is nothing short of a hero for the Union and Angel of Andersonville. Dorence was from Terryville, Connecticut in Litchfield, County nearby to the city of Bristol. He enlisted when he was just sixteen, lying about his age.

His father was furious that he lied and brought him up to Hartford to confess his life. But Atwater was convinced that he was to fight and go to war. There was a calling to him. He enlisted in the 2nd New York Cavalry and served a courier running messages from the unit. Dorence was captured in the aftermath of Gettysburg. He was exercising his horse when he was captured by Confederates dressed as Yankees. and sent to prison at Richmond where he was held at Belle Isle and became sick with diarrhea and went to the hospital three times. Prison would kill the teenager, so to save his own life, he became useful to his captors and accepted a parole to work for the Confederacy. Still technically a prisoner, he worked as a clerk in the office that was charged with distributing supplies from the north to prisoners. He saw firsthand the misuse and mismanagement of the system and that clothing and blankets were being sent to Confederate guards. "Enough clothing was received to have furnished every prisoner with a complete suit and change of under-clothing, blankets, and over-coat, but no prisoner received these articles; if he were furnished with a blouse he must go without a shirt; if with pants he had to go without drawers..." he testified in 1869. He also witnessed a Confederate officer with a stolen amount of $50,000. After this post, Atwater was sent to Andersonville to Camp Sumter which would become the infamous prison camp simply called Andersonville. Once more as a prisoner he had chronic diarrhea/dysentery and had to be hospitalized. He knew the drill and sked the doctor about a parole to work as a clerk for the prison hospital. He got his wish and was charged with the maintenance of the death register that June. By August, he began to make a copy, in secret of the death list in fear that the record would not actually be kept or released by the Confederacy at the war's conclusion. When Andersonville was transferred out of Andersonville in February 1865, he smuggled with him his copy knowing that the repercussions for being caught with it would be incredibly severe. He made it back to Connecticut a month later and notified the Union of the record. Though he was safe at home, he was sick with diphtheria, typhoid and scurvy, visibly thin and weak but he recovered from all of it and took the train to Washington DC to bring the list. Lincoln was killed while he was on the train and so did his father who had gotten ill with the diphtheria. It was planned right away that the graves of the prison at Andersonville would be marked. Atwater wasted no time in gaining assets and help and reached out to Clara Barton who was notifying families of missing soldiers of any information and he offered to help. Atwater and Barton teamed up with the army expedition and went through all burial records, identified the graves and wrote letters to the families of the dead. A doctor and

Andersonville Relics from Atwater (Courtesy of the Library of Congress)

42 headboard carvers went to mark the graves at Andersonville.

After the expedition, Atwater refused to say where the list was and went to prison for larceny for a few months until he was released to help Clara in her Missing Soldier's Office. She had consulted President Andrew Johnson for his pardon. By 1866, the New York Tribune published the death register and making Atwater famous. The National Park Service names Dorence Atwater as "one of the most important enlisted soldiers of the Civil War." Around half of Civil War dead were unknown or unmarked, with higher proportions ins southern prison, but because of Atwater over 95% of the graves are marked. He was just nineteen when he smuggled out the list and seventeen to eighteen when he had the foresight to keep the list, to bring the souls peace. Atwater later had a career as a US consul to Tahiti where he married an island princess and established a shipping line. But he came home to Terryville in 1908 to see the monument built for him in Baldwin Park where Clara Barton had attended its dedication in 1907. Atwater would forever remember Andersonville and the place he came to know as hell itself.

Today you can visit the site of Andersonville where replicas of the stockade remains and a memorial to the Providence Spring where sudden water appeared in 1864 as some sort of miracle for the men. It lies next to the path where the prisoners would have been walked up to the stockades for the first time. And the site is next to the Andersonville Cemetery where the 13,000 dead are buried, where each state has a memorial to their beloved dead and where the spirits of those who lost their lives continue to tell their story. A beautiful monument sits for Connecticut among the graves designed and constructed between 1906 and 1907. Nearly 50 years after his stay there, George Whitney of Connecticut's 16th and 5 other former prisoners from the 16th visited the site where they had been. The men were said to have seen the flag of "Old Glory," flying above the site instead of the "bars and stars," that had haunted them years before. They looked at the flag, "wiped tears from their eyes and scattered across the field to revisit the memories." They came, they said, to honor the memory of Connecticut men who remained loyal to their cause in the face of degradation. The men of the 16th were appointed to the commission for the monument and dedication ceremony as they had had more members held captive than any other regiment. They picked the design by sculptor and Norwich native, Bela Lyon Pratt which sits there today. The same sculptor, who had attended Yale is also known for his statue of Connecticut state hero, Nathan Hale. It was the same year that the commission declared that there would be a second casting of the same memorial placed on the Connecticut State Capitol Grounds and it is entitled "Andersonville Boy." The statue is meant to show the men how they would want to be pictured and remembered, not beaten down by the ordeals of prison. Hartford's Outdoor Sculpture" quotes, without source, the statement that the young man "portrays a Union soldier with dejected but unconquered mien." Be it in Hartford or Andersonville, the young man looks to us all and urges us to Remember.

Andersonville Boy Connecticut Mon, GA (Martin Reardon Jr. photo)

And what of the other notable prisons?

Libby Prison in Richmond was set up in an old warehouse on Tobacco Row next to the James River and occupied an entire city block. Like Salisbury, it was somewhat different than the stockade prison of Andersonville. At the beginning of the war Libby was used as both a prison and a hospital. Union surgeons kept records of the poor diet, lack of food lack of clothing and the ill treatment of men who were not officers. The prisoners at Libby created a newsletter filled with bitter sentiments toward their own government as well as their captors. By 1864 the prisoners were all moved to Georgia. The remains of the prison can be seen at the American Civil War Center in Richmond.

Other prisons such as Salisbury, which received a great deal of prisoners from Richmond had similar painful experiences for the inhabitants. Salisbury Prisons held not only those captured in war but also a great deal of Yankee deserters and dissident Confederates. Salisbury had an old textile mill that was fitted for the purpose of being a prison. Between October 1864 and February 1865, nearly 28 percent of all prisoners would die of disease and starvation to their dead house which was a nearby old cornfield over a series of 18 trenches now marked as the Salisbury National Cemetery. Salisbury was the first and only Civil War prison in North Carolina. Salisbury had a slightly higher success rate with escape with over 100 able to escape through dug tunnels and more prisoners defected at Salisbury to the Confederacy as galvanized rebels.

One of the major contributors to the hell-hole of Andersonville was the Commandant of the stockade, Henry Wirz. It's perhaps no coincidence that Wirz has become one of the most famous ghost and restless spirits of the Civil War. Wirz was one of a small group who would be tried for war crimes in the Civil War because of his behavior at the prison and he would be found guilty and sentenced to die of execution by hanging; one of just a few executed by the government in connection with the Civil War. Others executed for war crimes had executed captured Union soldiers for no reason or planted explosives around New York City. Ultimately, execution was a rare consequence at the time with most other war criminals being held in prison or charged with hard labor including James Duncan who worked the Quartermaster Office at Andersonville. It's perhaps not shocking with a death toll of 13,000, many deaths which arguably could have been prevented and a public who needed to hold someone accountable. Henry Wirz was from Switzerland and emigrated to Russia and then the United States. He first resided in Massachusetts before settling in Hopkinsville, Kentucky for a time and finally after marriage in 1854, moving to Louisiana, deep in the Confederacy. He worked as a plantation overseer and physician. Wirz was 37 when the Civil War started and enlisted as a private in the Louisiana infantry. After receiving an injury, Wirz was promoted to Captain and assigned to the staff of General Winder in charge of the Confederate POW camps and served as his adjutant. In February of 1864, Wirz had his home at Andersonville as the post Commandant of the stockade and it's interior. Wirz realized quickly that there was lack of sanitary conditions, overcrowding and no food or medicine and petitioned for more and was denied. After this, he seemed to take on the position of a cruel prison commandant who took joy in the death and mistreatment of the Union men. He would even allow his men to use the prisoners as target practice and the deadline that surrounded the prison was the line that if crossed by men would result in them immediately being shot by the guards and this was something he advocated with zeal. On May 7th, 1865 Wirz was arrested by the 4th U.S. Cavalry in Andersonville and brought to Macon, Georgia where he was put on a train to Washington, DC and held in the Old Capitol Prison until trial by a special Military Commission. Wirz was charged with "combining, confederating, and conspiring together," with several other Confederate officers, "and others unknown, to injure the health and destroy the lives of soldiers in the military service of the United States, then held and being prisoners of war within the lines of the so-called Confederate states and in the military prisons thereof, to the end that the armies of the United States might be weakened and impaired, in violation of the laws and customs of war and for violation of the laws of war to impair and injure their lives – buy subjecting to torture and great suffering, by confining in unhealthy and unwholesome quarters; by exposing to the inclemency of winter and to the dews and burning summer, by compelling the use of impure water, and by furnishing insufficient and unwholesome food – of large numbers of Federal Prisoners. Accusations amounted to thirteen acts of personal cruelty and murder by revolver, by physically stomping/kicking a victim, confining in stocks, beating with a revolver and chaining prisoners together. Wirz was also charged with ordering guards to fire on prisoners and have dogs attack escaped prisoners. Wirz was found guilty of all except for one murder by revolver. 158 witnesses testified at the trial including prisoners and ex-Confederate soldiers and town residents. One witness, a descendant of Marquis de Lafayette even identified one of the victims having been shot. Judge Advocate General Joseph Holt said of Wirz,

"His work of death seems to have been a saturnalia of enjoyment for the prisoner, (Wirz) who amid these savage orgies evidenced such exultation and mingled with them such nameless blasphemy and ribald jest, as at times to exhibit him rather as a demon than a man."

He was sentenced to death, and when he asked for clemency from President Andrew Johnson, his letter went unanswered. Wirz was executed in November of 1865 at the Old Capitol Prison next to the Capitol however, as fate or karma would have it, his hanging was not the most efficient or quick death. His neck didn't break in the fall and he writhed and died by slow by strangulation. Over 200 spectators and 120 soldiers watched the event. Wirz was one of only two men, the other being a Confederate guerilla who was tried and executed for war crimes during the civil war. The commandant of Salisbury Prison was also charged with violations of laws and war but was acquitted of charges. Wirz was initially buried alongside the Lincoln assassins before being moved (burial at Mount Olivet Cemetery). In body transfer, body parts including his head were reported missing, having been removed during the autopsy. As of the late 1990's the National Museum of Health and Medicine claimed ownership of two vertebrae. For obvious reasons, Wirz has become one of the most frequently sighted ghosts of the Civil War with sightings at Andersonville, in Washington DC and even speaking at seances in New York City. Wirz is reported to be seen haunting the Old Brick Capitol in Washington where he was executed but more commonly, he is seen walking along the road near Andersonville. The *Houston Tri-Weekly Telegraph* reported just one month after his execution,

"Wirz's ghost is a regular attendant at the spiritual sessions in New York State."

To be sure, there are many reasons Wirz may be restless but it the spirit one least wants to encounter at Andersonville.

If you visit the National Park at Andersonville near to sunset, look to the wood line, where you can see the Union soldiers, perhaps trying to escape even in the afterlife, running through the woods. Many report to see them standing among the trees. Others say when a storm washes over the property you can hear the cries of agony at the prison site and among the tombstones. Remember to honor them, bring them peace as the ghosts of Andersonville and the prisons may be some of the most haunting for any visitor.

Museums, Monuments & More: Honoring Service and Sacrifice of Connecticut's Sons in their Home State

"To perpetuate the memory of its dead for all time." - GAR Hall by Civil War Veterans of Burpee Post #71 & New England Civil War Museum

"And when in God's good time our lives are spent,

Our children here shall come in proud array

With spring-time flowers, on filial duty bent,

To deck, with grateful hearts, the Soldier's Monument" – D.B. Lockwood

Connecticut is a state steeped into history since it's early days as a colony but there's perhaps no time period that Connecticut mourned more and simultaneously remembered more than that of the American Civil War. As the Victorian era took place, so did the ideals of commemorating the beloved dead and the events that changed citizens as a people. Throughout Connecticut, there were thousands of men who called Connecticut home that would never return, whose families grieved their loss, and whose workplaces forever missed their talent and contributions. Many would return and be forever changed, and Connecticut knew to honor and

Back Soldier & Sailor Arch Hartford (Martin Reardon Jr. photo)

remember was the least that could be done for these soldiers. Monuments started being erected to great acclaim, parades, ceremonies, famous speakers and more remembering the stories of the men of Connecticut. Most of this took place from late 1800's into the early 1900's and survivors were present. The survivors also traveled to battlefields to unveil memorials built to their regiments and those lost. Gettysburg, Antietam, Chattanooga and more boast Connecticut monuments. The statues, ornate are meaningful and meant to tell a story and honor the spirits of all the men. Connecticut's parks and streets are filled with unique memorials, that we often take for granted but are meant to make us reflect on the lives and sacrifices of those who came before. Monuments are not the only memories of the Civil War in our little corner of New England. Museums throughout the state house artifacts, letters, clothes, weapons and stories of the Connecticut men and our State buildings house reminders of our mid-19th century history throughout their halls. From monuments to museums, the ghosts of Connecticut's Union men are felt in every town and city. This chapter highlights some of the most haunting but next time you drive through Connecticut or go on a walk in your local park, be sure to take a moment to speak the men of the Civil War, wherever you may find yourself. They will be certain to hear you.

Bristol

Newton Manross Monument - Remembering the Academic Who Gave His Life at Antietam
Forestville Cemetery, Bristol, Connecticut 06010

The 16th Connecticut had some hard luck and the survivors often wanted to honor their fallen. This was no different when it came to Captain Newton Manross, a Yale graduate with a PhD from University of Gottingen in Germany and well-traveled man, he even wrote for the American Journal of Science. Working as a professor at Amherst College, when the Civil War began, the 37-year-old academic knew that he had to take up arms and serve. He was killed at Antietam the same year by a cannonball. Buried in his hometown of Bristol at the Forestville, Cemetery, it seemed a fitting place for the survivors of his company, Company K, to build a monument there which is an 8-foot brownstone honoring their Captain.

9th CT 1887 Bristol Manross Monument (Courtesy of Bristol Historical Society)

Cornwall

Major General John Sedgwick Memorial – Honoring Uncle John at Home
400 Cornwall Hollow Road, West Cornwall, Connecticut 06976

Major General John Sedgwick is remembered in memorial at Gettysburg, at West Point, at the Connecticut State Capitol and in his hometown of Cornwall Hollow. The man affectionately called, "Uncle John," by his troops is honored with the John Sedgwick Monument at the intersection of Cornwall Hollow Road and

Hautboy Hill Road in Cornwall Hollow. The monument is a large granite slab depicting Sedgwick. The inscription includes a fitting sentiment for the brave officer, "A skilled soldier, a brave leader, a beloved commander and a loyal gentleman" and

"The fittest place where man can die is where man dies for man."

There is an 1839 cannon with a bronze eagle on the south face and wreaths on east and west. There are six pyramids of concrete cannonballs. Schoolchildren planted a tree near the site in 1950. So, if you are a Nutmeg native and a road trip to the other monuments is a bit distant, be sure to add the Cornwall Hollow monument to your list!

Eastford

General Lyon Monument – Remembering Connecticut's Fiery General who Prevented the Secession of Missouri
General Lyon Cemetery/Phoenixville Cemetery, General Lyon Road, Eastford, Connecticut 06242

General Nathaniel Lyon Grave Eastford (Martin Reardon Jr. photo)

The General Lyon Monument at the burial site of General Nathaniel Lyon sits in the General Lyon Cemetery on General Lyon Road. As one can tell by the utilization of the General's name, he is Eastford's most famous son. General Lyon was credited with stopping the secession of Missouri, so despite dying so early in the war at the Battle of Wilson's Creek, his legacy is incredibly important. He is also recorded as the first Union General to die in the Civil War. His monument includes commemoration for the Civil War battles, a depiction of his last moments holding his hat on horseback and a list of his battles in the Mexican-American war. The work is carved into marble and sits about 12 foot high, sculpted by Sanford Grasser. Three Civil War cannon guard the plot. The memorial dates to about 1907 when a commission was set to improve the monument. Much of the evidence we acquired in our paranormal investigations came from the General's burial and site of his home less than two miles away. At his burial site, it's almost hard to imagine the sight of the Governors of Connecticut and Rhode Island serving as pall bearers as the mourners numbering in the tens of thousands gathered at the tiny cemetery but it was a service and now a monument fitting for such a memorable General. *We like to leave the General Mustard from time to time at his grave as it's his favorite food and fitting tribute that seems to appease his spirit.

Nathaniel Lyon Memorial State Park – Walking the Grounds where Connecticut's Red-Headed General was born...with his ghost that visits after Sunset
Natchaug State Forest, Eastford, Connecticut 06242

To honor the man who inspired so many Union men to join the war and who rallied troops with vigor, be sure to include a visit the Nathan Lyon Memorial State Park in the Natchaug State Forest. Established as a park in 1920 when the state purchased 216 acres of land around it, the park is named for Lyon and the chimney remains showing hearts on every side from the heart of the house which according to the Hartford Courant in 1903, was dilapidated and in ruins. General Lyon told us that he visits the home usually in the evening hours in his spirit form, so keep an eye out for him after sunset.

General Lyon Homestead& Park Eastford (Martin Reardon Jr. photo)

Hartford

Connecticut Historical Society Museum & Library – From Lincoln's Whitehouse to Andersonville Prisons, a Home for Artifacts and Research with a Haunting Civil War Past
1 Elizabeth Street, Hartford, Connecticut 06105

The Connecticut Historical Society has perhaps one of the most comprehensive collections of Civil War artifacts and collections as they relate to Connecticut with regular programs regarding the importance of the time period and its long-lasting effect on our state. Starting in the 1990's the Historical Society participated and developed the Civil War Manuscripts Project which is ongoing to ensure names, dates, and record of service for as many Connecticut men as possible. They also have a complete list of the monuments statewide in honor of the Civil War and the men who proudly served from the Nutmeg State. In the early 2000's an exhibit at Connecticut Historical Society entitled "Civil War Treasures" told the story of Connecticut at home and on that battlefield with a display of letters, images, clothing and soldier's supply and having at the centerpiece the Treasury Guard National flag that was in Lincoln's Box at Ford's Theater when he was assassinated. Reports state that it was the last thing he grasped and consciously touched as he was shot. They house a collection of letters from the 29th Colored Regiment by way of Joseph Cross of Griswold and a drinking cup made by prisoners at Andersonville as well as a bent spoon hit by a bullet in the war. One thing is for sure, any items attached to the war and specifically Lincoln can come with their own haunting effect. The most famous Civil War ghost in all of America is none other than President Abraham Lincoln who has sightings across the country, notably the White House and who even had a premonition of his own death and participated in seances. For a step back in time and a look at some chilling artifacts, it's worth a visit to the Society's programs, exhibits and research library to see what they have to offer.

Museum of Connecticut History – Authentic Civil War Artifacts and the history of Colt Firearms in the Heart of Connecticut
231 Capitol Ave. Hartford, Connecticut 06106

The Museum of Connecticut History is located within the 1910 State Library and Supreme Court Building across the street from the State Capitol in Hartford. Of notable display related to the Civil War and our state roots are Civil War Uniforms that can be seen in the Connecticut Collections State military history exhibits which also holds weapons and diaries from soldiers including some from those who were at Andersonville Prison. Also of great prominence is the Colt Firearms Collection including Colt prototypes, factory models, experimental firearms, gatling guns, shotguns and automatic weapon as well as the Rampant Colt statue from the original factory. You can also visit the Quilt Collection honoring Connecticut's Freedom Trail, sharing the story of the African American experience in Connecticut and honoring Harriet Beecher Stowe, the Underground Railroad and the Amistad. Historic properties across the state can be seen with this purpose as well. Eli Whitney's invention is honored in the Connecticut collections as well and house a portrait of each state Governor including War Governor Buckingham in the collection of Governor's Portraits. The Museum of Connecticut History is a wonderful time capsule of many centuries and wars, particularly the Civil War and Connecticut's role within and of spectacular note, the museum entry is free – so be sure to mark a day in your calendar to stroll and study it's halls!

Connecticut State Library – Collections of Manuscripts and Letters from the Connecticut Men of the War

231 Capitol Ave. Hartford, Connecticut 06106

The Connecticut State Library across the street from the Museum of Connecticut history houses an enormous Civil War collection of documentation including manuscripts of families, chaplains and soldiers complete with letters, maps, correspondence, muster rolls and receipts. The George Whitney Collection houses many recollections of the 16th Connecticut as well as some photographs. Political records regarding the war and reports of death can be found at the library as well which has an abundance of resources.

Connecticut State Capitol Sculptures of native Civil War Generals Align the High Victorian Gothic Structure in our State's Capital City
Connecticut State Capitol, 210 Capitol Ave. Hartford, Connecticut 06106

The State Capitol of Hartford houses several notable Civil War memories. At the State Capitol, a renowned sculptor named Hermon MacNeil sculpted Civil War heroes that sit on the Capitol. At the Capitol there is a sculpture of General John Sedgwick of Cornwall who was killed at Spotsylvania Courthouse after having led his men of the VI Corps of the Army of the Potomac in lethal battles. General Alfred Howe Terry of Hartford, Connecticut was also depicted in sculpture – notably one of the only Generals to receive a Thank you from Congress due to his capture of Fort Fisher, North Carolina during the War which made Wilmington a safe shipping for Confederates no longer. He went on to survive the war and fight with Colonel Custer at Little Big Horn. Both Sedgwick and MacNeil are on the south elevation of the Capitol in full standing form. They are also in the company of one of Lincoln's cabinet members, U.S. Secretary of the Navy, Gideon

Welles of Glastonbury, Connecticut whose statue is also on the south side of the capitol, second elevation. The Civil War heroes sit with notable revolutionaries also sculpted by MacNeil including Oliver Wolcott, David Humphreys and General David Wooster. General Joseph Hawley has a relief sculpture located in the east side of the North Porch of the Capitol which is bronze in color with an ornate marble surrounding unlike the other standing sculptures, this one sits on the wall and is a three-quarter length portrait inscribed "The First Volunteer in Connecticut 1861 Brevet Major General 1865/ Governor 1866 1867 Representative in Congress 1881 1905 with the State Seal of Connecticut. You may recall that Terry was Hawley's mentor and its quite fitting that they are both featured in the Capitol sculptures.

Andersonville Boy – Hartford, Connecticut – A Lasting Memorial for those Connecticut Men who suffered as Prisoners in Andersonville Prison, Georgia.

Connecticut State Capitol, 210 Capitol Ave. Hartford, Connecticut 06106

Andersonville Boy Monument Hartford (Martin Reardon Jr. photo)

This statue is a copy of the Andersonville Boy Statue at the Andersonville National Cemetery in Georgia. This is the second casting, sculpted by Bela Pratt and stands at 6 foot, 11 inches. The statue was dedicated on October 23rd, 1908 and is a Bronze figure on a pink base, meant to be realistic, in many ways it's a piece of abstract art, showing a soldier holding no provisions, looking forward, we must imagine the starved, disheartened and demoralized men sitting in southern prisons during the war when we look at the statue. For more details on the Andersonville Boy at Hartford and National Cemetery, please see the chapter on Prisons.

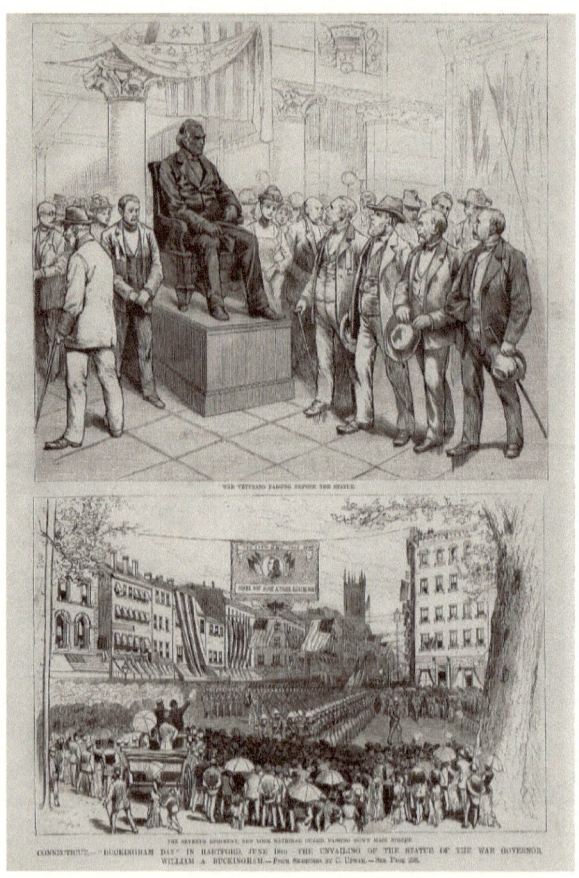

Buckingham Day Unveil Statue (Frank's Illustrated 1884)

Governor William Buckingham Statue at Hartford State Capitol – Honoring the Man who took care of Connecticut's Men and became known as Connecticut's War Governor and Identifying the Ghost of Room 362
Connecticut State Capitol, 210 Capitol Ave. Hartford, Connecticut 06106

Let us not forget that the William Buckingham Statue sits in the State Capitol as well. As mentioned in the Regiments Chapter, Buckingham was considered the state's War Governor and got a lot of recognition from Lincoln and the Union for assuring provisions and money for the men of Connecticut even if it came from his own pocket. Buckingham, a native of rural Lebanon, and graduate of the Bacon Academy in Colchester was everything from a surveyor, store owner and schoolteacher as well as retail worker, all giving him great experience in navigating the state during the war. His statue sits at the State Capitol's Hall of Flags and was unveiled posthumously at the first June 18th Buckingham Day in his honor. Sitting in the battle flag vestibule is a particular honor for the Governor who did so much to protect Connecticut's own. The statue was unveiled after a two-hour parade with 70,000 onlookers. The statue is life-size, made of bronze and sits atop marble, designed by Olin Warner. He is in sitting position. Buckingham is remembered as friendly, approachable, heroic and one of the most popular Governors in state history. The most well-known haunting at the State Capitol is thought to be the Governor himself who has been seen walking the halls and room 324. See the Regiments Chapter for details or better yet, visit the Governor's likeness and see if you don't see the real thing peering out from behind the corner.

Petersburg Express Mortar – Hartford – State Capitol – Honoring the Heavies and the Artillery that stunned the

Confederates at Petersburg

Connecticut State Capitol, 210 Capitol Ave. Hartford, Connecticut 06106

Petersburg Express Mortar Hartford

In the 11-month long Siege at Petersburg, the First Connecticut Heavy artillery known as the Heavies placed their new artillery support traveling mortar at the Chesterfield Battery where the Confederate army has been threatening the Union lines. The mortar sitting at 13-inchest arrived in Petersburg in July of 1864 via rail car that it sat on and fired on Confederate positions. The first fired over 63,940 rounds and 1,200 pounds of iron at Petersburg with help from the mortar which fired 19 shells at Battle of the Mine on July 30th. Since it sat upon a railcar for its deadly firing it received the nickname the "Petersburg Express." By the 1890's it was decided that the Heavies should be honored, and the consensus became of the General Committee and Regimental Association that it was best to do so with the Petersburg Express which was found at Fort Monroe where it had been left in Hampton, Virginia. The correct mortar was identified and brought to Bridgeport in 1896 where it stayed for many years. The mayor of Bridgeport offered at one time to donate a great amount of money to play the mortar at Seaside Park however regimental historian John Taylor, who also assisted in photographing body recovery at The Wilderness site, explained that the Fourth Connecticut, mustered in Hartford and having ties to the city, wanted the mortar on Capitol grounds and to symbolize Connecticut's commitment. Funds were raised to place the mortar and its carriage on a pedestal of granite at the State Capitol and it was dedicated on September 25th, 1902, the muster anniversary date and over 50,000 in attendance. It was claimed to be the original though there are some who debate its authenticity, thinking that perhaps they brought back the wrong one. Regardless, the mortar symbolizes memory and will forever be a Connecticut mystery of the Civil War.

Griffin A. Stedman Memorial & Griffin A. Stedman Monument– A Seasoned Career, A successful Officer, Lost at the War's End is buried in a Beautiful Ornate Sarcophagus and the Campgrounds of the Unlucky Regiment are Remembered
Memorial: Cedar Hill Cemetery, 453 Fairfield Ave, Hartford, Connecticut 06114
Monument: Barry Square, 10 Campfield Avenue, Hartford, Connecticut 06106

Another monument to a Connecticut General sits in the prominent Cedar Hill Cemetery of Hartford and that is the Griffin A. Stedman Monument honoring the Hartford native and Trinity college graduate who had just begun his law career in Philadelphia when the Civil War began. Directly after Fort Sumter, General Stedman joined the 14th U.S. Infantry in Hartford, which was later disbanded, and he took on his appointment as a Captain in the 5th Regiment of Connecticut Volunteers. Stedman fought at Antietam, Fredericksburg and Cold Harbor and became commander of the 11th Connecticut Infantry receiving his mortal wound in a skirmish at the second battle of Petersburg. He lay in pain, dying for nearly

24 hours and during those hours of August 6th, 1864, he was promoted to General. His body was placed in New London, CT at the Stedman Summer home for a few days before being moved to Cedar Grove in New London. It was in 1875 that he was re-interred from Cedar Grove, New London to Cedar Hill in Hartford in a beautiful sarcophagus with a flag and the names of his battles as well as a sword. "Brave, just, generous and pure, without fear and without reproach," reads the monument. Also, in Hartford, stands the Campfield Monument made in the likeness of Griffin Stedman and sitting at the mustering-in point and camping place for Connecticut Regiments.

Soldiers and Sailors Memorial Arch – The first American Triumphal Arch honoring Connecticut's Civil War Dead and Interring its Architect
Memorial Park, 15 Trinity State, Hartford, Connecticut 06106

Soldier & Sailors Memorial Arch, Hartford (Martin Reardon Jr. photo)

The Soldiers and Sailors Memorial Arch in Hartford's Memorial Park is the first permanent triumphal arch built in

America. In 1879, a committee formed to sponsor a competition to come up with the scheme for the memorial arch and then two years later didn't approve any of the schemes. In 1884, the commission was awarded to a Hartford architect named George Keller who designed the Soldiers and Sailors Memorial arch honoring 4,000 Hartford citizens who served in the Union Army in the Civil War and the nearly 400 who died for the cause. The design is two Norman towers flanking a Gothic arch and decorate with statues and classical frieze modeled by Swiss sculptor Entress. The arch was built with Portland, Connecticut brownstone and was completed in 1886. On the north frieze is a story of the war and a figure of General Ulysses S. Grant surveying his troops and on the left marines are depicted leaping from a boat rushing Confederate troops whereas the South frieze is a story of peace and depicts a soldier's homecoming. The ashes of the architect and his wife are interred in the memorial since he had a horror of cemeteries. The arc h also depicts symbols of all four military services.

Weld Monument – Remembering African-American Soldiers who were Leaders representing Connecticut in the Civil War
Old North Cemetery, 1821 Main Street, Hartford, Connecticut 06120

In Hartford, Connecticut at the Old North Cemetery on Main Street, also part of the Freedom Trail, there are several notable plots including those of some men from the 29th Connecticut though all but 2 graves of theirs are destroyed. There is also a monument called the Weld Monument which is a memorial to two brothers, Charles and Lewis Weld who were African American soldiers in the Civil War. Lewis was notably a leader in the 41st U.S. Colored Infantry. The Weld Monument appears as a grave with a funerary cloth engraved and a woman afront with their names inscribed. The monument is in good company with notable families such as the Colts and Wards as well as with over two-dozen men from Connecticut's 29th.

Kensington/Berlin

Kensington Soldier's Monument (1st) CT

Civil War Monument – The First Civil War Monument of Connecticut and an American Example of Honoring the Union Soldiers

Kensington Congregational Church, 312 Percival Ave, Kensington, Connecticut 06037

Connecticut boasts the home of one of the oldest memorials to the American Civil War in the United States and the oldest memorial in the Nutmeg States. The Kensington Soldier's Monument sits on the grounds of the Kensington Congregational Church in Berlin, CT. A Brownstone obelisk with accompanying cannon, the monument originated in 1862 when six local men were reported dead in Civil War battles Nelson Moore, a Connecticut sculptor designed the moment and used brownstone from Portland. The monument was dedicated just weeks after the Battle at Gettysburg on July 28th, 1863 with a speech by a U.S. Senator.

Middletown

Middlesex County Historical Society – Middletown,

Connecticut – The Home of General Joseph Mansfield and his Family Spirits Among Central Connecticut's Historic Archives 151 Main St. Middletown, Connecticut 06457

Gen Joseph Mansfield House Middletown (Martin Reardon Jr. photo)

As mentioned prominently in the chapter on Connecticut Men, the Middlesex County Historical Society has its headquarters in the General Mansfield House in the oldest remaining residential structure on Main Street in Middletown. The house dates to 1817 and originally belonged to Samuel and Catherine Livingston Mather. The Mather family links directly back to Richard Mather, born in England 1596 who was a Puritan minister in Boston and who was father to Increase Mather and grandfather to Cotton Mather of Salem Witch Trials fame, though, Samuel's line moved to Connecticut before the Witch Trials and descends a different line. Samuel and Catherine's daughter, Louisa married Joseph Mansfield and together they lived in the Federal Style Brick Mansion and raised their children. They also had two Irish servants residing in the house. They had five children, though, one would die as a baby. The four surviving children were aged 23, 21, 17 and

12 at the time of their father's death. Eldest son, Samuel had just enlisted into the military himself months before his dad's passing. The house stayed in the Mansfield's family through to his grandchildren and some great-grandchildren until the direct descendants of the General gave the house to the Middlesex County Historical Society where its headquarters have been ever since. The General never met any of his grandchildren or great-grandchildren and by all accounts, Louisa and the General had their children a bit later in life than was average for the time, with some of the children still being quite young when the General neared 60 years of age. The couple didn't marry until the General was 35 and Ms. Mather, 30, so that could explain some of the delay. Judging by the letters of the couple, there was great love between them and throughout the family. The General would have been away at war a lot but the house would have been bustling with activity with such a prominent family. Today you can visit changing exhibits on the first floor of the house and envision the family as they went about their business. During our paranormal investigation of the house, our cameras found shapes of people when we tried to take photos and captured many voices. What we made note of, that was quite funny, is that when we asked the General if he had a favorite room of the house, his response on the spirit box was, "The Kitchen." The Historical Society and house are a remarkable resource for history, and it can be felt at every turn.

General Mansfield Monument and Mansfield Post Civil War Monument - Remembering a man with a Storied Military Past in Central Connecticut, complete with a Spirit Animal
Indian Hill Cemetery, 383 Washington Street, Middletown, Connecticut 06457

General Mansfield, the oldest Connecticut General to pass in the war is honored throughout the state and luckily, his house unlike Lyon's still stands at the Middlesex County Historical Society. His ornate sandstone burial monument is in the middle of Indian Hill Cemetery with inscriptions bearing the name of him and his family. The monument is topped by a carving of a flag, a sword, and a hat. And diagonally across the way is the 1884 monument of the Mansfield Post, the local Grand Army of the Republic depicting an infantry soldier and rifle and dedicated to deceased soldiers and sailors of that post. General Mansfield burial place and GAR monument is breathtaking and perhaps you'll see the young buck, that we believe is the General's spirit animal and who likes to roam the grounds of the cemetery.

Gen. Joseph Mansfield Grave Middletown (Courtney McInvale photo)

24th Connecticut Regiment Monument – Honoring the Central Connecticut Men of the Western Theater

Veteran's Memorial Green/Park, Washington Street, Middletown, Connecticut 06457

At the Veteran's Memorial Green on Washington Street in Middletown there are several monuments and perhaps one of the most beautiful is the monument built in 1904 near to the western end of the Park in honor of the 24th Connecticut Volunteers who served many engagements in Louisiana. The monument is a short column with two curved benches and topped by a bronze eagle. The Battle of Port Hudson is noted on the monument and a plaque indicates that the monument was made by survivors of the war and regiment as well as local residents and the state. Also listed in addition to Port Hudson is the battle of Irish Bend, battle of Donaldsonville and Battle of Baton Rouge. About 75 men were lost to the engagements and are honored here.

New Haven

Knight Hospital Monument, Evergreen Cemetery, New Haven, Connecticut – New England's Premier Civil War Hospital for Soldiers at the heart of Yale New Haven Hospital is honored with a Monument to being a Military Hospital and many of the dead are buried around the monument at Evergreen Cemetery in New Haven.
769 Ella T Grasso Blvd. New Haven, Connecticut 06519

The General Hospital Society of Connecticut founded in 1826 opened in 1833 on seven-and-a-half acres of land between Cedar Street and Howard Avenue and Davenport and Congress Avenues in New Haven. The Hospital was small, having 13 beds and was called the State Hospital. The role of the hospital was charitable – to care for the poor and eventually, the whole community. Early on, the hospital was frequented by local sailors. But things changed

Knight Hospital Memorial New Haven (Martin Reardon Jr. photo)

at State Hospital during the Civil War. "Lincoln-care," was established during the Civil War which was a national provision of healthcare providing service for sick and wounded soldiers. 130 hospitals and 130,000 beds would be federally operated for this purpose One of the Union Military Hospitals established was the Knight U.S. General Hospital in New Haven at the site of the State Hospital. The Hospital was named after Jonathan Knight, a Professor at Yale College and President of the General Hospital Society Board. The Hospital cared for over 25,000 U.S. Army soldiers between 1861 and 1865. After the war had ended the Hospital was re-named New Haven Hospital and in 1913 became the Yales School of Medicine and New Haven Hospital. Today the original building still sits in the Yale New Haven Hospital and remembers their days as Knight Hospital and the years that followed where they still served as a designated military hospital. A monument to the hospital and the 204 soldiers who died there sits in the Evergreen Cemetery on Winthrop Avenue in New Haven. The Monument was dedicated not long after the end of the war in 1870. Around the monument are the graves of approximately 130 of the deceased from varying regiments around the region. The monument sits an impressive 25-foot height and bears the name of battles such Gettysburg, New Berne, Fort Fisher and Fredericksburg, honoring some of the battles where Connecticut sacrificed so many in battle or to disease. Atop is Union soldier depicted with beard, mustache, cap, overcoat and cape holding a musket in his left hand and right hand over the barrel. On the east side is depicted flags, cannons, ramrods and the Connecticut seals. It reads "Dedicated A.D. 1870 By the State of Connecticut, to Commemorate the Services and Perpetuate the Memory of the Two Hundred and Four Union Soldiers Who Died in Knight Hospital in New Haven, in the years 1862, 3, 4, & 5 and were buried in these grounds. A complete history of the Knight General Hospital, its founders, it's doctors, it's patients and its newspapers which the men produced regularly along with poetry can be found in a book by Dr. Ira Spar, M.D. entitled "New Haven's Civil War Hospital." There are heartbreaking letters and accounts of the surgeon Pliny Adams Jewett, Johnathan Knight and Timothy Beers. The Jewett family who rests in Evergreen Cemetery not far from the Memorial is particularly devastating to the reader. But their assistance and their value for human life and the meaningful life of each soldier cannot be overstated. Of spooky note, near to the Knight Hospital Monument is the grave of Midnight Mary, a local legendary woman and spirit who was buried alive and has been related as the cause of missing people in the cemetery at night.

9th Connecticut Infantry Monument – Honoring the Irish-American Regiment Motivated by Meagher and Trained in New Haven
Bayview Park, New Haven, Connecticut 06511

Built in 1903, the large granite monument with soldier depicted atop in sculpture is a monument to the 9th CT Regiment of Irish American volunteers and sits in Bay View Park in New Haven, Connecticut. Like the 29th's monument, this sculpture stands at the park where the 9th Regiment trained. The State seal and name of the regiment as well as names of their battles is on the monument as well as the names of nearly 100 men who died in the Battel of Baton Rouge. The monument is surrounded by four cannons known as boat howitzers. There is also a monument to the 9th Connecticut in Mississippi at the Vicksburg National Military Park.

9th CT Monument New Haven (Martin Reardon Jr. photo)

The Regiment's History Honor's this monument and it's everlasting meaning with a poem entitled *The Soldier's Monument* by D.B. Lockwood,

"How many hearts will leap with swelling pride,
How many eyes will fill with burning tears,

To see, at last, above the swelling tide,
The monument, foretold these many years;
Foretold with hope deferred and anxious fears,
Till comrades living, feared that comrades dead
Might be forgot; and all that so endears
Their mem'ry to the land for which they bled
Would fade away from earth with time's unceasing tread.

Proud emblem of the men who bravely fell
Who only counted dear the nation's life,
Who blanched not at the sound of shot or shell,
Rememb'ring duty, country, home and wife,
Each volunteer a hero in the strife.
Ready to fight, as only fight the brave
Or meet in midnight the assassin's knife,
In prison-pen to die, their land to save
A land as fair as free, that owns no more a slave.

Reminder of the days of bloody strife,
Of fierce contending hots in stern array,
Battling for dear bought liberty and life,
And all that makes us glorious to-day
A Union! From Alaska's ice-bound shore
To Ponce de Leon's fragrant land of flowers!
Long may it stand, deying Time's decay!
Long may its soldier-sailor mantled towers
Keep watch and ward above this goodly land of ours

Hither shall come in each succeeding year
Bringing the fairest, freshest flowers of May,
The comrades left behind; who'll drop a tear
For consecrated dust that's far away
And keep with pride our "Decoration Day."

And when in God's good time our lives are spent,
Our children here shall come in proud array
With spring-time flowers, on filial duty bent,
To deck, with grateful hearts, the Soldier's Monument

A hundred years of earnest labor done
Of arts improved, of progress near and far
In civil strife a thousand battles won;
IN peace more conquests than in bloody war!
O, who shall draw the horoscope afar
Of cent'ries hence, when nations ne'er shall know
The lust of cruel strife, but when the star
Of Peace o'er all the world shall brightly glow
And man shall conquer self, his greatest earthly foe"

9th CT Veterans early 1900s New Haven

*29th Connecticut Infantry Monument – Honoring Connecticut's
Colored Regiment where they Trained
Criscuolo Park, New Haven, Connecticut 06513*

29th CT Colored Reg Mon, New Haven (Wiki Commons)

6th, 7th, 1st L Battery Monument New Haven

In Criscuolo Park in New Haven, Connecticut you can visit the monument of Connecticut's 29th Regiment, the monument is dedicated to the 900 African American Civil War Veterans of the regiment and is a large polished black graine monument with eight smaller monuments listing members and regiments. On the west face you can see a depiction of soldiers carrying the U.S. flag and the units colors as well an engagement list. The monument stands on the ground where the 29th trained.

Broadway Civil War Monument – Honoring the New Haven Regiments and Artillery who Mustered from Across the State
318 Elm Street at Broadway, New Haven, Connecticut 06511

The third Civil War monument to be established in New Haven

following the Soldiers and Sailors Monument and the 9th Regiment Monument, this monument was built to honor the First Connecticut Light Battery as well as the Sixth, Seventh and Tenth Connecticut volunteers. As with many dedications, this was a major local event where the crowds were immense, and buildings were covered with flags. The mayor of New Haven and dean of Yale Law School spoke at the event. He monument was designed and supplied by Smith Granite Company of Westerly, RI. The monument is atop a granite pedestal with bronze plaques atop the cylindrical shape and a large eagle sits at the top of the 31-foot-high monument.

Soldiers and Sailors Monument – A prestigious monument to remember Connecticut's beloved dead and service members
East Rock Park, New Haven, Connecticut 06511

Located on a summit of East Rock in New Haven, Connecticut, the monument is visible for miles and can be seen from the Long Island Sound. The monument honors soldiers of the Revolutionary War, the War of 1812, the Mexican War and the Civil War and was dedicated in June of 1887 with over 175,000 attendees including General Sherman and General Sheridan as guests of honor. They attended the ceremony after a large parade of nearly 20,000 attendees. The Civil War battles honored on the monument include Gettysburg, Port Hudson and Fort Fisher. The monument is a long column from a square base with sculptures depicting war scenes including the surrender of Lee at Appomattox. There are also inscribed the names of 520 local soldiers and sailors of New Haven who died in the Civil War. Atop the monument sits the Angel of Peace holding an olive branch in the left arm.

Yale Civil War Memorial – Students and Soldiers Remembered
Memorial Woolsey Hall Rotunda, Yale University, Intersection of Grove & College Streets, New Haven, Connecticut 06520

Yale students joined the war in large numbers and the University recognizes the role of its graduates in the Civil War with the Yale Civil War Memorial. Nearly 500 men serve in the Union Army that were Yale Graduate, but the memorial also honors the Yale graduates who served the Confederacy. The committee was appointed by President William Howard Taft by 1909 and it was dedicated on June 20th, 1915 where the marble hallways with names on the walls between figures was unveiled. The figures signify courage, devotion, memory and peace and the floor is engraved with poetry. The sculptor was Henry Hering. The hall with the memorial is thought to be haunted by two university organists according to paranormal researcher, Hans Holzer and randomly enough Jimi Hendrix who played music at Woolsey Hall.

New London

Fort Trumbull – New London, Connecticut – A Civil War Recruitment Center with Phantom Soldiers Practicing their March Fort Trumbull, New London, Connecticut 06320

Fort Trumbull served as Union fort for inducting and training recruits during the Civil War and became the setting for Connecticut native, Mark Twain's short thriller series set at the location during the Civil War and entitled *A Curious Experience*. The work confronts wartime tensions in Connecticut. Fort Trumbull had recently undergone extensive fortification work after the War of 1812 when the city of New London avoided what was almost imminent attack. By the Civil War, the fort had walls of Waterford granite that were massive. It made for a perfect recruitment center for the men. The post was also considered a headquarters for the 14th U.S. Infantry who had been organized with 8 other infantry regiments under Lincoln's call for military.

The 14th was organized at Fort Trumbull ins May of 1861 and participated straight away in the Peninsula Campaign before being moved to 1st Brigade, 2nd Division, 5th Corp Army of the Potomac and participating in deadly engagements in four of the top ten deadly engagements – Antietam, Chancellorsville, Gettysburg and the Wilderness as well as the Siege of Petersburg. General George Meade even awarded them the place of honor at the "right of the Line," in the Grand Review of the Armies, giving the regiment the motto, "The Right of the Line." Fort Trumbull is a spectacular place to think of the courage and award-winning U.S. Infantry with men from across the country who supported its brave cause. At the war's conclusion, Fort Trumbull continued in it's very Provision State purpose by serving as a supply post. Today, visitors can walk the grounds of Fort Trumbull with a beautiful view of the Thames River, in the footsteps of training soldiers and the men of the 14th U.S. Infantry and can almost hear them marching back and forth in practice as you gaze upon Fort Griswold and Connecticut's Revolutionary roots across the way. Many have claimed to see shadowy figures move in and around the fort before vanishing and to actually see them marching outside with the same phantom vanish. Today, Fort Griswold is a Connecticut State Park.

Grave of Major General G.W. Smith -- A Grave of a Confederate General in southeastern Connecticut
Cedar Grove Cemetery, 638 Broad St. New London, Connecticut 06320

One of the most peculiar Civil War Gravestone reminders in Connecticut, perhaps lies in Cedar Grove Cemetery in New London, Connecticut and belongs to Confederate General Gustavus Woodson Smith. Smith was a West Point graduate who worked as an engineer during the construction of Fort Trumbull after his West Point graduation nearly two decades before the Civil

War in 1842. Though, a Kentucky native, he found love in New London and married his wife, Lucretia Bassett of the city, daughter of a local whaling merchant. During the Civil War as a northern woman with a Confederate husband, Lucretia found herself in Savannah, Georgia when it was captured by Union General Sherman who noted in his memoirs that he was glad to extend courteous protection to the "very handsome," Mrs. Smith. Her was buried in the family plot at Cedar Grove when he died in 1896 at age 74 in an unmarked grave. His wife had passed in 1881, some years earlier. In 1977, a family member and descendent, Robert Smith put up a stone for his Confederate ancestor.

21st Connecticut Infantry Monument – Honoring the Soldiers of Eastern CT in the Whaling City
Williams Memorial Park, New London, Connecticut 06320

A large granite obelisk sits in New London's Williams Memorial Park near to the north corner in honor of the soldiers of the 21st regiment founded in 1862. This regiment recruited mostly from eastern Connecticut towns and served from 1862-1865. The monument was erected in 1898 by the State of Connecticut and "in honor of her citizen soldiers." The monument lists battles such as Drewry's Bluff, Petersburg, Fort Harrison, Richmond, Fredericksburg and Cold Harbor. Though regiment survivors wanted the monument to sit in Willimantic, CT, local officials disagreed on its placement and New London became the monument's home.

Norwich

Andersonville Memorial Gun – Remembering Norwich Natives imprisoned at Hell on Earth & the Local Cemetery Ghost Who Resides with them

Yantic Cemetery, 68 Lafayette St. Norwich, Connecticut 06360

In the middle of Norwich's Yantic Cemetery there is a large Cannon, a 4.2 inch, 30-pound Parrott Rifle dated in 1862 dedicated to veterans, with specific honor to the fifteen residents who died as war prisoners at Andersonville, Georgia. The bodies of nine Norwich men were recovered and re-interred in Yantic Cemetery on February 1st, 1866 in a day of ceremony and parade and were buried in circular pattern. On the day of their re-interment, businesses closed in support and residents participated in an eight-course dinner at the Chelsea Hotel. It is noted that Norwich was the first northern city to retrieve its Andersonville dead and sent representatives after the war to claim their dead. They could identify ten, the one that is not at Yantic Cemetery is at the family's plot in Center Cemetery. Legend states that in the same cemetery, glowing lights can be beheld by local residents and passerby and the grave with the blue lady statue holds different objects in her hand depending on what day you visit – rose, rosary, bible, inkwell, cloak...and she keeps watch over the men, the veterans and the residents of Yantic Cemetery.

William Buckingham House -The Home of the Esteemed and Beloved War Governor and Meeting Place of Veterans
307 Main Street, Norwich, Connecticut 06360

If you're following Governor Buckingham's trail, don't miss a visit the Buckingham Memorial Hall/William A Buckingham House in Norwich CT. It was built by the man himself in 1847 in the city where he would later serve as mayor, before becoming state governor. In the impressive 2-and-a-half story brick structure with a hip roof and a steep gable, Buckingham hosted both Abraham Lincoln and Ulysses S. Grant, so you'd be walking in famous footsteps. His house was purchase in 1898 by the Grand

Army of the Republic and since then it has housed veterans and service organizations. As late as the 1980's Sons of Union Veterans of the Civil War met there. Currently there is a joint project between United War Veterans Grand Army of the Republic, Buckingham Memorial Association, New England Civil War Museum and Sedgwick Camp #4, Sons of Union Veterans of the Civil War to restore the house and open it as a museum.

26th Connecticut Regiment Monument –Honoring the Eastern Connecticut Men of the Western Theater
Little Plain Park (Broadway/Union/Crossway Streets), Norwich, Connecticut 06360

At Little Plain Park in Norwich, CT between Broadway and Union Street is a tall, sectioned obelisk dedicated to the memory of the 26th Connecticut Volunteer Infantry. The monument honors their contribution at Port Hudson. Crossed rifles and cross symbols can be seen around the monument as well as the casualty rate of the regiment. The 26th was mostly men from Norwich whose major engagement was the capture of Port Hudson and capture of Vicksburg.

Plymouth

Dorence Atwater – Honoring the Angel of Andersonville and POW who Gave Memory to thousands of Union POW's
2 Park St. Terryville, Connecticut 06786

Dorence Atwater, better known to me as the Angel of Andersonville, the young man who endured hardship and imprisonment and kept the list of the dead at Andersonville so that they could receive proper burial went on to live an impressive life after the war and was a true story of overcoming tragedy and

Dorence Atwater Memorial Terryville (Martin Reardon Jr. photo)

having triumph in life. Lying about his age to join the military upset his parents but proved to be a blessing the Union wouldn't know they needed until some years later and in Connecticut we are enormously proud of our native son. At Baldwin Park on Main Street in Terryville (Plymouth) is the Dorence Atwater monument consisting of a plaque and cannon. Clara Barton attended its dedication on Memorial Day 1907. Atwater returned from his post in Tahiti to see it in 1910. Atwater even became inspiration for author Robert Louis Stevenson, who used Atwater in his book, *The Ebb-Tide*. His parent's graves are in Hillside Cemetery of Plymouth, CT. His mother died before his imprisonment and his father just after he returned home. The family homestead still stands at 192 South Eagle Street Terryville as a private residence. It is a remarkable place to pay respects to a man who knew he was meant to join the war and to help others no matter what happened.

Vernon

New England Civil War Museum – A Civil War Time Capsule with a Resident Ghost from its Construction

14 Park Place, Vernon, Connecticut 06066 Memorial Hall

The New England Civil War Museum is located in the historic Memorial Hall of Vernon, Connecticut and is the only surviving Grand Army of the Republic (GAR) Hall in Connecticut and one of the longest running GAR Hall's in the country with beautiful stained-glass windows that remain from its old meeting post. The museum location was originally picked as the GAR Hall by Civil War Veterans of Burpee Post #71 by 1896 and it was utilized by them between 1890 to 1934. Their mission statement was

"To perpetuate the memory of its dead for all time."

Today, the museum has exhibits of artifacts relevant to the people and places of the Civil War and specifically Union and Connecticut soldiers. Collections remain from individual soldiers including musket balls that they were shot with and Sharp's rifles and Springfield rifles that were utilized. The museum boasts its own supernatural activity as well with flickering lights and phantom footsteps being a reportedly not so rare occurrence. The staff thinks they may know who the ghost is and relate the phantom's behavior to the construction of the Memorial Hall tower. In late September of1889 during the construction of the tower, Antoine Coulombe was a 35-year-old married bricklayer who had been working on the construction of the Memorial Tower when he was killed in a 60-foot fall from the top of the tower where they had been working. Antoine had stepped on the end of a plank projecting over the wall and fell inside the tower, straight through the other floors. He struck the iron rod connecting the beams across the first story breaking his neck and fracturing his skull. It was reported that he was instantly killed, and his body appeared as if nothing happened,

"Not a mark on the face and it presented a calm and life-like appearance."

That day, the men working with him accompanied his body to the local railroad station. They had all been working on the building since April. Work was halted on the hall for a couple days to allow everyone time to mourn. Of course, construction resumed but the story of Antoine would be told for decades to come and is still remembered today. Many assume the strange goings on at the hall relate to his spirit still inhabiting the establishment, but it's not ruled out that perhaps some of those Civil War relics can be contributing to the supernatural activity as well.

Statewide/Nationwide

Route 6 – Grand Army of the Republic Highway – America's Roads Remember
Nationwide

Running Across the Country and through Connecticut is the Grand Army of the Republic Highway honoring the American Civil War Veterans Association. It is considered the main road of the U.S. Highway System and runs from Bishop, California to Provincetown, Massachusetts. In Connecticut, Route 6 runs from Danbury, Waterbury Bristol and Hartford over the Connecticut River and connects to Rhode Island through cities such as Willimantic and Danielson.

The heartbeats of Connecticut's Union boys and men, privates and officers can be heard and felt throughout the small street. Be sure to listen to their whispers as they guide us from their graves.

EPILOGUE

The spirits of the Civil War and the men of Connecticut in the Civil War are felt in every corner of the state, in each town that honors their memory, in the cemeteries where they are buried and  across the eastern United States where the men fought bravely and endured immense hardship in prisons. From battlefields to hospitals and prisons, paranormal activity can be accounted for and attributed to the brave men of the Union. This book, serves in many ways as a mere glimpse at the tragedy of the American Civil War and the Nutmeg State's role within but it is my firm hope that you can feel the human link to each of the men you met in this book, be they officers or soldiers and know that

Grave Corporal William Brooks

they were loved and more importantly that they are remembered. The Civil War itself will always haunt American history, the cause, the event and the death are something that we should all carry with us and the souls will forever share their story.

Thank you for joining me on this journey of history, investigations and stories as we traversed the Civil War landscape together with the ghosts of Civil War Connecticut.

Sincerely,

Courtney McInvale

BIBLIOGRAPHY

Books

Author, Unknown. *Personal Reminiscences and Fragments of the Early History of Springfield and Greene County, Missouri: Related by Pioneers and Their Descendant.* Forgotten Books, 2015.

Banks, John. *Connecticut Yankees at Antietam.* Charleston, SC: The History Press, 2013.

Banks, John. *Hidden History of Connecticut Union Soldiers.* Charleston, SC: The History Press, 2015.

Berthelson, Robert L. "Connecticut's Role in the War of the Rebellion, 1861-1865." Trumbull, Connecticut: RLB Images, n.d.

Blakeslee, B. F. *History of the Sixteenth Connecticut Volunteers.* Hartford, CT: Case, Lockwood & Brainard Co., 1875.

Cole, Garold L. *Civil War Eyewitnesses: an Annotated Bibliography of Books and Articles.* Columbia, SC: Univ. of South Carolina Press, 1988.

Freiheit, Laurence H. *Major General Joseph King Fenno Mansfield: a Soldier from Beginning to End.* Press Of the Camp Pope, 2019.

Gordon, Lesley J. *A Broken Regiment: the 16th Connecticut's Civil War.* Baton Rouge, LA: Louisiana State University Press, 2014.

Gould, John Mead. *Joseph K.F. Mansfield: Brigadier General of the U.S. Army.* Portland, CT: Stephen Berry, Printer, 1895.

Grant, Ulysses S. *Personal Memoirs of Ulysses S. Grant.* Astor Place, NY: J. J. Little & Company, 1885.

Hamilton, Michelle. *Civil War Ghosts*. Middletown, DE: Haunted Road Media, 2019.

Hansen, Harry, John Jakes, and Gary W. Gallagher. *The Civil War: a History*. New York, NY: New American Library, 2002.

Hubbard, Robert, and Kathleen Hubbard. *Middletown*. Charleston, SC: Arcadia Publishing, 2009.

Kellogg, Robert H. *Life and Death in Rebel Prisons: Giving a Complete History of the Inhuman and Barbarous Treatment of Our Brave Soldiers by Rebel Authorities, Inflicting Terrible Suffering and Frightful Mortality, Principally at Andersonville, Ga. and Florence, S.C., Describing Plans of Escape, Arrival of Prisoners, with Numerous and Varied Incidents and Anecdotes of Prison Life*. Hartford, CT: L. Stebbins, 1865.

Longley, Dione, and Buck Zaidel. *Heroes for All Time: Connecticut Civil War Soldiers Tell Their Stories*. Middletown , CT: Wesleyan University Press, 2015.

Marvin, Edwin E. *The Fifth Regiment, Connecticut Volunteers: a History Compiled from Diaries and Official Reports*. Hartford, CT: Press of Wiley, Waterman & Eaton, 1889.

Murray, Thomas Hamilton. *History of the Ninth Regiment, Connecticut Volunteer Infantry, "the Irish Regiment," in the War of the Rebellion, 1861-65, Etc*. New Haven, CT: Price, Lee & Adkins Co, 1903.

Niven, John. *Connecticut for the Union: the Role of the State in the Civil War*. New Haven (etc.), CT: Yale University Press, 1965.

Page, Charles D. *History of the Fourteenth Regiment, Connecticut Vol. Infantry*. Salem, MA: Higginson, 1998.

Phelps, M. William. *The Devil's Right Hand: the Tragic Story of the Colt Family Curse*. Guilford, CT: Lyons Press, 2012.

Phillips, Christopher. *Damned Yankee: the Life of General Nathaniel Lyon*. Baton Rouge , LA: Louisiana State University Press, 1996.

Richardson, Albert D. *The Secret Service, the Field, the Dungeon and the Escape*. Chicago, IL: American Publishing Co., 1865.

Roberts, Nancy. *Civil War Ghosts & Legends*. New York, NY: Barnes & Noble Books, 1996.

Robertson, James I., and Neil Kagan. *The Untold Civil War: Exploring the Human Side of War.* Washington, DC: National Geographic, 2013.

Roll of Honor: Names of Soldiers Who, in Defense of the American Union, Suffered Martyrdom in the Prison Pens throughout the South. Washington, DC: G.P.O., 1868.

Saunders, Lisa M. *Mystic Seafarer's Trail: Secrets behind the 7 Wonders, Titanic's Shoes, Captain Sisson's Gold, and Amelia Earhart's Wedding.* CreateSpace, 2012.

Schechter, Harold. *Killer Colt: Murder, Disgrace and the Making of an American Legend.* New York, NY: Ballantine, 2010.

Spar, Ira. *New Haven's Civil War Hospital: a History of Knight U.S. General Hospital, 1862-1865.* Jefferson, NC: McFarland & Company, Inc., Publishers, 2014.

Stowe, Harriet Beecher. *Uncle Tom's Cabin; or, Life among the Lowly.* Boston, MA: John P. Jewett & Company, 1852.

Taylor, Jeremiah. *Memorial of General Mansfield,* Boston, MA: Press of T.R. Marvin & Son, 1862. Eulogies

Taylor, Troy. *Spirits of the Civil War: a Guide to the Ghosts & Hauntings of America's Bloodiest Conflict.* Alton, IL.: Whitechapel Productions Press, 1999.

Toney, B. Keith. *Battlefield Ghosts.* Berryville, VA: Rockbridge Pub., 1997.

Trumbull, H. Clay. *The Knightly Soldier: a Biography of Major Henry Ward Camp, Tenth Conn. Vols.* New York, NY: Nichols and Noyes, 1865.

Walkley, Stephen W. *History of the Seventh Connecticut Volunteer Infantry: Hawley's Brigade, Terry's Division, Tenth Army Corps, 1861-1865.* Hartford, CT, 1905.

Warner, Elizabeth A. *A Pictorial History of Middletown.* Norfolk, VA: Donning Co., 2001.

Warshauer, Matthew. *Connecticut in the American Civil War: Slavery, Sacrifice, and Survival.* Middletown, CT: Wesleyan University Press, 2012.

Wesley, Zachary. "A Slaughter Forgotten: A Reflection on the Wayside on Iverson's Assault." Web log. *The Gettysburg Compiler: On the Front Lines of History* (blog). Civil War Institute, n.d.

https://gettysburgcompiler.org/2018/05/11/a-slaughter-forgotten-a-reflection-on-the-wayside-on-iversons-assault/.

White, Kristopher D. "Gettysburg Off the Beaten Path: The 27th Connecticut Monuments at Gettysburg." Web log. *Emerging Civil War* (blog). WordPress, June 27, 2016. https://emergingcivilwar.com/2016/06/27/gettysburg-off-the-beaten-path-the-27th-connecticut-monuments-at-gettysburg/.

Whittemore, Henry. *History of Middlesex County, Connecticut: with Biographical Sketches of Its Prominent Men.* New York, NY: J.B. Beers & Co., 1884.

Woodward, Ashbel. *Life of General Nathaniel Lyon.* Hartford, CT: Case, Lockwood & Co., 1862.

Dissertations

Amico, Michael. "The Forgotten Union of the To Henrys: A History of the 'Peculiar and Rarest Intimacy' of the American Civil War," n.d.

Interviews

McInvale, Courtney. Interview with Matt Reardon. Personal, December 1, 2020.

McInvale, Courtney. Interview with Michael Amico. Personal, December 26, 2020.

Letters

Brady, Major Allen G. Letter to Lieut. H. Whitney Chatfield. "Field Report from Gettysburg."

17th Connecticut   Headquarters: 17th Connecticut Headquarters, July 4, 1863.

Chet. "Dear Wife." New Petersburg, Virginia: Battery D, 1st C.V.A., September 2, 1864.

Dyer, C.H. Letter to Mrs. Louisa Mansfield. "Remains of General Mansfield Telegram," September 19, 1862.

Dyer, C.H. Letter to Mrs. Louisa Mansfield. "Return of Mansfield's Belongings." Vicksburg, MS: Headquarters 14th Division, June 7, 1863.

Edwards, Charles. "Account of Michael Farley at Andersonville." New London, Connecticut: Clerk of the Superior Court, Connecticut, January 11, 1865. Provided by Matt Reardon

Farley, Michael. "Pension Deposition for Michael Farley." Westerly, RI, December 18, 1879. Provided by Matt Reardon

Flood, P.H. Letter to Mrs. Louisa Mansfield. "Surgeon's Report of General Mansfield." Hope Landing, VA, April 28, 1863.

"General Mansfield Collection." Middletown, CT: Middlesex County Historical Society, n.d.

Gould, John M. "Recollection of Mansfield's Death." Berlin, MD: Headquarters Fourth Maine Regiment, December 2, 1862.

Merwin, Henry Czar. Letter to Ruby Sophia Merwin (Osborn). "My Dear Sister." Headquarters 27th Connecticut: Headquarters 27th Connecticut, January 27, 1863

Stanton, Edwin M. Letter to Benjamin Douglas. "Your Telegram Just Received (Mansfield's Death Telegram)." Washington, DC, September 18, 1862.

Magazines & Journals

"The 29th Connecticut Infantry." *Main Street Magazine*, October 3, 2019.

"Connecticut Explored," November 2003.

Ethier, Eric. "Firebrand in a Powder Keg: Nathaniel Lyon in St. Louis." *Civil War Times*, June 2005.

Frick, Allison. "The Mingled Dust of Both Armies." *Yale Alumni Magazine*, 2011.

Gordon, Lesley J. "Bad Luck Regiment: The 16th Connecticut Infantry." *Civil War Times*, April 2015.

Kaplan, Johnna. "The Three Lives of Fort Trumbull." *Connecticut Explored*, n.d.

Lowry, Thomas P. "The Incredible Dorence Atwater Story." *The Surgeon's Call*, 2016.

Morris, Roy. "Battle of the Wilderness." *Military History*, April 1997.

Nelson, Dean E. "Connecticut Arms the Union." *Connecticut Explored*, 2011

Ofgang, Erik. "Isabella Beecher Hooker: Mother, Medium, Suffragist." *Connecticut Magazine*, May 12, 2016.

Ofgang, Erik. "The Fighting Irish: Revisiting the Civil War's 9th Regiment." *Connecticut Magazine*, February 19, 2018.

Petty, Adam H. "This Place Is Called the Wilderness." *America's Civil War*, May 2020.

Sacco, Nick. "The Contested Memories of General Nathaniel Lyon in St. Louis." *The Journal of the Civil War Era*, May 28, 2019. https://www.journalofthecivilwarera.org/2019/05/the-contested-memories-of-general-nathaniel-lyon-in-st-louis/.

Music & Television

Foster, Stephen Collins, Charles Magnus, and Charles Magnus. *Better Times Are Coming*. New York: Published by Chs. Magnus 12 Frankfort St, N.Y., 1862.

Greenleaf, James E.. *John Brown's Body*. American Folk Song. 1856.

Whiskey Myers. *Bury My Bones*. MP3. *Whiskey Myers*. Wiggy Thump Records: Whiskey Myers, 2019.

Whole. *Grant* 1, no. 1-3. History Channel, May 25, 2020.

Newspaper Articles

"A Soldier Murder's Remorse." *Dayton Daily Empire*, May 5, 1864.

Appel, Allan. "A Hero's Descendant Keeps History Alive." *New Haven Independent*, June 18, 2012.

"Brigadier General Mansfield (and Various Articles)." *Connecticut War Record*. September 1863.

Collins, David. "A Confederate General Is Buried in New London." *The Day*. June 20, 2020.

Condra, Amy. "Looking for Ghosts at Cold Harbor." *Richmond Times-Dispatch*, May 15, 2008.

Drury, David. "Called to Arms in Civil War, Connecticut's Black Soldiers Respond." *Hartford Courant*, January 18, 2014.

Drury, David. "Connecticut Soldiers Revealed True Toll At Civil War's Andersonville Prison." *Hartford Courant*, March 28, 2014.

Drury, David. "Gov. William Buckingham, Faded From History, Played National Role During Civil War." *Hartford Courant*, April 7, 2012.

Drury, David. "Local Hero: Eastford Man First Union General to Die in Civil War." *Hartford Courant*, September 17, 2011.

Drury, David. "Study in Contrasts: Connecticut And Civil War." *Hartford Courant*, May 15, 2011.

Farrington, Connie Harris. "Who Were the Brooks Brothers from Haddam Who Served in the Civil War?" *Haddam Killingworth Now*, May 1, 2020.

Finnegan, Lauren. "Commentary: McDonogh Teachers Set Antietam Story Straight." *Aberdeen Proving Ground News*, October 6, 2016

Ganley, Michelle. "October Road Trip? Creepiest Places in Virginia Guaranteed to Haunt Your Dreams." *Click Orlando*, October 2017.

Gentile, Gary. "Site At Risk Where Civil War Hero Died." *Hartford Courant*, August 29, 1994.

Gould, John Mead, and John McElroy. "Army of the Cumberland and Grand Central Campaign: Brig-Gen Joseph K.F. Mansfield." *National Tribune*. May 24, 1906.

Hines, Patricia. "Black Soldiers from Westport Fought for Union in Civil War." *Westport News*, August 9, 2011.

"The Late General Mansfield; Funeral Services at Middletown, Conn." *The New York Times*, September 23, 1862.

Leavenworth, Jesse. "Restoring a Memory of the 16th Regiment." *Hartford Courant*, November 21, 1997.

Leff, David K. "Connecticut Has Its Own Civil War Sites." *Hartford Courant*, October 12, 2012.

Malley, Richard C. "Behind the Stockade: Andersonville Prison." *WNPR*, March 14, 2014. https://www.wnpr.org/post/behind-stockade-andersonville-prison.

Marteka, Peter. "Hiking a Path from Civil War General's Birthplace to Final Resting Place." *Hartford Courant*, December 12, 2015.

McNally, Owen. "Arms & The Man & Woman." *Hartford Courant*, September 8, 1996.

O'Neil, Tim. "Look Back 250: Civil War Explodes in Street Riots, but Union Hangs on to St. Louis." *St. Louis Post-Dispatch*, June 14, 2014.

"Personal," *Houston Tri-Weekly Telegraph*, December 13, 1865.

S, Claudia. "Ghosts March Through Time at Battlefield, Legend Says." *The Washington Post*, October 26, 1989.

Sommer, Carol. "More About Thomas Wolfe's Great Escape." *The Day*. March 4, 2018.

Sommer, Carol. "Saved by Courage, Kindness and a Star." *The Day*. January 14, 2018.

"Stonewall Jackson," *Muscatine Weekly Journal*, July 24, 1862.

Tipple, Stephanie. "Civil War Soldiers Never Left Stone House." *Potomac Local News*, October 9, 2012.

Walsh, Tobi. "Lynchburg-Area Ghost Stories and Urban Legends to Get You in the Halloween Spirit." *The News & Advance*. October 27, 2016.

Blogs

Allen, Jonathan R. "Civil War Army Organization and Order of Rank." Web log. *The Civil War: Civil War History and Stories* (blog). Learn Civil War History, n.d. http://www.nellaware.com/blog/civil-war-army-organization-and-order-of-rank.html.

Bacon, Karl. "The Wilderness - May 6, 1864." Web log. *Fourteenth Connecticut Volunteer Infantry: The History of the Fighting Fourteenth in the American Civil War* (blog), 2014. http://www.kbacon.com/wordpress/blog/2014/05/06/the-wilderness-may-6-1864/.

Bacon, Karl. "Tribute to a Fallen Hero." Web log. *Fourteenth Connecticut Volunteer Infantry: The History of the Fighting Fourteenth in the American Civil War* (blog). WordPress, May 16, 2014. http://www.kbacon.com/wordpress/blog/category/wilderness-spotsylvania/.

Banks, John. "Antietam Dead: Lieutenant William Horton." Web log. *John Banks' Civil War Blog* (blog). Blogspot, April 8, 2012. http://john-banks.blogspot.com/2012/04/antietam-dead-lieutenant-william-horton.html.

Banks, John. "Antietam Dead: 18-Year-Old Private Daniel Tarbox." Web log. *John Banks' Civil War Blog* (blog). Blogspot, April 5, 2012. https://john-banks.blogspot.com/2012/04/antietam-dead-18-year-old-private.html

Banks, John. "Antietam Photo Journal: Evidence of a Family's Pain." Web log. *John Bank's Civil War Blog* (blog). Blogspot, July 6, 2013. http://john-banks.blogspot.com/2013/07/antietam-photo-journal-evidence-of.html.

Banks, John. "Faces of the Civil War: Private Daniel Tarbox." Web log. *John Banks' Civil War Blog* (blog). Blogspot, April 14, 2012. http://john-banks.blogspot.com/2012/04/faces-of-civil-war-private-daniel.html.

Banks, John. "Gettysburg: Death of 17th Connecticut Lt. Colonel Fowler." Web log. *John Banks' Civil War Blog* (blog). Blogspot, May 14, 2014. http://john-banks.blogspot.com/2014/05/gettysburg-death-of-17th-connecticut-lt.html.

Banks, John. "Letter to Mrs. Mansfield: 'Depths of Pandemonia'." Web log. *John Banks' Civil War Blog* (blog). Blogspot, January 24, 2012. http://john-banks.blogspot.com/2012/01/letter-to-mrs-mansfield-depths-of.html.

Banks, John. "'No Sweet Dream': Remarkable Life of a Gettysburg Casualty." Web log. *John Banks' Civil War Blog* (blog). Blogspot, October 30, 2016. http://john-banks.blogspot.com/2016/10/no-sweet-dream-remarkable-life-of.html.

Banks, John. "Reading Private Tarbox's Final Letter." Web log. *John Banks' Civil War Blog* (blog). Blogspot, April 22, 2012. http://john-banks.blogspot.com/2012/04/antietam-reading-private-daniel-tarboxs.html.

Banks, John. "Seldom-Seen circa-1877 Photo of Main Street in Sharpsburg." Web log. *John Banks' Civil War Blog* (blog). Blogspot, July 31, 2017. http://john-banks.blogspot.com/2017/07/.

Bendici, Ray. "The State Capitol, Hartford." Web log. *Damned Connecticut* (blog). Damned Connecticut, n.d. https://www.damnedct.com/the-state-capitol-hartford/.

"Chaplain, I Will Die Like a True and Loyal Soldier." Web log. *The Chaplain Kit* (blog). WordPress, n.d. https://thechaplainkit.com/history/chaplains-at-war/civil-war/chaplain-i-will-die-like-a-true-and-loyal-soldier/.

"Chapman, 2 September 1864." Web log. *Spared & Shared 20* (blog), n.d

"The Civil War in the East, with Unit Histories, Biographies and Timelines (Various Articles)." The Civil War in the East, February 26, 2020. https://civilwarintheeast.com/.

"Civil War Manuscripts Project Alphabetical Name List K - L." Civil War Manuscripts Project - K - L, November 11, 2011. http://chs.org/finding_aides/kcwmp/cwkl.htm.

"Connecticut's Civil War Monuments (Various Articles)." Connecticut's Civil War Monuments. Connecticut Historical Society & Museum, December 7, 2010. https://chs.org/finding_aides/ransom/townlist.htm.

"The Curious Case of the 27th Connecticut - Part 2 & Part 3." Web log. *Battlefield Back Stories - Thoughts on the Civil War, Its Battlefields and Public History* (blog). Blogspot, May 30, 2012. http://battlefieldbackstories.blogspot.com/2012/05/curious-case-of-27th-connecticut-part-3.html.

"Explore over 50 Battlefields in the Eastern Theater of the Civil War." Stone Sentinels, February 14, 2020. https://stonesentinels.com/.

Finlay, Nancy. "One of the Honored Dead: General J.K.F. Mansfield." Web log. *Connecticut History* (blog). Connecticut Humanities, June 22, 2019. https://connecticuthistory.org/one-of-the-honored-dead-general-j-k-f-mansfield/.

Finlay, Nancy. "'An Admirable Portrait' of Frederick Douglass." Web log. *Connecticut History* (blog). Connecticut Humanities & Your Public Media, February 3, 2021.

"Four National Park Ghost Stories." Web log. *The Clymb* (blog). The Clymb, n.d. https://blog.theclymb.com/out-there/5-national-park-ghost-stories/.

"General Nathaniel Lyon." *New England History* (blog). Gatehouse Media, February 7, 2014. http://blogs.gatehousemedia.com/newenglandhistory/2014/02/07/general-nathaniel-lyon/.

Glory, Erica Sweeney. "Most Haunted Places in Baton Rouge." Baton Rouge Events, Things To Do, Restaurants, & Hotels. Visit Baton Rouge, September 12, 2019. https://www.visitbatonrouge.com/blog/post/most-haunted-places-in-baton-rouge/.

Gordon, Lesley J. "The Union Army Regiment That Survived Andersonville." Web log. *Zocal Public Square* (blog). ASU Knowledge, November 1, 2018. https://www.zocalopublicsquare.org/2018/11/01/union-army-regiment-survived-andersonville/ideas/essay/.

Griff. "1863: Henry Czar Merwin To Ruby Sophia Merwin Osborn." Web log. *Spared & Shared 18* (blog). WordPress, January 30, 2019. https://sparedshared18.wordpress.com/2019/01/30/1863-henry-czar-merwin-to-ruby-sophia-merwin-osborn/.

Groeling, Meg. "Gettysburg Memories: Devil's Den 125!" Web log. *Emerging Civil War* (blog). WordPress, July 11, 2013. https://emergingcivilwar.com/2013/07/11/gettysburg-memories-devils-den-125/.

Hawley, Charles Ben. "Connecticut's Black Civil War Regiment." Web log. *Connecticut History* (blog). Connecticut Explored, November 23, 2015.

"Hidden Nearby: Terryville's Dorence Atwater Monument." Web log. *Hidden in Plain Sight* (blog). WordPress, May 28, 2014. https://hiddeninplainsightblog.com/2014/05/.

Hudyma, Evelyn. "A Memorial to General Hawley at the State Capitol." Web log. *Connecticut History* (blog). Connecticut Humanities, October 24, 2019. https://connecticuthistory.org/a-memorial-to-general-hawley-at-the-state-capitol/.

Insalaco, Jeanne Bryan. "Oct. 26, 2014: The Knight Hospital Civil War Monument." Web log. *Everyone Has a Family Story to Tell: Tell Their Stories* (blog). WordPress, November 1, 2014. https://everyonehasafamilystorytotell.wordpress.com/2014/11/01/knight-hospital-civil-war-monument-new-haven-ct/.

Hickman, Kennedy. "American Civil War: Major General William F. 'Baldy' Smith." Web log. *ThoughtCo.* (blog). ThoughtCo., July 3, 2019. https://www.thoughtco.com/william-f-baldy-smith-4053790.

"John C. Colt, Samuel Colt's 'Bad' Brother, Commits a Macabre Murder." *New England Historical Society: Connecticut* (blog). New England Historical Society, n.d. https://www.newenglandhistoricalsociety.com/john-c-colt-samuel-colts-bad-brother-commits-a-macabre-murder/.

Jones, Todd. "29th Regiment Connecticut Volunteers Fought More than One War." Web log. *Connecticut History* (blog). Connecticut Humanities, November 23, 2016. https://connecticuthistory.org/the-29th-regiment-connecticut-volunteers-fought-more-than-one-war/.

Kaller, Seth. "A Union Officer's Commission and Field Report from the 17th Connecticut Regiment at the Battle of Gettysburg." Web log. *Historic Documents & Legacy Collection* (blog). Seth Kaller, Inc., n.d. https://www.sethkaller.com/item/394-21808-A-Union-Officer%E2%80%99s-Commission,-and-Field-Report-from-the-17th-Connecticut-Regiment-at-the-Battle-of-Gettysburg.

Leininger, Daniel Neil. "Connecticut History Statues by H.A> MacNeil - 'General Alfred Howe Terry' and 'Major General John Sedgwick.'" Web log. *Hermon A. MacNeil: American Sculptor: 1866-1947* (blog). Daniel Neil Leininger, 7AD. https://hermonatkinsmacneil.com/2011/05/07/connecticut-history-statues-by-h-a-macneil-general-alfred-howe-terry-and-major-general-john-sedgwick/.

"Little Sorrel, Connecticut's Confederate War Horse." Web log. *Connecticut History* (blog). Connecticut Humanities, November 12, 2019. https://connecticuthistory.org/little-sorrel-connecticuts-confederate-war-horse/.

Lucian, David. "Connecticut's War Governor, William A. Buckingham." Web log. *Connecticut History* (blog). Connecticut Humanities, June 18, 2020. https://connecticuthistory.org/connecticuts-war-governor-william-a-buckingham/.

Malley, Richard. "Disaster at Cold Harbor: Connecticut's Second Volunteer Heavy Artillery Regiment." Web log. *Connecticut History* (blog).

Connecticut Humanities, October 26, 2019. https://connecticuthistory.org/disaster-at-cold-harbor-connecticuts-second-volunteer-heavy-artillery-regiment/.

Mark. "The Seacoast Mortar Called 'The Dictator' at the Siege of Petersburg 1864." Web log. *Iron Brigadier: Civil War Info & Resources* (blog). Iron Brigadier, December 13, 2011. https://ironbrigader.com/2011/12/13/seacoast-mortar-called-the-dictator-siege-petersburg-1864/.

McCain, Diana. "Fighting Sons of Erin: Connecticut's Irish Regiment in the Civil War." Web log. *Connecticut History* (blog). Connecticut Humanities & Your Public Media, March 17, 2019. https://connecticuthistory.org/fighting-sons-of-erin-connecticuts-irish-regiment-in-the-civil-war/.

Muston, Kimit. "Off to the Races." Web log. *The Public "I": History in Context Every Day* (blog). Blogspot, November 19, 2014. http://thepublici.blogspot.com/2014/11/off-to-races.html?m=1.

"Nathaniel Lyon: Colorful Commander from Connecticut." *Connecticut History* (blog). Connecticut Humanities & Your Public Media, April 12, 2013. https://connecticuthistory.org/nathaniel-lyon-colorful-commander-from-connecticut/.

Nesbitt, Mark. "Hidden, Haunted, Hotspots of Gettysburg." Web log. *Mark Nesbitt* (blog). WordPress, August 20, 2019. https://markvnesbitt.wordpress.com/2019/08/20/hidden-haunted-hotspots-of-gettysburg-east-cavalry/.

Pelland, Dave. "CT Monuments (Various Articles)." CT Monuments: Connecticut History in Granite and Bronze. WordPress, n.d. http://ctmonuments.net/.

Pelland, Dave. "General Mansfield and GAR Monuments, Middletown." CT Monumentsnet, June 18, 2009. http://ctmonuments.net/2009/06/general-mansfield-and-gar-monuments-middletown/.

Pelland, Dave. "Soldiers' Monument, Danbury." CT Monumentsnet, March 23, 2009. http://ctmonuments.net/2009/03/soldiers%E2%80%99-monument-danbury/.

"Photos, Text and Locations of the Union Monuments at Gettysburg." The

Battle of Gettysburg, December 26, 2019. https://gettysburg.stonesentinels.com/union-monuments/.

Posted by blogger in Civil War Ghosts. "Hauntings at Devil's Den - Civil War Ghosts - Battle of Gettysburg." Civil War Ghosts, March 23, 2020. https://civilwarghosts.com/hauntings-at-devils-den/.

Posted by blogger in Civil War Ghosts. "Most Haunted Spots on the Gettysburg Battlefield." Civil War Ghosts, December 17, 2020. https://civilwarghosts.com/most-haunted-spots-on-the-gettysburg-battlefield/.

Potter, John. "Nathaniel Lyon: Colorful Commander from Connecticut." Web log. *Connecticut History* (blog). Connecticut Humanities & Your Public Media, April 12, 2013. https://connecticuthistory.org/nathaniel-lyon-colorful-commander-from-connecticut/.

Randy. "Private George Warner, 20th Connecticut." Web log. *The Battle of Gettysburg & The American Civil War* (blog). Blogspot, December 3, 2006. http://gettysburg-acw.blogspot.com/2006/12/private-george-warner-20th-connecticut.html.

Sanders, Jack. "John Rowley: Murderer on A Monument." Web log. *Old Ridgefield* (blog). Blogger, May 17, 2018. http://www.naturegeezer.com/2018/05/.

Schaff, Morris. "Morris Schaff's Wilderness, Pt. 2: Spirits, Ghosts and Talking Plants on the Battlefield." Web log. *Mysteries & Conundrums: Exploring the Civil War-Era Landscape in the Fredericksburg & Spotsylvania Region* (blog). WordPress, August 11, 2014. https://npsfrsp.wordpress.com/2014/08/11/morris-schaffs-wilderness-pt-2-spirits-ghosts-and-talking-plants-on-the-battlefield/.

Schecter, Harold. "The Colt-Adams Affair, 1841." *The Yale Review* (blog). Yale University, n.d. https://yalereview.yale.edu/colt-adams-affair-1841.

Staub, Jerry. "Sherman's Inability to Liberate the South's Most Notorious Prison." Web log. *Ohio State University: Department of History: Ehistory* (blog). Ohio State University, n.d. https://ehistory.osu.edu/articles/shermans-inability-liberate-souths-most-notorious-prison.

"Suffolk, VA 1863: The Lads from Connecticut." Web log. *Hartford in the Civil War* (blog). WordPress, January 18, 2017. http://hartfordinthecivilwar.com/wordpress1/2017/01/18/suffolk-va-1863-connecticut-lads-south/.

Sullivan, Austin. "A Monument Memorializes the Fallen." Web log. *Connecticut History* (blog). Connecticut Humanities, September 25, 2020. https://connecticuthistory.org/a-monument-memorializes-the-fallen/.

Sweeney, Gary. "Traces of the Dead: The Haunted Battleground of Cold Harbor." Web log. *The Lineup* (blog). The Lineup, May 25, 2016. https://the-line-up.com/cold-harbor-haunted.

Taylor, Troy. "Hell Hole of the Confederacy: Horror and Hauntings at Andersonville." Web log. *American Hauntings: Ghosts, Gangsters, Murder* (blog). American Hauntings Ink & Troy Taylor, February 24, 2014. http://troytaylorbooks.blogspot.com/2014/02/hell-hole-of-confederacy.html.

Taylor, Troy. "The Colt Family Curse." *American Hauntings: Ghosts, Gangsters, Murder & Mayhem in American History* (blog). American Hauntings Ink & Troy Taylor, January 4, 2013. http://troytaylorbooks.blogspot.com/2013/01/the-colt-family-curse.html.

Ural, Susannah J. "The War In Their Words: 'I Hope You Will Come Home'." Web log. *HistoryNet* (blog). HistoryNet, February 2019. https://www.historynet.com/war-words-hope-will-come-home.htm.

Warshauer, Matthew. "The Complicated Realities of Connecticut and the Civil War." *Connecticut History* (blog). Connecticut Humanities, December 30, 2020. connecticuthistory.org/connecticut-and-the-civil-war.

Wilkosz, Jennifer. "Remembering Civil War Prisoners of War." Web log. *Connecticut History* (blog). Connecticut Humanities, September 17, 2016. https://connecticuthistory.org/remembering-civil-war-prisoners-of-war/.

Woodward, Walter W. "From the State Historian: Final Journey of Nathaniel Lyon." Web log. *Connecticut History* (blog). Connecticut Humanities & Connecticut Explored, September 5, 2020. https://connecticuthistory.org/from-the-state-historian-the-final-journey-of-nathaniel-lyon/.

Electronic Sources

"10 Facts: Cold Harbor." American Battlefield Trust, November 23, 2020. https://www.battlefields.org/learn/articles/10-facts-cold-harbor.

"10th Connecticut Infantry Regiment." Wikipedia. Wikimedia Foundation, January 21, 2021. https://en.wikipedia.org/wiki/10th_Connecticut_Infantry_Regiment.

123rd NY Infantry Regiment - Civil War Newspaper Clippings - NY Military Museum and Veterans Research Center, n.d. https://dmna.ny.gov/historic/reghist/civil/infantry/123rdInf/123rdInfCWN.htm.

"14th Connecticut Infantry Regiment." Wikipedia. Wikimedia Foundation, September 6, 2020. https://en.wikipedia.org/wiki/ 14th_Connecticut_Infantry_Regiment.

"16th Connecticut Infantry Regiment." Wikipedia. Wikimedia Foundation, June 29, 2020. https://en.wikipedia.org/wiki/16th_Connecticut_Infantry_Regiment.

18, Richard Scott |July, Duff Conner | July 27, and Chris Kelly | September 23. Hartford In The Civil War, n.d. http://hartfordinthecivilwar.com/wordpress1/.

"1st Connecticut Cavalry Regiment." Wikipedia. Wikimedia Foundation, June 29, 2020. https://en.wikipedia.org/wiki/1st_Connecticut_Cavalry_Regiment.

"29th Connecticut Colored Infantry Regiment." Wikipedia. Wikimedia Foundation, June 29, 2020. https://en.wikipedia.org/wiki/ 29th_Connecticut_Colored_Infantry_Regiment.

"2nd Connecticut Heavy Artillery." Wikipedia. Wikimedia Foundation, July 1, 2020. https://en.wikipedia.org/wiki/2nd_Connecticut_Heavy_Artillery.

"31st United States Colored Infantry Regiment." Wikipedia. Wikimedia Foundation, January 31, 2021. https://en.wikipedia.org/wiki/ 31st_United_States_Colored_Infantry_Regiment.

"7th Connecticut Infantry Regiment." Wikipedia. Wikimedia Foundation, January 16, 2021.

https://en.wikipedia.org/wiki/7th_Connecticut_Infantry_Regiment.

"8th Connecticut Infantry Regiment." Wikipedia. Wikimedia Foundation, September 19, 2020. https://en.wikipedia.org/wiki/ 8th_Connecticut_Infantry_Regiment.

Alexander, Errol D., "CTMQ's Town Guides." CTMQ, n.d. http://www.ctmq.org/hartford-10/.

"Alfred Terry." Wikipedia. Wikimedia Foundation, January 15, 2021. https://en.wikipedia.org/wiki/Alfred_Terry.

"American Civil War Prison Camps." Wikipedia. Wikimedia Foundation, December 23, 2020. https://en.wikipedia.org/wiki/American_Civil_War_prison_camps.

"The American Civil War." History Learning Site, n.d. https://www.historylearningsite.co.uk/the-american-civil-war/.

Ancestors of Commander James Harmon Ward - Family Tree, n.d. http://searchtrees.com/tree/15298.htm.

"Andersonville Raiders." Wikipedia. Wikimedia Foundation, December 20, 2020. https://en.wikipedia.org/wiki/Andersonville_Raiders.

Antietam Sequence of Events, n.d. https://civilwarhome.com/antietamevents.htm.

"Antietam Union Order of Battle." Wikipedia. Wikimedia Foundation, January 24, 2021. https://en.wikipedia.org/wiki/Antietam_Union_order_of_battle.

Bai, Xiaoyan. "Poems from the Knight Hospital Record." UConn Health Sciences Library, September 15, 2017. https://lib.uconn.edu/health/research-assistance/hartford-medical-society-library/hms-library-collections/archival-collections/poems-from-the-knight-hospital-record/.

"Battle of Antietam Facts & Summary." American Battlefield Trust, December 15, 2020. https://www.battlefields.org/learn/civil-war/battles/antietam.

"Battle of Antietam." Wikipedia. Wikimedia Foundation, January 15, 2021. https://en.wikipedia.org/wiki/Battle_of_Antietam.

"Battle of Cold Harbor." Wikipedia. Wikimedia Foundation, February 2, 2021. https://en.wikipedia.org/wiki/Battle_of_Cold_Harbor.

"Battle of Drewry's Bluff." Wikipedia. Wikimedia Foundation, August 7, 2020.

https://en.wikipedia.org/wiki/Battle_of_Drewry%27s_Bluff.

"Battle of Gettysburg, Second Day." Wikipedia. Wikimedia Foundation, August 4, 2019. https://en.wikipedia.org/wiki/Battle_of_Gettysburg,_Second_Day.

"Battle of Gettysburg." Wikipedia. Wikimedia Foundation, December 26, 2020. https://en.wikipedia.org/wiki/Battle_of_Gettysburg.

"Battle of North Anna." Wikipedia. Wikimedia Foundation, January 15, 2021. https://en.wikipedia.org/wiki/Battle_of_North_Anna.

"Battle of the Wilderness." Wikipedia. Wikimedia Foundation, January 21, 2021. https://en.wikipedia.org/wiki/Battle_of_the_Wilderness.

"Battle of Yellow Tavern." Wikipedia. Wikimedia Foundation, January 31, 2021. https://en.wikipedia.org/wiki/Battle_of_Yellow_Tavern.

"Battlefront." Middlesex County Historical Society, August 6, 2016. https://mchsct.org/exhibits-displays/hard-stirring-times-online-exhibit/battlefront/.

Blair, Dan. "Plymouth, Battle Of." NCpedia, n.d. https://www.ncpedia.org/plymouth-battle.

Bloody Angle - Spotsylvania Court House Battlefield VA - Ghosts and Hauntings on Waymarking.com, n.d. http://www.waymarking.com/waymarks/WM96DX_Bloody_Angle_Spotsylvania_Court_House_Battlefield_VA.

Brown, Louis A. "Confederate Prison (Salisbury)." NCpedia, n.d. https://www.ncpedia.org/confederate-prison-salisbury.

"Burnside's Bridge." Wikipedia. Wikimedia Foundation, June 13, 2020. https://en.wikipedia.org/wiki/Burnside%27s_Bridge.

"Causes of Death at Camp Sumter." National Parks Service. U.S. Department of the Interior, n.d. https://www.nps.gov/ande/learn/historyculture/causesofdeath.htm.

"Cedar Hill Cemetery Foundation " General Griffin A. Stedman (1838 – 1864) -." Cedar Hill Cemetery Foundation. Connecting with our past. Protecting our future., n.d. http://cedarhillfoundation.org/notable-residents/general-griffin-stedman/.

"Cedar Hill Cemetery Foundation " Henry Ward Camp (1839 – 1864) -." Cedar Hill Cemetery Foundation. Connecting with our past. Protecting our future., n.d. http://cedarhillfoundation.org/notable-residents/henry-ward-camp/.

"Chancellorsville Union Order of Battle." Wikipedia. Wikimedia Foundation, December 9, 2020. https://en.wikipedia.org/wiki/ Chancellorsville_Union_order_of_battle.

"Christopher Flynn (Medal of Honor)." Wikipedia. Wikimedia Foundation, January 14, 2021. https://en.wikipedia.org/wiki/ Christopher_Flynn_(Medal_of_Honor).

"Civil War Facts." American Battlefield Trust, October 1, 2020. https://www.battlefields.org/learn/articles/civil-war-facts.

Civil War Plymouth Pilgrims Descendant Society :: Imprisonment, n.d. http://cwppds.org/index.php/imprisonment/.

"Civil War Prisons," n.d. civilwarpirsoners.com.

"Clara Barton and Andersonville." National Parks Service. U.S. Department of the Interior, n.d. https://www.nps.gov/ande/learn/historyculture/ clara_barton.htm.

Coe, Alexis. "That Time Charlotte Brontë's Ghost Haunted Harriet Beecher Stowe." Lenny Letter, n.d. https://www.lennyletter.com/story/charlotte-brontes-ghost-haunts-harriet-beecher-stowe.

"Cold Harbor Union Order of Battle." Wikipedia. Wikimedia Foundation, November 17, 2020. https://en.wikipedia.org/wiki/ Cold_Harbor_Union_order_of_battle.

"Colonel Elisha Kellogg." The Confederation of Union Generals, May 30, 2019. https://uniongenerals.org/meet-the-generals/colonel-elisha-kellogg/.

"Columbia Military Prison Richland County Jail." Richland County Jail, n.d. https://www.sciway3.net/cmp-csa/camps/colajail.html.

Connecticut State Library. Connecticut State Library, n.d. https://ctstatelibrary.org/.

"Connecticut." National Parks Service - Petersburg National Battlefield. U.S. Department of the Interior, n.d. https://www.nps.gov/pete/learn/ historyculture/connecticut.htm.

Connelly, Lt. Col. Kevin T. "Strategy Research Project: The 14th Regiment, Connecticut Volunteers, Infantry." Defense Technical Information Center. U.S. Army, January 12, 2000.

https://apps.dtic.mil/dtic/tr/fulltext/u2/a374955.pdf.

Cutler, James C. "Civil War: Connecticut Volunteers from Thompson." Thompson, CT: Thompson Historical Society, n.d.

"Daniel Tarbox Jr. (1844-1862) - Find A Grave..." Find a Grave, n.d. https://www.findagrave.com/memorial/78809603/daniel-tarbox.

The Death of Sedgwick, n.d. http://www.cornwallhistoricalsociety.org/exhibits/ civilwar/sedgdeath.html.

"Dorence Atwater Monument." Plymouth historical society, March 31, 2014. https://plymouthhistoricalsociety.org/other-historic-sites-in-plymouth/dorence-atwater-monument/.

"Dorence Atwater." National Parks Service. U.S. Department of the Interior, n.d. https://www.nps.gov/ande/learn/historyculture/dorence_atwater.htm.

"Dorence Atwater." Wikipedia. Wikimedia Foundation, July 6, 2020. https://en.wikipedia.org/wiki/Dorence_Atwater.

"Elijah W. Bacon." Wikipedia. Wikimedia Foundation, October 1, 2020. https://en.wikipedia.org/wiki/Elijah_W._Bacon.

"Elijah William Bacon (1836-1864) - Find A Grave..." Find a Grave, n.d. https://www.findagrave.com/memorial/19045/elijah-william-bacon.

"Elisha Strong Kellogg (1824-1864) - Find A Grave..." Find a Grave, n.d. https://www.findagrave.com/memorial/6577008/elisha-strong-kellogg.

"Fort Fisher." American Battlefield Trust, September 15, 2020. https://www.battlefields.org/learn/articles/fort-fisher.

"Fort Trumbull - Long Island Paranormal Investigators," n.d. http://www.liparanormalinvestigators.com/haunted-places-on-li/connecticut-2/fort-trumbull/.

"General Joseph Mansfield." Middlesex County Historical Society, November 19, 2016. https://mchsct.org/local-stories/general-joseph-mansfield/.

General Joseph Roswell Hawley - Hartford, CT - Relief Art Sculptures on Waymarking.com, n.d. https://www.waymarking.com/waymarks/ wmQ9K0_General_Joseph_Roswell_Hawley_Hartford_CT.

"Gettysburg Union Order of Battle." Wikipedia. Wikimedia Foundation, December 29, 2020. https://en.wikipedia.org/wiki/ Gettysburg_Union_order_of_battle.

"Gettysburg." American Battlefield Trust, December 10, 2019. https://www.battlefields.org/learn/articles/gettysburg.

"Ghost Stories: Spotsylvania Court House." Stevenson Ridge, October 26, 2018. http://stevensonridge.net/blog/ghost-stories-spotsylvania-court-house/.

"Ghosts and Hauntings at Woolsey Hall of Yale University!" Ghosts of New Haven: Facebook. Facebook, July 1, 2017. https://www.facebook.com/GhostsOfNewHaven/posts/ghosts-and-hauntings-at-woolsey-hall-of-yale-university-the-auditorium-woolsey-h/1511015022291039/.

"Ghosts of Gettysburg." American Hauntings, n.d. https://www.americanhauntingsink.com/gettysburg.

Gideon Welles - Hartford, CT - Statues of Historic Figures on Waymarking.com, n.d. https://www.waymarking.com/waymarks/wmHZ5D_Gideon_Welles_Hartford_CT.

"Gideon Welles." Wikipedia. Wikimedia Foundation, January 5, 2021. https://en.wikipedia.org/wiki/Gideon_Welles.

Gnam, Carl, C. David Coyle, November 6, C. David Coyle, James Vinski November 6, James Vinski, and T. J. "Battle of Antietam: Clash in the Cornfield." Warfare History Network, May 23, 2020. https://warfarehistorynetwork.com/2018/12/21/battle-of-antietam-clash-in-the-cornfield/.

Governor William A. Buckingham House. Facebook, n.d. https://www.facebook.com/Governor-William-A-Buckingham-House-202198830361615/.

"Grant's Canal." National Parks Service. U.S. Department of the Interior, n.d. https://www.nps.gov/vick/learn/historyculture/grants-canal.htm.

"Harriet Beecher Stowe House." CTHauntedHouses.com, n.d. https://www.cthauntedhouses.com/real-haunt/harriet-beecher-stowe-house.html.

"Hartford War Monuments." Hartford Preservation Alliance, n.d. https://hartfordpreservation.org/monuments/.

HauntedPlaces.org. "Connecticut State Capitol." Haunted Places, n.d.

https://www.hauntedplaces.org/item/connecticut-state-capitol/.

"Henry Clay Trumbull." Wikipedia. Wikimedia Foundation, September 4, 2020. https://en.wikipedia.org/wiki/Henry_Clay_Trumbull.

"Henry Czar Merwin (1839-1863) - Find A Grave..." Find a Grave, n.d. https://www.findagrave.com/memorial/5845029/henry-czar-merwin.

"Henry W. Wessells." Wikipedia. Wikimedia Foundation, January 5, 2021. https://en.wikipedia.org/wiki/Henry_W._Wessells.

"Henry Wirz." Wikipedia. Wikimedia Foundation, December 23, 2020. https://en.wikipedia.org/wiki/Henry_Wirz.

"History and Heritage." Yale New Haven Hospital: History and Heritage. Yale New Haven Health, n.d. https://www.ynhh.org/about/hospital-overview/history-heritage.aspx.

"History of the Andersonville Prison." National Parks Service. U.S. Department of the Interior, n.d. https://www.nps.gov/ande/learn/historyculture/camp_sumter_history.htm.

"History of the First Regiment Connecticut Volunteer Cavalry." CT.gov, n.d. https://portal.ct.gov/MIL/MAPO/History/Units/History-of-the-First-Regiment-Connecticut-Volunteer-Cavalry.

"The History of the Seventh Regiment." Olustee, n.d. https://battleofolustee.org/letters/history_7th_nhv.htm.

History.com Editors. "Emancipation Proclamation." History.com. A&E Television Networks, October 29, 2009. https://www.history.com/topics/american-civil-war/emancipation-proclamation.

Hollis, Nicholas E. "Longstreet at Antietam: Profile of a Commander." The Agribusiness Council. Agribusiness Council, Inc., n.d. https://www.agribusinesscouncil.org/Longstsreet/Battle%20of%20Antietam.htm.

"The House & Gardens." Middlesex County Historical Society, July 18, 2017. https://mchsct.org/aboutmchs/general-mansfield-house/.

"Irish." Middlesex County Historical Society, July 22, 2016. https://mchsct.org/exhibits-displays/their-own-stories-online-exhibit/irish/irish/.

"Isaac P. Rodman." Wikipedia. Wikimedia Foundation, June 26, 2019. https://en.wikipedia.org/wiki/Isaac_P._Rodman.

"James H. Ward." Wikipedia. Wikimedia Foundation, October 10, 2020. https://en.wikipedia.org/wiki/James_H._Ward.

"Jedediah Chapman (1759-1848) - Find A Grave..." Find a Grave, n.d. https://www.findagrave.com/memorial/80932008/jedediah-chapman.

"John Brown's Raid on Harpers Ferry." Wikipedia. Wikimedia Foundation, January 29, 2021. https://en.wikipedia.org/wiki/John_Brown%27s_raid_on_Harpers_Ferry.

"John Sedgwick." American Battlefield Trust, September 10, 2019. https://www.battlefields.org/learn/biographies/john-sedgwick.

"John Sedgwick." Wikipedia. Wikimedia Foundation, January 7, 2021. https://en.wikipedia.org/wiki/John_Sedgwick.

"Joseph Hooker." Wikipedia. Wikimedia Foundation, January 5, 2021. https://en.wikipedia.org/wiki/Joseph_Hooker.

"Joseph K. Mansfield." Wikipedia. Wikimedia Foundation, January 26, 2021. https://en.wikipedia.org/wiki/Joseph_K._Mansfield.

"Joseph Roswell Hawley." Wikipedia. Wikimedia Foundation, January 11, 2021. https://en.wikipedia.org/wiki/Joseph_Roswell_Hawley.

"June 1st, Cold Harbor Evening." American Battlefield Trust, August 9, 2018. https://www.battlefields.org/learn/articles/june-1st-cold-harbor-evening.

"Kensington Soldier's Monument." Wikipedia. Wikimedia Foundation, October 5, 2020. https://en.wikipedia.org/wiki/Kensington_Soldier%27s_Monument.

Krick, Robert E.L. "Control of Cold Harbor Crossroads." American Battlefield Trust, October 23, 2018. https://www.battlefields.org/learn/articles/control-cold-harbor-crossroads.

Lamoureux, Aimee. "This Civil War General Uttered History's Most Ironic Last Words Just Before Getting Shot." All That's Interesting. All That's Interesting, September 25, 2019. https://allthatsinteresting.com/general-john-sedgwick.

Legends of America, n.d. https://www.legendsofamerica.com/va-civilwarbattles/16/.

"Libby Prison." Wikipedia. Wikimedia Foundation, February 3, 2021. https://en.wikipedia.org/wiki/Libby_Prison.

Liebenson, Bess. "Civil War Unfolds Item by Item." *The New York Times*, September 9, 2001.

"Lieut Frank M Chapman (1841-1903) - Find A Grave..." Find a Grave, n.d. https://www.findagrave.com/memorial/135345510/frank-m-chapman.

"List of American Civil War Battles." Wikipedia. Wikimedia Foundation, January 22, 2021. https://en.wikipedia.org/wiki/List_of_American_Civil_War_battles.

"List of Connecticut Civil War Units." Wikipedia. Wikimedia Foundation, January 30, 2021. https://en.wikipedia.org/wiki/List_of_Connecticut_Civil_War_units.

"Little Sorrel (1850-1886) - Find A Grave Memorial." Find a Grave, n.d. https://www.findagrave.com/memorial/2247/little_sorrel.

Longfellow, Ricky. "Back in Time: Ghosts of Antietam's Battlefield and the Bloody Lane." Highway History. U.S. Department of Transportation: Federal Highway Administration, June 27, 2017.

"Maj Henry Ward Camp (1839-1864) - Find A Grave..." Find a Grave, n.d. https://www.findagrave.com/memorial/9337347/henry-ward-camp.

Maranzani, Barbara. "How Ulysses S. Grant Earned the Nickname 'Unconditional Surrender Grant'." Biography.com. A&E Networks Television, July 28, 2020. https://www.biography.com/news/ulysses-s-grant-nickname-unconditional-surrender-grant.

McManus, Hailey. "The 17th Connecticut: The Battle of Gettysburg," 2014.

McNamara, Robert. "Significance of the Battle of Gettysburg: 5 Reasons the Battle Mattered." Web log. *ThoughtCo. History & Culture* (blog). ThoughtCo., September 12, 2019. https://www.thoughtco.com/significance-of-the-battle-of-gettysburg-1773738.

"Michael Farley (1840-1917) - Find A Grave..." Find a Grave, n.d. https://www.findagrave.com/memorial/11054083/michael-farley.

"Myth: General Ulysses S. Grant Stopped the Prisoner Exchange, and Is Thus Responsible for All of the Suffering in Civil War Prisons on Both Sides." National Parks Service. U.S. Department of the Interior, n.d.

https://www.nps.gov/ande/learn/historyculture/grant-and-the-prisoner-exchange.htm.

"Myth: Henry Wirz Was the Only Person Tried for War Crimes in the Civil War." National Parks Service. U.S. Department of the Interior, n.d. https://www.nps.gov/ande/learn/historyculture/wirztribunal.htm.

"Nathaniel Lyon (1818 – 1861)." Nathaniel Lyon - Historic Missourians - The State Historical Society of Missouri, n.d. https://historicmissourians.shsmo.org/historicmissourians/name/l/lyon/.

Nathaniel Lyon (1818-1861), n.d. http://www.thelatinlibrary.com/chron/civilwarnotes/lyon.html.

"Nathaniel Lyon Memorial State Park." Explore Connecticut, January 5, 2021. https://explorect.org/nathaniel-lyon/.

"Nathaniel Lyon." Wikipedia. Wikimedia Foundation, January 5, 2021. https://en.wikipedia.org/wiki/Nathaniel_Lyon.

"Not Even Past: Social Vulnerability and the Legacy of Redlining." History Engine 3.0, n.d. https://historyengine.richmond.edu/episodes/view/3960.

"Our Story." NE Civil War Museum, n.d. https://www.newenglandcivilwarmuseum.com/our-mission.

"Private George Simon Brooks (1844-1865) ." Find A Grave. Find A Grave, n.d. https://www.findagrave.com/memorial/30512922/george-simon-brooks.

"Pvt George W. Warner (1832-1923) - Find A Grave..." Find a Grave, n.d. https://www.findagrave.com/memorial/13408068/george-w.-warner.

"Rev Samuel Wheelock Fiske (1828-1864) - Find A..." Find a Grave, n.d. https://www.findagrave.com/memorial/65881920/samuel-wheelock-fiske.

"Richard Mather." Wikipedia. Wikimedia Foundation, January 28, 2021. https://en.wikipedia.org/wiki/Richard_Mather.

Roos, Dave. "The Ghosts of Gettysburg's Devil's Den." HowStuffWorks. HowStuffWorks, August 27, 2019. https://history.howstuffworks.com/american-civil-war/devils-den.htm.

"Second Manassas Hikes." National Parks Service. U.S. Department of the Interior, n.d. https://www.nps.gov/mana/planyourvisit/second-manassas-hikes.htm.

"Sgt. Maj. Robert H. Kellogg, 'I Wonder If They Know at Home of Our Real Condition Here.".'" Wethersfield Historical Society, December 30, 2018. https://www.wethersfieldhistory.org/articles/sgt-maj-robert-h-kellogg-i-wonder-if-they-know-at-home-of-our-real-condition-here/.

"Society for Psychical Research." Society for Psychical Research | Psi Encyclopedia, n.d. https://psi-encyclopedia.spr.ac.uk/articles/society-psychical-research.

"Soldiers and Sailors Memorial Arch." Wikipedia. Wikimedia Foundation, October 14, 2018. https://en.wikipedia.org/wiki/Soldiers_and_Sailors_Memorial_Arch.

"Spotsylvania Court House Union Order of Battle." Wikipedia. Wikimedia Foundation, January 15, 2021. https://en.wikipedia.org/wiki/Spotsylvania_Court_House_Union_order_of_battle.

"Spotsylvania Court House." Colonial Ghosts, May 9, 2020. https://colonialghosts.com/spotsylvania-court-house/.

"St. Louis Arsenal." St. Louis Arsenal – Legend of the Blue Man", n.d. http://www.militaryghosts.com/arsenal.html.

"The Stamford Historical Society Presents." The Stamford Historical Society, Civil War Exhibit 2003, Regimental Histories, n.d. https://www.stamfordhistory.org/cw_reghist.htm.

State Capitol Preservation & Restoration, n.d. https://www.cga.ct.gov/cprc/history.asp.

"Strange Events." Baton Rouge Civil War Round Table, n.d. https://www.brcwrt.com/strange-events.html.

"The Surrender Meeting." National Parks Service. U.S. Department of the Interior, n.d. https://www.nps.gov/apco/learn/historyculture/the-surrender-meeting.htm.

Tappan, Nancy. "12 Forgotten Heroes of Gettysburg." HistoryNet. HistoryNet, June 19, 2019. https://www.historynet.com/12-forgotten-heroes-of-gettysburg.htm.

"Tour Stop 10." National Parks Service. U.S. Department of the Interior, n.d. https://www.nps.gov/anti/learn/photosmultimedia/tour-stop-10.htm.

"Two Centuries at the Front Lines of Defending Our Freedoms!" FORT

TRUMBULL HISTORY, n.d. http://www.fortfriends.org/history.htm.

"U.S. Route 6." Wikipedia. Wikimedia Foundation, January 11, 2021. https://en.wikipedia.org/wiki/U.S._Route_6.

"Uncle Tom's Cabin." Wikipedia. Wikimedia Foundation, January 19, 2021. https://en.wikipedia.org/wiki/Uncle_Tom%27s_Cabin.

"Union Order of Battle." National Parks Service. U.S. Department of the Interior, n.d. https://www.nps.gov/mana/learn/historyculture/order-of-battle.htm.

Union Provost Marshal, n.d. https://www.tnsos.net/TSLA/provost/index.php.

Wagner, Stephen. "Reported Encounters With Gettysburg Ghosts." LiveAbout, n.d. https://www.liveabout.com/ghost-encounters-at-gettysburg-2594202.

"Welcome to the Museum of CT History." Museum of Connecticut History, July 28, 2020. https://museumofcthistory.org/.

"Wilderness Union Order of Battle." Wikipedia. Wikimedia Foundation, December 9, 2020. https://en.wikipedia.org/wiki/Wilderness_Union_order_of_battle.

"William Alfred Buckingham." Wikipedia. Wikimedia Foundation, January 21, 2021. https://en.wikipedia.org/wiki/William_Alfred_Buckingham.

"William B. Hincks." Wikipedia. Wikimedia Foundation, August 26, 2020. https://en.wikipedia.org/wiki/William_B._Hincks.

"William Bliss Hincks (1841-1903) - Find A Grave..." Find a Grave, n.d. https://www.findagrave.com/memorial/7766252/william-bliss-hincks.

"William Danforth Brooks (1842-1864) - Find A..." Find a Grave, n.d. https://www.findagrave.com/memorial/51151996/william-danforth-brooks.

"William Danforth Brooks (1842-1864) - Find A..." Find a Grave, n.d. https://www.findagrave.com/memorial/51151996/william-danforth-brooks.

"William Farrar Smith." Wikipedia. Wikimedia Foundation, January 5, 2021. https://en.wikipedia.org/wiki/William_Farrar_Smith.

"William Hincks - Recipient." The Hall of Valor Project, n.d. https://valor.militarytimes.com/hero/3219.

"Yantic Cemetery and the Blue Lady." Locations of Lore, June 2, 2020. https://locationsoflore.com/2018/07/13/yantic-cemetery-and-the-blue-lady/.

ABOUT THE AUTHOR

Courtney McInvale Reardon is the founder of Seaside Shadows based out of Mystic, Connecticut and offering walking tours and boat tours throughout the southern New England region. She is a licensed tour guide, published author and actual descendant of accused witches. She is a Connecticut native and Courtney spent 5 years in DC after completing her studies at Catholic University of America and the University College Dublin where she studied abroad, majoring in International Relations. After earning her degree, she worked for the FBI as an analyst -- having been influenced by her time interning at NCIS for the Cold Case Homicide Unit -- She then spent 2 years in Vermont working for Dept of Homeland Security and honing her investigative skills. Courtney also spent many months in Ireland in study and visiting, a place rich with histories and hauntings alike! She avidly studies histories of Celtic cultures, specifically Ireland and Scotland, specializing in rebellions. Her love for rebellion history dates to the studies of the American Civil War that began in childhood. Her father, a history major at the University of Georgia, had Courtney memorize the names of Civil War Generals by photograph before she turned seven. She lost many ancestors to the Civil War on both sides and researching and writing about War between the States seemed to be her destiny. Courtney is an empathic spirit medium -- able to feel, see and communicate with spirits. She has frequently had experiences involving the paranormal. In Courtney's childhood home in central Connecticut, in a town called East Hampton numerous paranormal occurrences happened. The events were so extreme that the Warren family came to investigate and exorcise the house during her teenage years there. Due to her haunting past, and ability to see and communicate with spirit, she has always taken an interest in the unknown and has now put her sensitivities, investigative skills, love of history, and writing aspirations to work. Courtney is also a realist amongst all things and believes no tour or book can be complete without corroborating information. Each book and tour she creates is inundated with historical facts to corroborate all the haunting occurrences surrounding the topic. Courtney has been featured as a historian and medium on Travel Channel's *Portals to Hell* and as a medium on Travel Channel's *Ghost Adventures*. She hosts paranormal investigations and historical site fundraisers annually. Courtney loves spending time with her husband, Marty, her loving pets, her sisters and wee niece & goddaughter. She is a sucker for a good period drama or true crime documentary and in free time can be found listening to classic rock or 90's pop and watching and obsessing over *Outlander* or *Vikings*.